Other Publications:

This volume is one of a series that explains and demonstrates how to prepare various types of food, and that offers in each book an international anthology of great recipes.

Fish

BY
THE EDITORS OF TIME-LIFE BOOKS

TIME-LIFE BOOKS/ALEXANDRIA, VIRGINIA

Cover: Swathed in a jacket of parboiled lettuce leaves and dotted with butter, a whole sea bass is sprinkled with white wine before being baked *(page 54)*. The leaf wrapping will help keep the fish moist in the oven's dry heat, and a vegetable stuffing will flavor it from within.

Time-Life Books Inc.
is a wholly owned subsidiary of
TIME INCORPORATED

Founder: Henry R. Luce 1898-1967

Editor-in-Chief: Henry Anatole Grunwald
President: J. Richard Munro
Chairman of the Board: Ralph P. Davidson
Executive Vice President: Clifford J. Grum
Chairman, Executive Committee: James R. Shepley
Editorial Director: Ralph Graves
Group Vice President, Books: Joan D. Manley
Vice Chairman: Arthur Temple

TIME-LIFE BOOKS INC.

Editor: George Constable. *Executive Editor:* George Daniels. *Board of Editors:* Dale M. Brown, Thomas H. Flaherty Jr., Martin Mann, Philip W. Payne, John Paul Porter, Gerry Schremp, Gerald Simons, Nakanori Tashiro, Kit van Tulleken. *Art Director:* Tom Suzuki; *Assistant:* Arnold C. Holeywell. *Director of Administration:* David L. Harrison. *Director of Operations:* Gennaro C. Esposito. *Director of Research:* Carolyn L. Sackett; *Assistant:* Phyllis K. Wise. *Director of Photography:* Dolores Allen Littles. *Production Director:* Feliciano Madrid; *Assistants:* Peter A. Inchauteguiz, Karen A. Meyerson. *Copy Processing:* Gordon E. Buck. *Quality Control Director:* Robert L. Young; *Assistant:* James J. Cox; *Associates:* Daniel J. McSweeney, Michael G. Wight. *Art Coordinator:* Anne B. Landry. *Copy Room Director:* Susan Galloway Goldberg; *Assistants:* Celia Beattie, Ricki Tarlow

President: Carl G. Jaeger. *Executive Vice Presidents:* John Steven Maxwell, David J. Walsh. *Vice Presidents:* George Artandi, Stephen L. Bair, Peter G. Barnes, Nicholas Benton, John L. Canova, Beatrice T. Dobie, Carol Flaumenhaft, James L. Mercer, Herbert Sorkin, Paul R. Stewart

THE GOOD COOK

The original version of this book was created in London for Time-Life Books B.V.
European Editor: Kit van Tulleken; *Design Director:* Louis Klein; *Photography Director:* Pamela Marke; *Planning Director:* Alan Lothian; *Chief of Research:* Vanessa Kramer; *Chief Sub-Editor:* Ilse Gray; *Production Editor:* Ellen Brush; *Quality Control:* Douglas Whitworth

Staff for Fish: *Series Editor:* Windsor Chorlton; *Series Co-ordinator:* Liz Timothy; *Text Editor:* Tony Allan; *Anthology Editor:* Liz Clasen; *Staff Writers:* Gillian Boucher, Norman Kolpas, Anthony Masters; *Designer:* Rick Bowring; *Researcher:* Ursula Beary; *Sub-Editors:* Jay Ferguson, Nicoletta Flessati; *Permissions Researcher:* Mary-Claire Hailey; *Design Assistant:* Mary Staples; *Editorial Department:* Anetha Bessidonne, Pat Boag, Debra Dick, Don Fragale, Philip Garner, Margaret Hall, Joanne Holland, Molly Sutherland, Julia West

U.S. Staff for Fish: *Editor:* Gerry Schremp; *Senior Editor:* Ellen Phillips; *Designer:* Peg Schreiber; *Chief Researchers:* Lois Gilman, Juanita Wilson; *Picture Editor:* Adrian Allen; *Writer:* Susan Bryan; *Researchers:* Cécile Ablack, Christine Dove, Barbara Fleming, Barbara Peters, Christine R. Schuyler; *Copy Coordinators:* Allan Fallow, Tonna Gibert; *Art Assistant:* Cynthia Richardson; *Picture Coordinator:* Alvin Ferrell; *Editorial Assistant:* Audrey Keir

CHIEF SERIES CONSULTANT

Richard Olney is an American who has lived and worked for some three decades in France, where he is highly regarded as an authority on food and wine. Author of *The French Menu Cookbook* and of the award-winning *Simple French Food,* he has also contributed to numerous gastronomic magazines in France and the United States, including the influential journals *Cuisine et Vins de France* and *La Revue du Vin de France.* He has directed cooking courses in both countries and is a member of several distinguished gastronomic and oenological societies, including L'Académie Internationale du Vin, La Confrérie des Chevaliers du Tastevin and La Commanderie du Bontemps de Médoc et des Graves. Working in London with the series editorial staff, he has been basically responsible for the planning of this volume, and has supervised the final selection of recipes submitted by other consultants. The United States edition of The Good Cook has been revised by the Editors of Time-Life Books to bring it into complete accord with American customs and usage.

CHIEF AMERICAN CONSULTANT
Carol Cutler is the author of a number of cookbooks, including the award-winning *The Six-Minute Soufflé and Other Culinary Delights.* During the 12 years she lived in France, she studied at the Cordon Bleu and the École des Trois Gourmandes, and with private chefs. She is a member of the Cercle des Gourmettes, a long-established French food society that is limited to just 50 members, and is also a charter member of Les Dames d'Escoffier, Washington Chapter.

PHOTOGRAPHERS
Alan Duns was born in 1943 in the north of England and studied at the Ealing School of Photography. He specializes in food, and has contributed to major British publications.
Aldo Tutino, a native of Italy, has worked in Milan, New York City and Washington, D.C. He has won awards from the New York Advertising Club.

INTERNATIONAL CONSULTANTS
GREAT BRITAIN: *Jane Grigson* has written books about food and has been a cookery correspondent for the London *Observer* since 1968. *Alan Davidson* is the author of *Mediterranean Seafood, Fish and Fish Dishes of Laos* and *North Atlantic Seafood.* FRANCE: *Michel Lemonnier,* co-founder and vice president of Les Amitiés Gastronomiques Internationales, is a frequent lecturer on wine and vineyards. GERMANY: *Jochen Kuchenbecker* was trained as a chef, but worked for 10 years as a food photographer in several European countries. *Anne Brakemeier* is the co-author of three cookbooks. THE NETHERLANDS: *Hugh Jans* has published several cookbooks and his recipes appear in a number of Dutch magazines. THE UNITED STATES: *François Dionot,* a graduate of L'École des Hôteliers de Lausanne in Switzerland, has worked as a chef, hotel general manager and restaurant manager in France and the U.S. He conducts his own cooking school. *José Wilson* wrote many books on food and interior decoration. *Kay Neil Noble,* special consultant for *Fish,* is a graduate of the professional cooking course of La Varenne École de Cuisine, Paris. *Judith Olney,* author of *Comforting Food* and *Summer Food,* received her culinary training in England and France. In addition to conducting cooking classes, she writes articles for gastronomic magazines.

Correspondents: Elisabeth Kraemer (Bonn); Margot Hapgood, Dorothy Bacon, Lesley Coleman (London); Susan Jonas, Lucy T. Voulgaris (New York); Maria Vincenza Aloisi, Josephine du Brusle (Paris); Ann Natanson (Rome).
Valuable assistance was also provided by: Jeanne Buys (Amsterdam); Hans-Heinrich Wellmann, Gertraud Bellon (Hamburg); Diane Asselin (Los Angeles); Bona Schmid, Maria Teresa Marenco (Milan); Carolyn T. Chubet, Miriam Hsia, Christina Lieberman (New York); Michèle le Baube (Paris); Mimi Murphy (Rome). The editors are indebted to Nancy Davis, Peggy Eastman, Wendy Murphy and Judy Oppenheimer, writers, for their help with this book.

For information about any Time-Life book, please write:
Reader Information, Time-Life Books
541 North Fairbanks Court, Chicago, Illinois 60611

Library of Congress CIP data, page 176.

CONTENTS

The Rich Harvest of the Waters

Fish exist in such astonishing variety that they can be a perpetual source of pleasure to cook and diner alike. More than 200 species of edible fish are caught in American waters, providing a choice ample to satisfy every taste. Some of these fish occupy a distinguished place in the culinary world: few dishes can match the sheer splendor of a whole poached salmon *(pages 32-33)*, for example, or of an airy mousseline of pike enclosed in a mold lined with fish fillets *(page 81)*. But humble and inexpensive fish can also do honor to the table: catfish wrapped in a jacket of cornmeal and fried to crisp perfection *(pages 70-71)* is a dish that richly deserves its status as an American tradition.

This volume aims to inspire the adventurous cook to make full use of the range of fresh fish available. On the next two pages, fundamental rules for buying and cooking fish are explained, and a chart lists the usual cookery methods for dozens of types of fish. An illustrated guide on pages 9-15 describes 80 of the principal fish caught or marketed in the United States and Canada. Step-by-step demonstrations of preparing fish and of techniques for cooking them follow the guide. These demonstrations will enable you to execute any of the 200 recipes in the anthology that makes up the second half of the book.

The route to market

With few exceptions—very hot thermal springs and Utah's Great Salt Lake are two—every natural body of water supports fish, and man has been eating fish since prehistory. The first fishermen captured fish in their bare hands—a practice still in use, and not only in primitive societies: when grunion, a small kind of silversides, swim onto California beaches to spawn, they are caught by hand in the thousands. But primitive societies quickly developed lines, nets and weapons that augmented their manual prowess. And when these devices were complemented by techniques of preserving fish—drying, salting and smoking—fishing became a true industry. By the Middle Ages, fleets of ships ranging into the Baltic Sea were catching herring by the ton to feed the populations of northern Europe.

The settlers of America hardly concerned themselves with deep-sea resources, since the waters of the New World seemed inexhaustible. The Reverend Francis Higginson of the Massachusetts Bay Colony wrote home to England in 1630, "The aboundance of Sea-Fish are almost beyond beleeving, and sure I whould scarce have beleevd it except I had seene it with mine owne Eyes." From Merry Mount, Massachusetts, a contemporary reported "such multitudes of sea bass that it seemed to me that one might goe over their backes dri-shod." And Captain John Smith, exploring near Jamestown, Virginia, found fish—

"more than could be devoured by Dog and Man"—schooling so densely he could scarcely push his boat through the water.

Overfishing and pollution gradually depleted the supply of fresh-water and coastal fish, so that modern-day fishermen have had to go farther and farther out to sea for big catches, sometimes ranging a thousand miles or more from their home ports. The ocean fishermen use large vessels equipped with electronic instruments to locate the fish, with large nets or long, many-hooked lines to catch them, and with refrigeration equipment to keep them fresh between fishing grounds and home.

The first stop for fish caught this way is a coastal processing center. On the East Coast, the major centers are Boston and Gloucester in Massachusetts and Hampton and Norfolk in Virginia; in the West, Kodiak and Dutch Harbor, Alaska, and San Pedro and San Diego, California; and in the South, Key West, Florida; Biloxi, Mississippi; and Brownsville and Port Isabel, Texas. In the plants the fish are sorted and cleaned (if they were not cleaned aboard ship). Then they are either packed in ice and shipped by plane to restaurants or markets in other cities, or they are frozen—whole or cut into one of the forms described on page 16—if the shipment is by truck. Freezing alters the texture of fish for the worse, but unfrozen fish are so perishable that they cannot withstand relatively slow journeys overland.

Fish from close-in coastal waters still form part of the fish supply, of course, and thanks to regulations that limit catches as well as to efforts to control pollution, sea fish will remain available, although not in their former abundance. Fresh-water fish are protected similarly by laws that help control pollution and limit the amount of commercial and amateur fishing permitted.

Atlantic salmon, whose annual migration from the sea to fresh-water spawning grounds has been recklessly interrupted by dams, log runs, poisonous chemical effluents and other man-made hazards, now are protected and are returning to some New England rivers where they have not been seen for decades. Furthermore, government programs supporting fish hatcheries have helped restock inland rivers and lakes. And fish farming has become an important industry; virtually every mature trout in the markets, for example, was raised on a trout farm, probably in Idaho, which specializes in trout breeding. In the Southern states, a vast number of ponds is devoted to breeding catfish.

Freshness: the key to quality

Shopping for as fragile a commodity as fish calls for special care. A reliable fish dealer is your best guarantee of quality, but you should also understand the characteristics of various fish and the signs that indicate prime condition.

The first rule of thumb in shopping is to buy the freshest fish available: for subtle flavor and texture, nothing can approach a fish that comes to you unmarred by freezing or canning. When a recipe requires a particular fish that is not available fresh, substitute another appropriate fresh fish, if possible, or choose a different recipe.

In selecting fish, reject any that have a fishy odor; this is an early sign of decomposition. A truly fresh fish will have a mild, almost sweet smell, faintly marine if it is an ocean fish. The exceptions are shark, skate and ray, which may briefly emit a smell of ammonia. This smell is natural and will disappear after about two days of storage.

Fresh fish have firm, elastic flesh that springs back when pressed with a finger. Other signs of freshness in whole fish are clear, protruding eyes with black pupils, bright red gills and shiny, tightly adhering scales. Fish fillets and steaks such as those shown on page 16 should have a moist, translucent appearance; if the flesh is dry-looking, milky white or discolored around the edges, reject the fish: it is past its prime.

On commercial fishing vessels, fish destined to be sold fresh are stored whole at a temperature cold enough to retard bacterial action, but not so cold as to freeze the fish. Sports fishermen have a harder time keeping their catches fresh, since few amateur fishing vessels are equipped with adequate refrigeration equipment. A fish should be gutted (page 19) the moment it comes off the hook. Gutting removes digestive organs containing the bacteria that start decomposition. Pack the cavity of a gutted fish with crushed ice, then store the fish in more crushed ice for its trip to the refrigerator at home—or to the campfire.

In some markets, you will find that frozen fish are your only choice. Sharp-eyed shopping is just as necessary in this second-best situation as it is when you are buying fresh fish. If a dealer is careless, frozen fish may thaw and freeze repeatedly, losing their flavor and risking spoilage. Reject any frozen fish packages that have torn wrapping, misshapen boxes or icy rimes around the edges. Blood in a package indicates that a fish has thawed and been refrozen; if the fish has not actually spoiled, it will be dry and tasteless.

At home, treat your fish with great solicitude. Ideally, fresh fish should be eaten immediately. If the fish must be stored, cover it loosely with plastic wrap and keep it in the coldest part of your refrigerator—but for no longer than two days. Frozen fish should be kept in a freezer rigorously maintained at 0° F. [–18° C.]; the storage period should be no longer than three months in the case of fatty fish (pages 12-13 and 14-15), six months for lean fish (pages 9-11 and 14-15).

Some useful principles

Fish are cooked by the same methods used for meat—frying, broiling, poaching, braising and so on. But many cuts of meat are tough and require long cooking to become tender; all fish, by contrast, are naturally tender and require relatively brief cooking. The amount of fibrous connective tissue in fish is much less than in meat and it breaks down more rapidly when exposed to

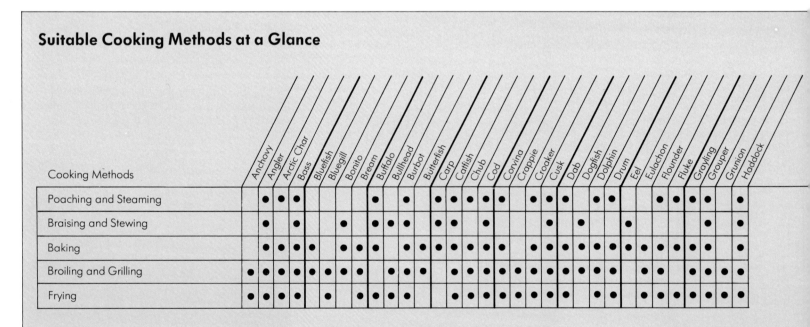

Suitable Cooking Methods at a Glance

An instant reference. The chart above indicates the cooking techniques commonly applied to particular fish. Designed as an aid in planning menus, the chart will prove especially helpful when you are selecting recipes from the anthology (pages 88-167); if the fish called for are not available, you can find substitutes on the chart. When experimenting with the techniques demonstrated in this volume, consult the chart to make sure the fish you have on hand lends itself to the preparation you want to try.

heat. By the same token, too much heat quickly damages the flesh, causing it to shrink, toughen and flake apart.

Fortunately, a simple and reliable method for estimating the proper cooking time for fish has been developed by the Canadian Department of Fisheries. Measure the fish at its thickest point and allow 10 minutes of cooking time for every inch [2½ cm.] of thickness if the fish is fresh, 20 minutes for every inch if it is frozen. (Except for fillets, which must be defrosted and separated, frozen fish may be cooked without defrosting; if you wish to defrost fish, thaw it in the refrigerator and calculate the cooking time as for fresh fish.)

The Canadian formula is a useful guide, but because fish is so delicate and because there are so many variables in cooking—inaccurate ovens, for example, or the temperature of the fish when cooking begins—you should always test a fish for doneness. The fish can be checked by cutting into the thickest part of the flesh with a knife; if the flesh is opaque and does not cling to the bones, the fish is done. You can check the internal temperature of a large whole fish with a rapid-response thermometer; it will register 140° F. [60° C.] when the fish is done. Other tests for doneness are described throughout this book.

Serving wine with fish

Most fish dishes will be enhanced by a white wine served well chilled. There are exceptions, of course. A rosé or a young, relatively light-bodied red wine is an excellent accompaniment to salmon, tuna, mackerel or other richly flavored fish, and a robust red wine can be exhilarating with a fish stew flavored with tomatoes, garlic and other assertive ingredients used in Mediterranean cooking. In general, however, red wines overwhelm the delicate taste of fish.

The light acidity of a dry white wine provides a pleasant contrast to the slight sweetness of most fish, and it is the best foil for the rich cream- or egg-bound sauces that marry so well with poached white fish. Suitable dry, white, French wines include Muscadet, Pouilly-Fuissé, Pouilly-Fumé and the Hermitage whites from the Rhône Valley. From Italy use Soave and Frascati, and from California a dry Chardonnay or a Fumé Blanc.

For special occasions, the rounder flavor of one of the finer white Burgundies—especially the first growths from the communes of Aloxe-Corton, Meursault and Puligny-Montrachet—is the perfect complement to sole, turbot or other fish of superior quality. Grand Cru Chablis, which comes from just north of Burgundy, has a slight green tint and a lingering, flinty taste that justifies its reputation as a classic accompaniment to fish. Particularly fine wines from outside France include the dry, delicate, but beautifully fragrant Moselles from Germany, and Chenin Blanc from California.

Although dry wines have a natural affinity for fish, some people prefer a more fruity wine with a hint of sweetness—a Vouvray from France, a Riesling or Gewürztraminer from Alsace or a German Spätlese or Auslese, for example. A California Riesling has similar qualities. The choice is yours: in choosing a wine, as in cooking itself, your own palate is the surest guide.

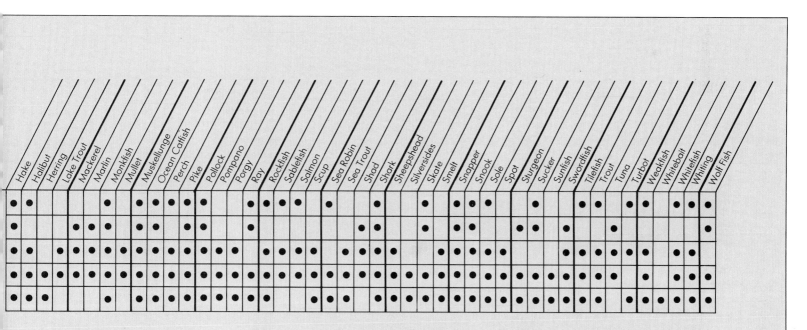

To use the chart, read across the top to locate the fish you want to cook — some fish are listed under two or more market names. Then read down: a black dot means that the cooking method listed in that row on the left side of the chart suits that fish.

A Prodigality of Options

On the following pages appear 80 of the food fish caught in America. This compendium is only a sampling (almost three times that many species are used in the United States and Canada), but it does include one or more important species in each of the major families, plus a scattering of odd but no less delicious offerings.

Within the illustrated guide, the fish are grouped mostly by family; in a few groupings—the flatfish shown opposite, for example—the fish belong to different families but share many important characteristics. The groupings are separated into two general categories—salt-water fish *(pages 9-13)* and fresh-water fish *(pages 14-15)*. Each fish is identified by its most commonly used market name. The guide also indicates regions where the fish is sold or caught, the season when it is likely to be available and any outstanding characteristics of the flesh —oiliness or leanness, firmness, taste and texture—that help determine how the fish should be cooked.

Because size, too, often affects the way a species is treated in the kitchen, the fish in the guide are drawn to scale— necessarily a sliding scale that accommodates the great range of fish sizes *(box, below)*. The dimensions of each fish represent its typical market size, which may not be the same as those the fish attains at maturity. Red snappers, for instance, have been known to measure up to 3 feet [about 1 m.] and weigh more than 30 pounds [14 kg.]. But because of aggressive harvesting and customer demand, a snapper in the market usually measures 14 to 16 inches [35 to 40 cm.] and weighs 4 to 6 pounds [2 to 3 kg.].

This guide is meant to be used in conjunction with other sections of the book. In the chapters demonstrating cooking methods, the text notes the qualities fish should have in order to suit a particular treatment; consult the guide to discover which fish fit the requirements.

The guide will also give you great latitude when consulting the recipes in the anthology that makes up the second half of the book. Enough fish species have similar characteristics so that a recipe hardly ever need be rejected because a particular fish is unavailable. For example, a recipe that calls for poaching a red snapper—an East and Gulf Coast fish—produces equally delicious results with a California corbina or even a fresh-water lake whitefish: as the guide shows, all these fish are similar, and will therefore respond the same way to poaching.

The guide can also serve as a valuable shopping aid simply by describing fish that may be unfamiliar. Most city markets now offer many kinds of fresh fish, some of them comparative newcomers. Pacific salmon and Greenland turbot, for example, now are routinely flown fresh to East Coast markets. In addition, species once confined to Atlantic or Pacific fisheries are being harvested far from their native environments: the Atlantic striped bass, for example, has been successfully transplanted to Pacific waters.

Yet another reason for the increase in the selection of fresh fish is a decline in the catches of such old favorites as the American shad and swordfish. This decline has forced fishermen to look again at species that once were tossed back; a case in point is the goosefish, or angler, once ignored but now much sought after for its lobster-like flavor and texture.

This broad choice of fish can only be an inspiration to the adventurous cook. Almost any fish found in the market—or caught on a line—belongs to one of the families described here. Once its family characteristics are understood, even an unfamiliar fish can be turned into a dish fit for the most demanding palate.

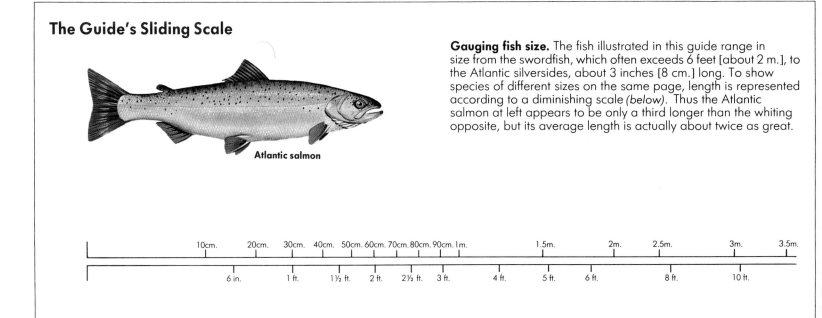

The Guide's Sliding Scale

Atlantic salmon

Gauging fish size. The fish illustrated in this guide range in size from the swordfish, which often exceeds 6 feet [about 2 m.], to the Atlantic silversides, about 3 inches [8 cm.] long. To show species of different sizes on the same page, length is represented according to a diminishing scale *(below)*. Thus the Atlantic salmon at left appears to be only a third longer than the whiting opposite, but its average length is actually about twice as great.

| 10cm. | 20cm. | 30cm. | 40cm. | 50cm. 60cm. 70cm. 80cm. 90cm. 1m. | 1.5m. | 2m. | 2.5m. | 3m. | 3.5m. |

| 6 in. | 1 ft. | 1½ ft. | 2 ft. | 2½ ft. | 3 ft. | 4 ft. | 5 ft. | 6 ft. | 8 ft. | 10 ft. |

Lean Sea Fish

The 33 fish shown on this and the next two pages represent the 10 main saltwater families or groups that are commonly classified as having lean flesh. Their fat content varies from 1 to about 5 per cent, and much of that fat is concentrated in the liver, which usually is removed in cleaning.

Almost all of these fish—exceptions have been noted in the captions—are netted throughout the year and have firm, mild-flavored, white flesh. Their lack of fat means that the flesh can dry out easily during cooking. Cooking methods that supply extra moisture—poaching, steaming and sautéing—are therefore the classic treatments for flounder, bass and other nonoily fish. However, as long as regular basting is part of the procedure, lean fish may be baked, broiled or even barbecued.

Among the most prized of lean saltwater fish are the oddly shaped flatfish shown at right below, all members of the sole and flounder families. A flatfish's eyes are located on the top of its head; it swims on its belly. Its internal structure differs from that of the more common roundfish *(diagrams, page 17),* and it is cleaned and cut up somewhat differently *(pages 19 and 22-23).*

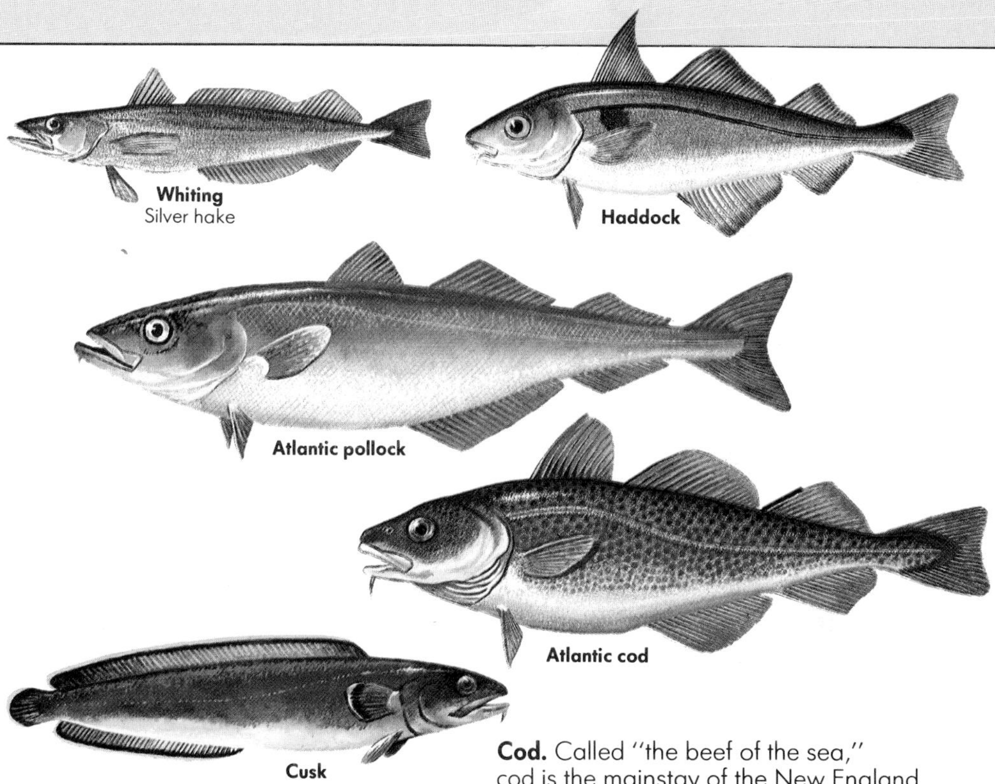

Whiting
Silver hake

Haddock

Atlantic pollock

Atlantic cod

Cusk

Cod. Called "the beef of the sea," cod is the mainstay of the New England fishing industry. The large Atlantic cod accounts for the bulk of the catch; it is somewhat coarser in texture than the others. Among this group of fish, haddock has the most delicate flavor and whiting has the softest flesh.

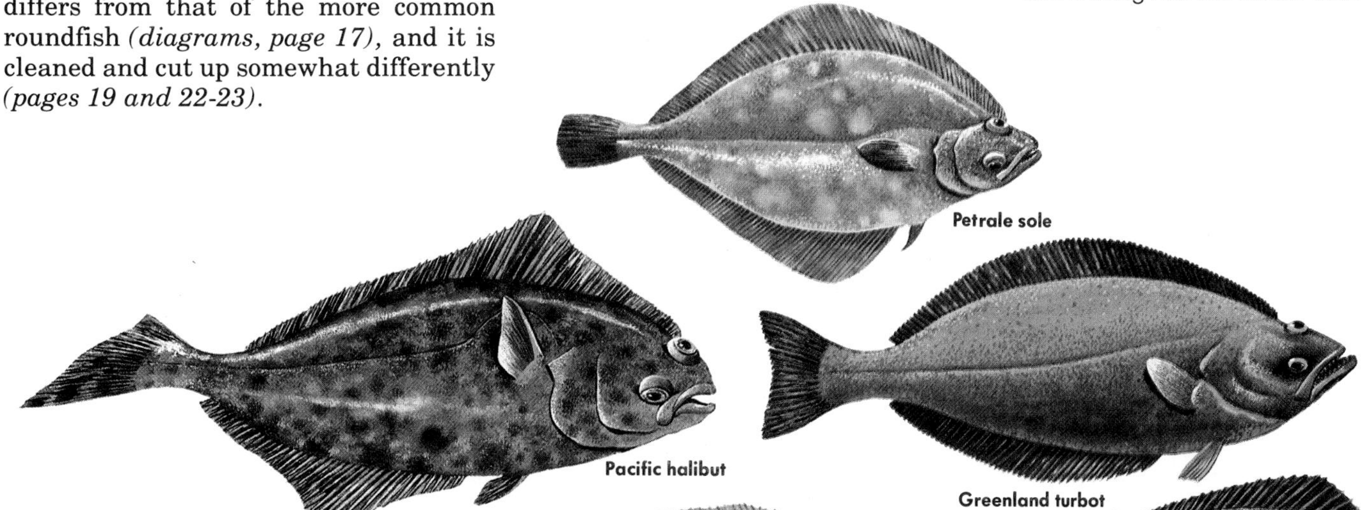

Petrale sole

Pacific halibut

Greenland turbot

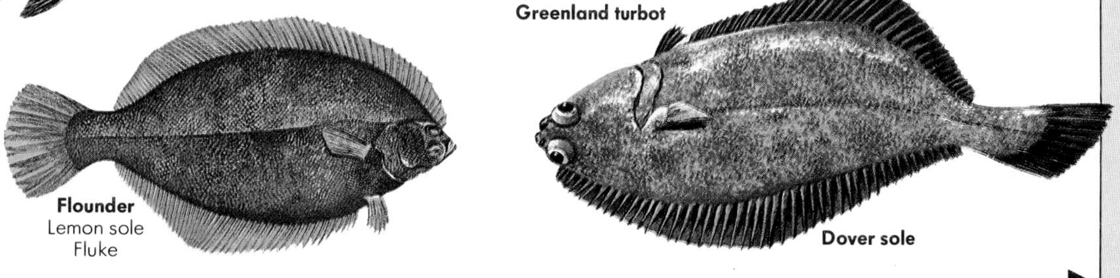

Flounder
Lemon sole
Fluke

Dover sole

Flatfish. The West Coast members of this group—all have fine-textured, delicate flesh—are the petrale and Dover sole and the Pacific halibut. Edible East Coast flatfish belong to the flounder family; they are known as winter or summer flounder, lemon sole or fluke.

▶

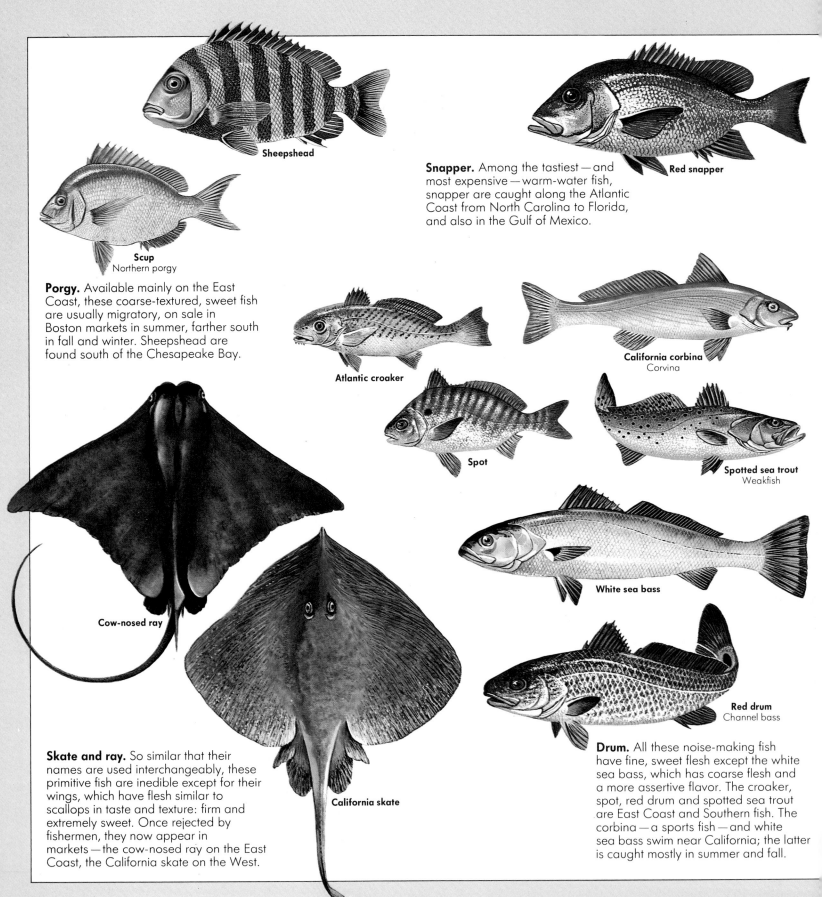

Sheepshead

Snapper. Among the tastiest—and most expensive—warm-water fish, snapper are caught along the Atlantic Coast from North Carolina to Florida, and also in the Gulf of Mexico.

Red snapper

Scup
Northern porgy

Porgy. Available mainly on the East Coast, these coarse-textured, sweet fish are usually migratory, on sale in Boston markets in summer, farther south in fall and winter. Sheepshead are found south of the Chesapeake Bay.

Atlantic croaker

California corbina
Corvina

Spot

Spotted sea trout
Weakfish

White sea bass

Cow-nosed ray

California skate

Red drum
Channel bass

Skate and ray. So similar that their names are used interchangeably, these primitive fish are inedible except for their wings, which have flesh similar to scallops in taste and texture: firm and extremely sweet. Once rejected by fishermen, they now appear in markets—the cow-nosed ray on the East Coast, the California skate on the West.

Drum. All these noise-making fish have fine, sweet flesh except the white sea bass, which has coarse flesh and a more assertive flavor. The croaker, spot, red drum and spotted sea trout are East Coast and Southern fish. The corbina—a sports fish—and white sea bass swim near California; the latter is caught mostly in summer and fall.

Striped bass
Rockfish

White perch

Nassau grouper

Black sea bass
Common sea bass

Giant sea bass
Giant black sea bass

Sea bass. White perch and black sea bass are Atlantic fish, as is the subtropic grouper; the giant sea bass lives in the Pacific, and the striped bass — sometimes called rockfish *(see below)* — is found on both coasts.

Vermilion rockfish

Ocean perch
Redfish

Rockfish. A major part of commercial catches, these fish range in flesh color from white to pink. The vermilion is a West Coast fish. Atlantic ocean perch lasts exceptionally long when frozen and provides much of the frozen fish marketed in the U.S.

Wolf fish

Wolf fish. This rarely seen northern fish often is sold as "ocean catfish." Its flavor is pronounced and it has very firm, white, coarse flesh.

Tilefish

Monkfish
Angler
Goosefish

Dolphin
Mahi Mahi

Northern sea robin

Uncommon market fish. The rarely marketed dolphin — a fish, not a mammal — is caught in semitropical waters on both coasts. Its flesh is sweet and juicy. The warm-water tilefish, found on both coasts, tastes like lobster. The delicate, mild-flavored sea robin and the firm-fleshed goosefish, or angler, are Atlantic fish little known in America.

A Rich-fleshed Catch

The fish shown on these pages contain enough fat or oil to make their flesh somewhat darker, richer and stronger tasting than that of very lean salt-water fish. Many of them are at their best—or available only—at certain times of the year, which are noted in the captions.

All these fish spend at least part of their lives in salt water but, like lean fish, many migrate with the seasons, and some live part time in fresh water. The salmon, shad and smelt, for example, are anadromous: they live in the sea but swim into fresh rivers and streams to spawn. Eels, on the other hand, are catadromous: they are spawned in the sea, but swim into East Coast fresh-water streams to live.

The fat or oil content in the salt-water fish shown here ranges from 5 to 35 per cent, varying not only from family to family but also within the same family—mainly because of their migrations and changing diets. The fat in these fish, unlike that in leaner fish, is distributed throughout their flesh. Because the fat melts during cooking and moistens the flesh, these fish are particularly suited to dry-heat cooking: broiling, baking and grilling. Frying a fat fish can yield too rich a dish; and only those lowest in fat—such as salmon—should be poached.

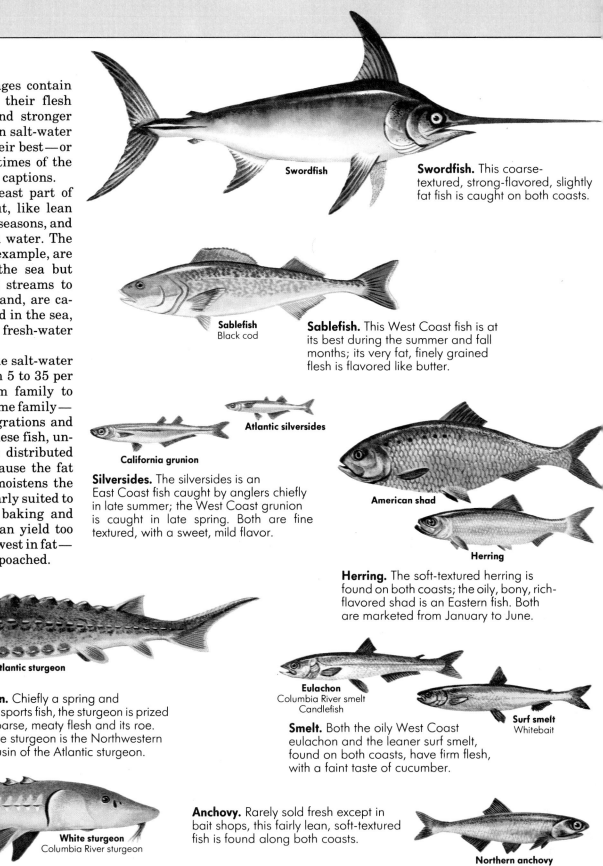

Swordfish

Swordfish. This coarse-textured, strong-flavored, slightly fat fish is caught on both coasts.

Sablefish
Black cod

Sablefish. This West Coast fish is at its best during the summer and fall months; its very fat, finely grained flesh is flavored like butter.

Atlantic silversides

California grunion

Silversides. The silversides is an East Coast fish caught by anglers chiefly in late summer; the West Coast grunion is caught in late spring. Both are fine textured, with a sweet, mild flavor.

American shad

Herring

Herring. The soft-textured herring is found on both coasts; the oily, bony, rich-flavored shad is an Eastern fish. Both are marketed from January to June.

Atlantic sturgeon

Sturgeon. Chiefly a spring and summer sports fish, the sturgeon is prized for its coarse, meaty flesh and its roe. The white sturgeon is the Northwestern river cousin of the Atlantic sturgeon.

White sturgeon
Columbia River sturgeon

Eulachon
Columbia River smelt
Candlefish

Surf smelt
Whitebait

Smelt. Both the oily West Coast eulachon and the leaner surf smelt, found on both coasts, have firm flesh, with a faint taste of cucumber.

Anchovy. Rarely sold fresh except in bait shops, this fairly lean, soft-textured fish is found along both coasts.

Northern anchovy

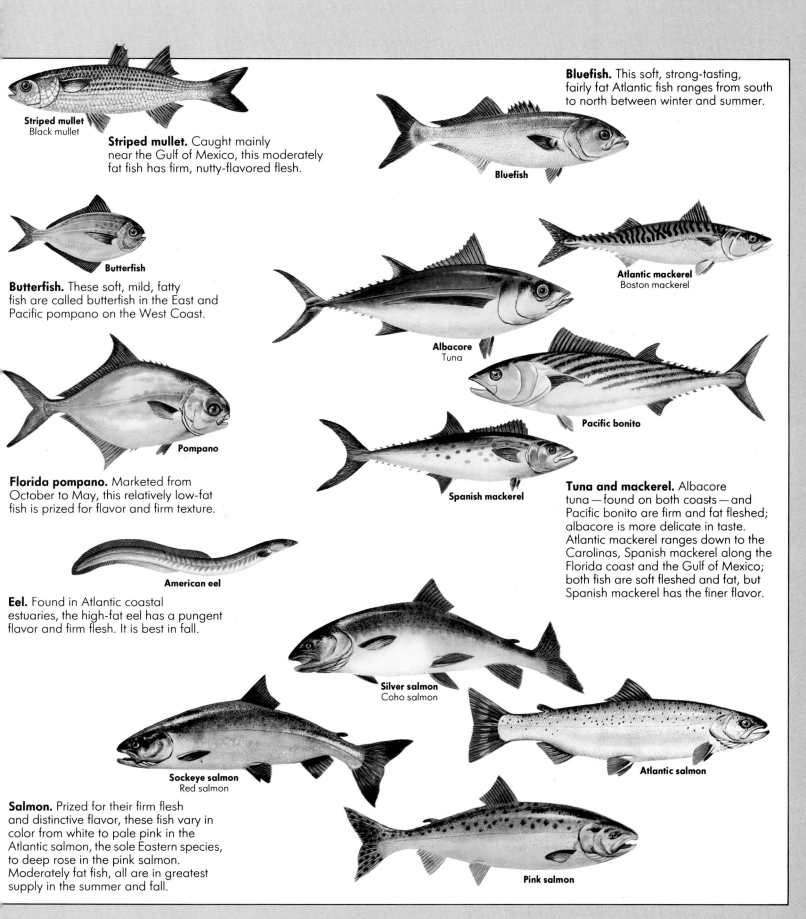

Striped mullet
Black mullet

Striped mullet. Caught mainly near the Gulf of Mexico, this moderately fat fish has firm, nutty-flavored flesh.

Butterfish

Butterfish. These soft, mild, fatty fish are called butterfish in the East and Pacific pompano on the West Coast.

Pompano

Florida pompano. Marketed from October to May, this relatively low-fat fish is prized for flavor and firm texture.

American eel

Eel. Found in Atlantic coastal estuaries, the high-fat eel has a pungent flavor and firm flesh. It is best in fall.

Salmon. Prized for their firm flesh and distinctive flavor, these fish vary in color from white to pale pink in the Atlantic salmon, the sole Eastern species, to deep rose in the pink salmon. Moderately fat fish, all are in greatest supply in the summer and fall.

Bluefish. This soft, strong-tasting, fairly fat Atlantic fish ranges from south to north between winter and summer.

Bluefish

Atlantic mackerel
Boston mackerel

Albacore
Tuna

Pacific bonito

Spanish mackerel

Tuna and mackerel. Albacore tuna—found on both coasts—and Pacific bonito are firm and fat fleshed; albacore is more delicate in taste. Atlantic mackerel ranges down to the Carolinas, Spanish mackerel along the Florida coast and the Gulf of Mexico; both fish are soft fleshed and fat, but Spanish mackerel has the finer flavor.

Silver salmon
Coho salmon

Atlantic salmon

Sockeye salmon
Red salmon

Pink salmon

Fresh-water Sampler

Although North America's inland waters shelter dozens of varieties of fresh-water fish, the fresh forms have stayed mostly in regional markets because of the impracticality of distributing them nationally. Many varieties are becoming more widely available, however, as regional fish are introduced to new habitats and commercial fish farms are established. Chief among these are trout farms and catfish ponds, which guarantee a copious supply of these popular fish.

Because of their diverse habitats and feeding grounds, it is difficult to generalize about the qualities of fresh-water fish. Wild fish are considered better tasting than fish that have been raised in farm ponds—where algae can give them a mossy taste—and fed on cereal mixtures. The fat content of fresh-water fish varies from 1.2 to 52 per cent depending on the species, habitat, diet and whether or not the fish are spawning. Fat content, flavor, and regional and seasonal availability—if applicable—are noted in the captions for each group of fish.

The cooking guidelines in the techniques demonstrations of this volume apply to these fresh-water fish just as they do to salt-water fish.

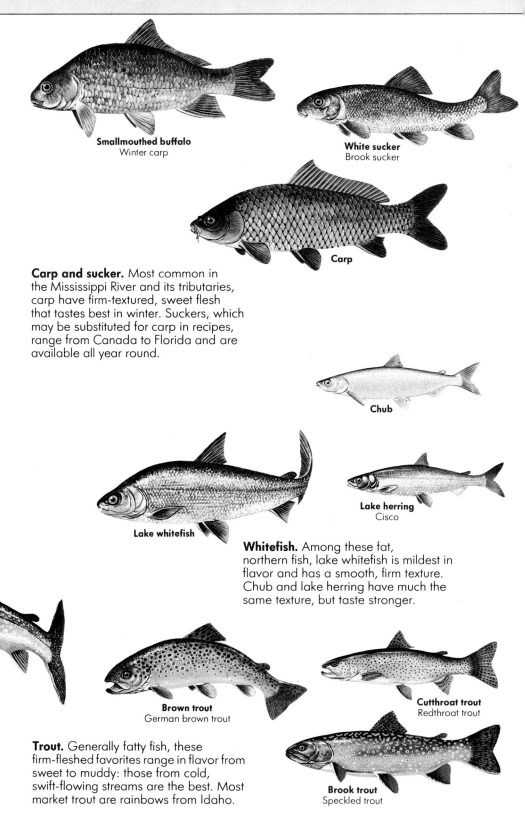

Smallmouthed buffalo
Winter carp

White sucker
Brook sucker

Carp

Carp and sucker. Most common in the Mississippi River and its tributaries, carp have firm-textured, sweet flesh that tastes best in winter. Suckers, which may be substituted for carp in recipes, range from Canada to Florida and are available all year round.

Chub

Lake whitefish

Lake herring
Cisco

Whitefish. Among these fat, northern fish, lake whitefish is mildest in flavor and has a smooth, firm texture. Chub and lake herring have much the same texture, but taste stronger.

Lake trout

Brown trout
German brown trout

Cutthroat trout
Redthroat trout

Rainbow trout

Trout. Generally fatty fish, these firm-fleshed favorites range in flavor from sweet to muddy: those from cold, swift-flowing streams are the best. Most market trout are rainbows from Idaho.

Brook trout
Speckled trout

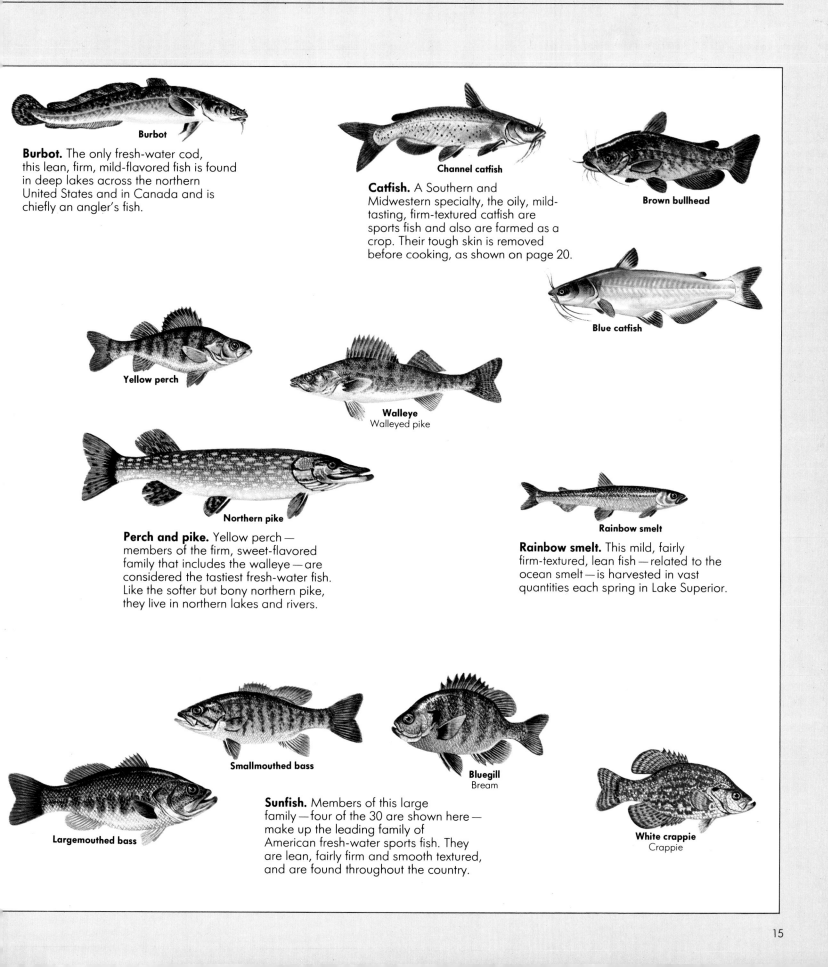

Burbot

Burbot. The only fresh-water cod, this lean, firm, mild-flavored fish is found in deep lakes across the northern United States and in Canada and is chiefly an angler's fish.

Channel catfish

Brown bullhead

Catfish. A Southern and Midwestern specialty, the oily, mild-tasting, firm-textured catfish are sports fish and also are farmed as a crop. Their tough skin is removed before cooking, as shown on page 20.

Blue catfish

Yellow perch

Walleye
Walleyed pike

Northern pike

Perch and pike. Yellow perch — members of the firm, sweet-flavored family that includes the walleye — are considered the tastiest fresh-water fish. Like the softer but bony northern pike, they live in northern lakes and rivers.

Rainbow smelt

Rainbow smelt. This mild, fairly firm-textured, lean fish — related to the ocean smelt — is harvested in vast quantities each spring in Lake Superior.

Smallmouthed bass

Bluegill
Bream

Largemouthed bass

Sunfish. Members of this large family — four of the 30 are shown here — make up the leading family of American fresh-water sports fish. They are lean, fairly firm and smooth textured, and are found throughout the country.

White crappie
Crappie

A Primer on Form — Natural and Commercial

When you buy whole fish and cut them up yourself just before cooking, as demonstrated on pages 18-25, you are guaranteed maximum succulence: the longer a fish keeps its bones and protective skin, the juicier and more flavorful it will be. But because such last-minute preparation is not always convenient, markets usually offer fish in a variety of forms that shorten your preliminary work — or present you with a finished job.

In the market as well as at home, the way a fish is cut up depends on whether it is flat or round. The upper and lower layers of flesh in a flatfish such as sole or flounder (*diagram, opposite, below*) are usually so thin that they can be divided along the backbone into only two pairs of narrow fillets. Except for halibut or turbot, which may be thick enough to cut into the crosswise sections called steaks, most flatfish are sold in only three forms: whole, pan-dressed (without the head or tail) or as single fillets.

Roundfish have two curved fillets that extend lengthwise along both sides of the backbone (*diagram, opposite, above*). Because their flesh is comparatively thick, roundfish can be divided crosswise as well as lengthwise, and they may be sold in the six distinct forms pictured below.

To some extent, the market form of a fish determines the amount you ought to buy. In a whole fish, almost half of the total weight is bone, head and tail: allow about 1 pound [½ kg.] of whole fish to a serving. For a pan-dressed fish, ¾ pound [⅓ kg.] to a serving should be enough. Fish steaks and fillets are almost completely edible flesh: allow only ⅓ to ½ pound [150 g. to ¼ kg.] to a serving.

Whole fish. In this form, the fish — here, a salmon — is usually sold scaled and gutted; you need only to remove the fins *(page 18)*. If you wish to gut the fish yourself *(page 19)*, ask for an uncleaned whole fish.

Pan-dressed fish. Whole cleaned fish like this striped bass sometimes are sold with their head and tail cut off so the fish will fit a pan more easily. Cook or cut up such a pan-dressed fish as if it were a whole fish.

Halved fish. A pan-dressed roundfish may be sold split in half along the backbone. Since its moisture-preserving skin and bones are left intact, a halved fish is especially suited to broiling or grilling.

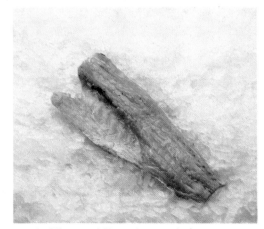

Single fillets. Sold boneless and often skinless, these strips of flesh are the most fragile fish cuts. They may be cooked by almost any method, but you must take care that the flesh does not dry out.

Butterfly fillets. Small roundfish — two spots *(left)* and a croaker are shown — are often pan-dressed, then opened flat like books. Remove the bones but not the skin. Cook them as if they were single fillets.

Steaks. Cross sections from large roundfish — in this case, sablefish — should be at least 1 inch [2½ cm.] thick. Each contains some backbone and is surrounded by skin. Steaks may be cooked by any method.

The Two Types of Structure

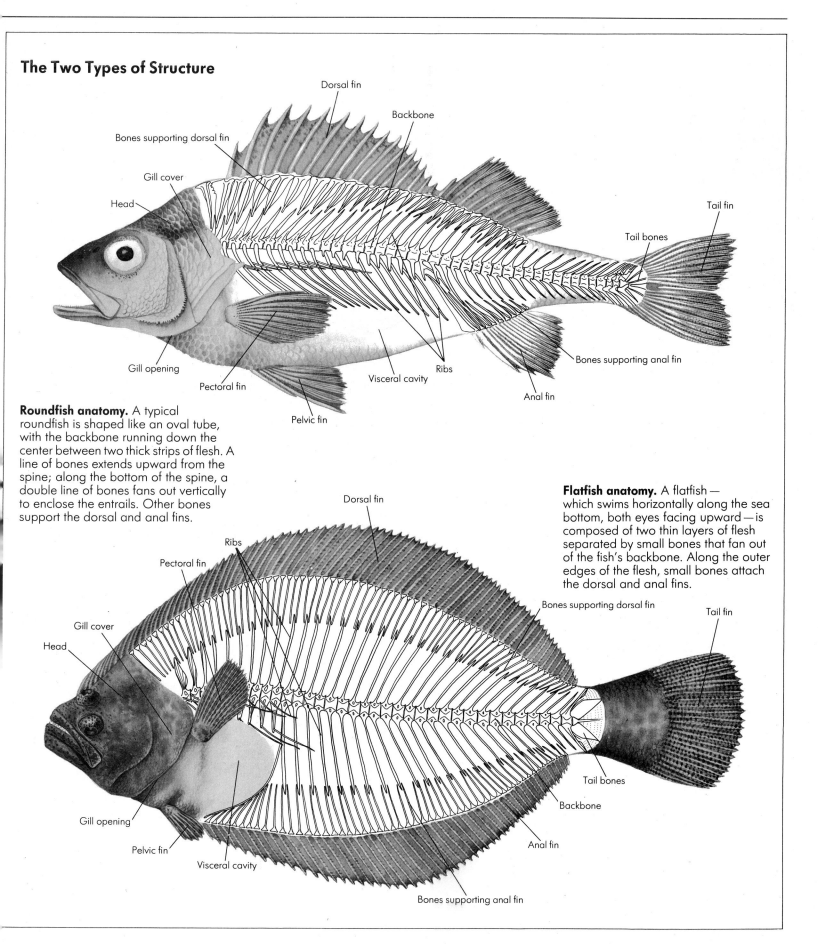

Dorsal fin

Backbone

Bones supporting dorsal fin

Gill cover

Head

Tail fin

Tail bones

Gill opening

Pectoral fin

Visceral cavity

Ribs

Bones supporting anal fin

Pelvic fin

Anal fin

Roundfish anatomy. A typical roundfish is shaped like an oval tube, with the backbone running down the center between two thick strips of flesh. A line of bones extends upward from the spine; along the bottom of the spine, a double line of bones fans out vertically to enclose the entrails. Other bones support the dorsal and anal fins.

Dorsal fin

Ribs

Pectoral fin

Gill cover

Head

Gill opening

Pelvic fin

Visceral cavity

Bones supporting anal fin

Flatfish anatomy. A flatfish — which swims horizontally along the sea bottom, both eyes facing upward — is composed of two thin layers of flesh separated by small bones that fan out of the fish's backbone. Along the outer edges of the flesh, small bones attach the dorsal and anal fins.

Bones supporting dorsal fin

Tail fin

Tail bones

Backbone

Anal fin

Cleaning and Trimming: The Essential First Steps

Whether fish are to be cooked whole, boned, filleted or cut into steaks, they must first be cleaned—a process that ordinarily includes removal of scales and fins and always calls for removal of the viscera, or internal organs. If you buy a whole fish in the market, it will probably be cleaned. You should learn to do the job yourself, however, so you can deal with a fresh fish when the occasion arises.

Almost all fish require scaling; among the few exceptions are catfish and eel, whose leathery skin must be removed altogether *(pages 20 and 45)*, and most trout, whose scales are an integral part of the skin. Scaling—simply scraping the scales from the skin—can be done with a knife or with the tool used below.

Fish fins are removed to make a fish more attractive and easier to serve and eat. The pectoral and pelvic fins can be clipped away with kitchen scissors at any stage of the cleaning process. The dorsal and anal fins, however, are not removed until after scaling: they are firmly attached to the flesh by bones *(diagrams, page 17)* and help keep the fish in one piece while you handle it. Cut them out before cooking if you plan to cut up *(pages 21-23)* or bone *(pages 24-25 and 56-57)* the fish. If, however, you intend to poach the fish whole and unboned, leave the dorsal and anal fins intact: they help hold the flesh together as the fish cooks and are easy to cut out when it is served.

The next step is gutting. For roundfish, there are two approaches: through the belly or through the gills *(box, right)*. Gutting through the belly is quick and convenient; use this method if you plan to bone or fillet a fish. Gutting through the gills—which better preserves the fish's shape—is preferred for fish that are to be stuffed and cooked whole *(pages 54-55)*, or served whole in aspic *(page 85)*.

To gut flatfish, simply make a small incision behind the gills and pull out the viscera; the organs occupy only a small portion of the fish's body.

Any fish to be cooked with its head on should have its cartilaginous gills removed after the gutting is done. Lift each gill cover and pull out the accordion-like gill; it will come away fairly easily.

Once fish have been cleaned, you can fillet *(pages 22-23)*, bone *(pages 24-25)* and skin them. Most roundfish are easiest to skin after they are filleted and cooked; the oil the fish exudes during cooking helps the skin and flesh separate. Flatfish may be skinned raw or cooked; because of their shape, the skin can be pulled off in one strip, providing the fish was recently caught and has never been frozen. If you are filleting a flatfish, skin it completely *(box, opposite)*. If you plan to cook the fish whole, remove only the tough dark skin on its upper side; the white skin on its lower side helps hold the flesh intact as it cooks.

Removing Fins and Scales

1 **Scaling.** Rinse the fish but do not dry it. Hold the fish by the tail on a flat surface. Beginning at the tail, scrape a knife blade or, as here, a multiedged fish scaler, against the scales in short, firm strokes. Work up to the head, removing the scales embedded there.

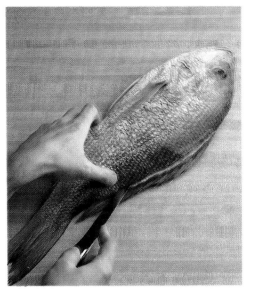

2 **Freeing the dorsal fin.** Rinse the fish again to wash off the loosened scales. With a sharp knife, slice down the fish's back on each side of the dorsal fin. Ease the knife into the cuts, angling it to free the short bones that connect the dorsal fin to the flesh.

3 **Finning.** Grasp the end of the dorsal fin nearest the tail and pull the fin toward the head of the fish. The fin and connected bones will pull free of the back. Repeat with the anal fin. With scissors, cut off the pectoral and pelvic fins. If you are cooking the fish whole, trim the tail to fit the cooking dish.

Techniques for Gutting Roundfish

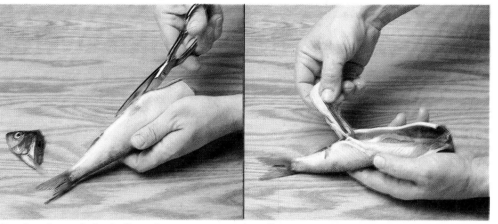

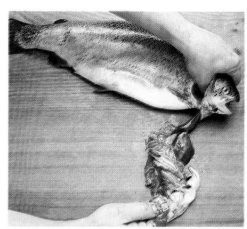

Gutting through the belly. When you want a headless fish, cut off the head behind the gill opening. Cut open the belly to the vent *(above)*. (If the fish head is left on, slice the belly open between the same two points.) Pull out the viscera *(above, right)*. Run a knife down both sides of the backbone inside the fish to release blood pockets. Rinse the fish.

Gutting through the gills. To gut a fish without opening it, hook one thumb into a gill to expand its opening, and pull out both the viscera and the gill. Check to be sure you have removed all of the organs, then rinse the fish.

A Rapid Method for Skinning Flatfish

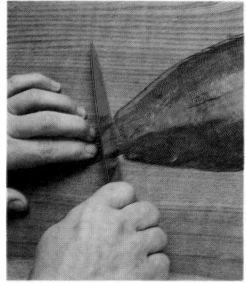

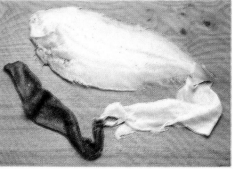

1 **Freeing the skin.** Lay the fish dark side up on a cutting board. With a sharp knife, cut across the skin where the tail joins the body *(above)*. Starting at the cut, use the knife point or your fingernails to prize a flap of skin away from the flesh until you can firmly grip the flap.

2 **Peeling the skin.** Grasp the flap of skin in one hand; with the other, hold down the tail, using a cloth to prevent slipping. Pull the skin toward, then over, the head. Turn the fish over and, holding the head, pull the skin down to the tail *(inset, right)*.

When and How to Skin Roundfish

As a rule, a fish cooked whole is not skinned beforehand: the skin protects the flesh from the heat, sealing in juices and flavor. Exceptions to the rule usually are made for convenience. Whole flatfish, for example, may be skinned before cooking, as shown on page 19. Roundfish baked in a pastry crust *(recipe, page 158)* will be easier to carve if they are skinned before being wrapped in pastry.

Skinning also eliminates undesirable qualities in certain roundfish. In butter-fish, for example, the oily layer beneath the skin—common to all fish but unnoticeable in most—can be unappetizing. Skinning removes much of this fat.

For fish with hard-to-remove scales—pike, carp and porgy, for instance—skinning is a useful shortcut: the scales come off with the skin. And some roundfish—catfish, cusk, grouper and shark among them—have tough skin that must be removed before cooking if you wish to fry the fish in a coating *(pages 70-71)*.

A skinned whole fish should not be poached or braised; the flesh would fall apart. Nor should it be broiled or grilled, since the exterior flesh would dry out before the fish cooked through. However, both baking and frying are suitable cooking methods, although the fish usually needs a coating—pastry or batter, for example—to seal in juices and flavor.

Only very fatty fish such as albacore or herring can be baked without a coating; their flesh renders enough fat to keep the fish from drying out as it cooks.

1 Cutting the skin. Gut the fish through the belly *(page 19)*. Without piercing the flesh, slit the skin across the body just behind the gills and just above the tail. Then slit the skin down the back between the head and tail cuts.

2 Separating skin and flesh. Work the knife blade under the skin behind the gills. Lifting with one hand and slicing away connective tissue with the other, separate the skin from the flesh, working toward the tail.

3 Removing the skin. As you lift the skin from the flesh, sever it where it is attached to the belly. When you reach the tail, discard the piece of skin, turn the fish over and repeat the procedure on the other side. Finally, cut out the anal and dorsal fins as described on page 18.

The Best Way to Skin a Catfish

Skinning catfish differs from skinning other fish because the catfish's flesh is formidably protected: its skin is too tough to peel off with a knife, its head bristles with whisker-like barbels, and its barbed fins inflict stinging wounds. In some species, the barbs contain a poison that makes wounds doubly painful.

To free a catfish's flesh, you will have to grip its slippery skin firmly in a pair of pliers and tear it off, as shown at right. To protect yourself from injury while you are skinning the fish, wear a thick glove. And to protect yourself as you handle the fish after skinning it, cut off its head and fins.

1 Slitting the skin. To provide an easy grip for skinning, cut a small "V" in the skin just behind the head. Cut all the way around the body, angling the knife to cut behind the pectoral fins.

2 Pulling off the skin. Hold the fish by the head with one gloved hand. With pliers, grasp the cut edge of the skin. Pull the skin firmly back toward the tail; it will peel off easily in large strips.

Dividing Fish into Steaks

Steaks—cross sections cut from a whole fish—are readily available in markets, but a do-it-yourself approach offers several advantages: you will have a wider choice in types of fish, you can control the size of the steaks, and the leftover fish head, tail and scraps will provide you with the makings of a fumet *(page 29)*.

With the exception of turbot and halibut, only roundfish can be sliced into steaks. Choose firm-fleshed fish that will not fall apart during cooking: the many candidates include swordfish, tuna, and —shown at right—salmon and cod. Do not try to make steaks from extremely bony fish such as shad: the steaks will be riddled with tiny bones. The fish you select must be large enough to provide serving-sized steaks: a 10-pound [4½-kg.] fish is the smallest practical size.

Use a large, sharp knife—such as the butcher knife shown here—or a meat cleaver. If you have difficulty in severing the fish's backbone with a knife, place the blade's sharp edge against the bone and sharply strike the top edge with a wooden mallet to force it through the bone. (Do not strike the blade with a metal tool, lest the knife be damaged.) Cut the steaks at least 1 inch [2½ cm.] thick: thin steaks have a tendency to dry out during cooking.

Steaks may be poached, braised, fried, baked, broiled or grilled. Usually, the skin and backbone are left in place; both help keep the flesh together during cooking, and both are easy to remove after cooking. If you plan to cook the steaks in a sauce, however, you may remove the band of skin beforehand *(right, bottom)*, since the job may be difficult and messy after the fish is cooked.

Slicing through the Backbone

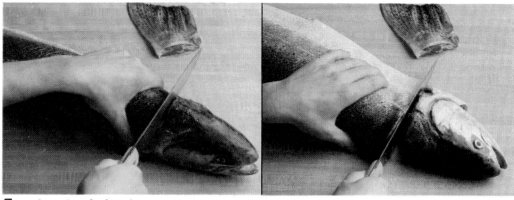

1 **Severing the head.** Lay a cleaned fish on its belly. Slice into the flesh just behind the gills *(left)* until you feel the blade slide between two vertebrae. Slice through the backbone, then turn the fish on its side and cut all the way through the body, severing the head.

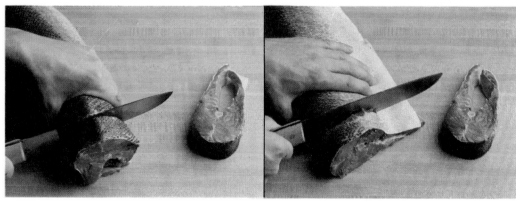

2 **Cutting steaks.** Turn the fish back on its belly. Cut through the backbone at least 1 inch [2½ cm.] behind the first cut. Turn the fish on its side and complete the cut as before to produce a steak 1 to 1½ inches [2½ to 4 cm.] thick. Repeat this step at even intervals.

Trimming the Portions

Skinning a steak. Insert the blade of a small, sharp knife between the skin and the flesh. Angle the blade against the skin *(left)* and cut through it to produce a small tag of skin. With this tag, pull the skin away from the steak and simultaneously slice under the tag, keeping the blade turned to avoid damaging the flesh.

Separating the Flesh from the Bones

Fillets—full-length sections of fish separated from the bones—are called for in most dishes where fish are to be served in a sauce or deep fried in batter, and they are the raw material for mousseline *(pages 78-79)*. In addition, fillets lend themselves to decorative presentations: they can be wrapped around a stuffing and poached, for example, or used to line a mold filled with mousseline or other stuffing *(page 81)*.

Most fish can be filleted, but the job is easiest and the results are best with fish that have well-defined bone structures, such as the sole and whiting shown here. Pike and other fish with hundreds of tiny bones embedded in their flesh do not easily produce neat fillets.

To separate fillets cleanly from the skeleton, you need a knife with a long, sharp blade that is flexible enough to ride over the fish's bones as you slice off the flesh above them. Flatfish and roundfish, because of their different anatomies *(diagrams, page 17)*, require slightly different methods of working. Flatfish, which are almost always skinned whole before filleting *(page 19)*, yield four fillets: two from the upper side of the body and two from the lower side. Roundfish, which can be skinned easily after filleting if a recipe calls for it, yield two fillets—one from each side of the backbone.

Cook fillets as soon as possible after you prepare them; exposing their flesh to air causes rapid drying. During the cooking, cover the flesh to prevent drying. Most commonly, fillets are sautéed gently in butter or poached briefly in a rich stock or sauce *(pages 36-37)*. They also may be coated with protective bread crumbs and pan fried *(pages 70-71)*, or covered with a wrapping of pastry and baked *(pages 82-83)*. Fillets may even be broiled or grilled with success, provided you baste them faithfully and pay close attention to the timing *(page 59)*.

Filleting Flatfish

1 **Freeing the flesh from the backbone.** Lay the skinned fish — a sole, in this case — on a cutting board with its eyes facing up and its tail toward you. With a sharp, flexible knife, cut down to the backbone along the center of the fish from the head to the tail. Insert the blade at a shallow angle between the head end of one fillet and the ribs. Lifting the fillet with one hand and cutting with short strokes, sever the head end of the fillet from the ribs.

Filleting Roundfish

1 **Cutting down the backbone.** Lay the cleaned fish on one side, with its tail toward you. Holding the fish steady with one hand, slice along the backbone from head to tail, cutting deep enough to expose the backbone.

2 **Removing the upper fillet.** Sever the fillet from the head by cutting down to the backbone behind the gill. Holding the head end of the fillet, insert the knife between the fillet and the ribs. With the blade of the knife parallel to the ribs, cut down the length of the fillet, using short strokes to detach it completely.

2 **Removing the first fillet.** When the head end of the fillet is detached, lift it clear of the ribs with your free hand and continue cutting away the fillet along its length. Let the fish's bone structure guide the knife. Cut off the fillet at the tail end, and trim any fins or ragged edges.

3 **Removing the second fillet.** Cut away the other fillet. If the fish has been caught in the spawning season, it will probably contain a sac of orange roe beneath one fillet, as shown here. You can save the roe for a fish stock, or it can be served poached or pan fried (pages 66-67) as a delicacy in its own right.

4 **A bonus for stock.** When the upper side of the fish has been filleted, turn the fish over and repeat the process on the underside. You will be left with four fillets and a cleanly picked skeleton (above). Save the skeleton for inclusion in a fumet (page 29).

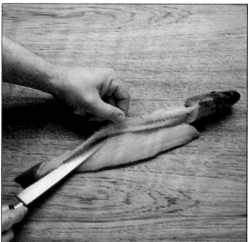

3 **Removing the lower fillet.** After separating the lower fillet from the head, hold the fish by its exposed backbone and use the knife to slice the fillet from the ribs. If you are filleting a fish with a delicate skeleton — a herring, for example — some bones may remain attached to the flesh. Carefully pull them out with your fingers or with tweezers.

4 **Skinning the fillets.** If you wish to skin the fillets, lay them skin side down and cut about ½ inch [1 cm.] of flesh away from the skin at the tail end. Pressing a finger on the exposed skin, insert the knife at a shallow angle beneath the flesh and, cutting away from you with short strokes, separate fillet and skin. Repeat for the second fillet. Trim the fillets neatly for cooking (inset).

Boning Roundfish through the Belly

Bones in a whole fish can be a nuisance to the diner, but with a little judicious cutting they can be removed before the fish is cooked. Because of their anatomy, flatfish such as flounder should be boned through the back, as shown on pages 56-57. For an elaborate dish, roundfish also may be boned through the back *(pages 56-57)*, but the simplest way to bone a roundfish—while preserving its shape—is through the belly, as shown here. You can then cook the whole fish au gratin *(pages 52-53)*, or fill the body cavity with a stuffing and bake or poach it by the methods on pages 30-33.

Most roundfish have simple skeletons composed of a backbone with ribs branching off it, as shown in the diagram on page 17. Removing the bones is a simple matter of opening the underside of the gutted fish from head to tail to expose the skeleton, then freeing the skeleton from the surrounding flesh. In the case of sea bass—shown here—and other big fish with large bones, you can use a knife to help free the ribs from the membrane that covers them, and then pick out each rib individually with your fingers.

The skeletons of finer-boned fish such as herring and shad should be pried loose with your fingers alone, since the bones are so tiny and closely spaced it is easy to damage the flesh with a knife. If you wish to bone very small fish such as anchovies, slit the belly open with your thumb and peel away the skeleton by hand.

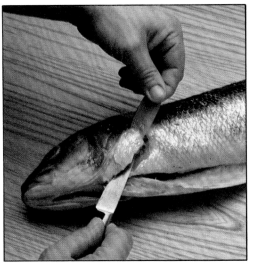

1 Gutting and finning. Check that the fish has been cleanly gutted; if not, first rinse out the belly cavity and wipe away any dried blood. Cut away the dorsal fins and the bones that support them *(page 18)*. Then slice off the pectoral fins *(above)*, cutting forward toward the gill apertures to remove them.

2 Opening the fish. The fish's belly will already have been sliced open for gutting. To remove the bones, extend the opening back along the length of the fish. Using a sharp knife, slit the underside all the way to the tail.

3 Cutting out the ribs. Hold the fish open to expose the backbone and the ribs that are embedded in the flesh and covered by membrane. Working down the fish, nick the membrane to expose each rib, and slide a small knife blade under the rib to lift it free of the flesh *(above)*. Then snap the rib off the backbone with your fingers *(right)*.

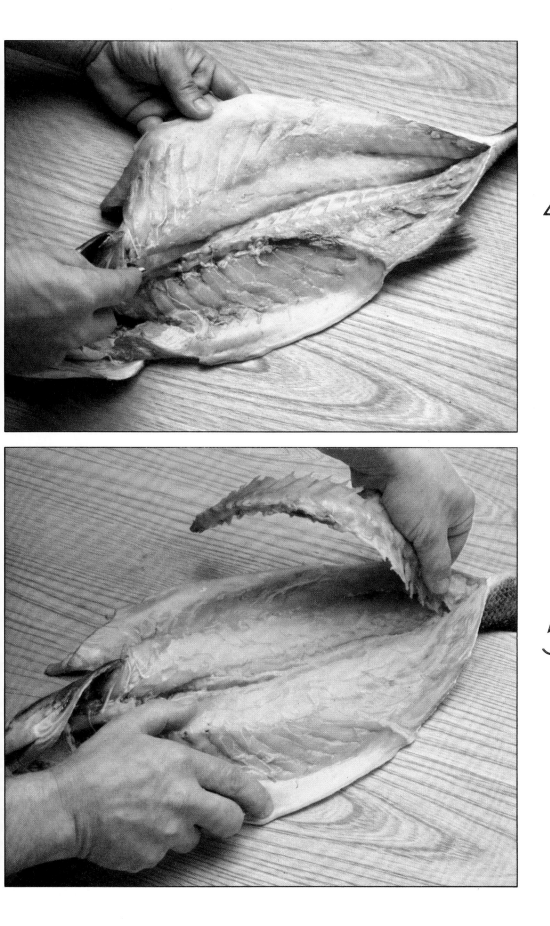

4 **Freeing the backbone.** The backbone will still be partly embedded in flesh. To free it, open the fish as wide as possible without tearing the flesh, and run the knife down both sides of the backbone. Do not press the knife so hard that you cut through the skin.

5 **Removing the backbone.** With a pair of kitchen scissors, sever the backbone as close to the head as possible. Grasp the severed end and pull the bone up; then, working toward the tail, lift the entire bone free of the flesh. Sever the bone as close to the tail as possible. The backbone may be included in a fumet *(page 29),* if you like.

1
Poaching and Steaming
Careful Handling and Controlled Cooking

Selecting a suitable liquid
Managing different fish sizes
Sauces to serve with hot and cold fish
Dealing with fillets
The virtues of steaming

A halibut steak is lowered into a milk-and-water court bouillon that is just at the frothing point. The fish's flesh, kept in shape by its bone and outer band of skin, will emerge with its flavor heightened by the acidity of lemon slices that have been added to the court bouillon.

A fish is poached by cooking it briefly in simmering liquid; the fish is steamed by cooking it for an equally short time suspended above boiling liquid. These two closely related methods could hardly be more simple, yet getting perfect results with them requires both care and skill.

One key consideration is the choice of fish. Firm-fleshed types such as salmon, trout or sole—whole or cut up—are the best candidates for poaching or steaming. Very fat fish such as butterfish, mackerel and herring tend to fall apart when cooked with liquid, as do soft-textured types such as bluefish or shad.

The size of the fish determines the cooking vessel. Steaks, fillets and small fish can be poached—or, with a perforated holder, steamed—in any covered vessel broad and deep enough to hold them. Large whole fish need outsized vessels like the poacher shown on page 32.

For either poaching or steaming, the liquid must be prepared ahead of time and flavored in a way that complements, but does not mask, the fish's flavor. Salted water will do, but most fish profit from being cooked in—or above—a court bouillon (page 28) made by simmering seasonings in water to which milk, wine or vinegar is added. If fish trimmings also are added, the court bouillon becomes a fish fumet, which not only makes a rich liquid for poaching delicate-tasting fish or fillets, but also furnishes the starting material for the sauces (pages 34-35) and aspic coatings (page 84) that may garnish the cooked fish.

Poaching, of course, is never synonymous with boiling: if fish are agitated in boiling liquid, their flesh breaks, ruining first their appearance, then their taste and texture. The liquid should therefore be kept around 175° F. [80° C.]; at this temperature, the surface will perceptibly tremble or shudder, but not bubble. By contrast, the liquid for steaming (pages 38-39) must be kept boiling vigorously to cook the flesh through evenly without ever coming in contact with it.

The best timing method for both techniques is the one developed by the Canadian Department of Fisheries: measure the fish, fillet or steak at its thickest point and allow 10 minutes cooking time for each inch [2½ cm.] of thickness. For absolute assurance that the fish is correctly done, you can check it with a skewer, trussing needle, rapid-response thermometer or even chopsticks, as described on the following pages.

Flavored Liquids for Cooking and Sauce-Making

A fish can, of course, be either steamed or poached with plain water, but the taste of any fish will be enhanced if the water is flavored. Sea water makes an excellent poaching medium for sea fish, and both fresh-water and salt-water fish can be poached or steamed in a court bouillon or a fish fumet *(recipes, pages 163-164)*.

A court bouillon usually combines water with wine or vinegar, but may be based on milk. A fumet is a fish stock: it is made with water, wine, and fish or fish trimmings. Both may be flavored with aromatic vegetables and herbs; the flavorings used will depend on the type of fish and how it is to be served, as well as on what ingredients are available.

Thyme, bay leaf, onion and carrot are usually present in a wine-and-vegetable court bouillon *(below, left)*. Parsley, fennel leaves, dill, garlic, leeks or celery are optional additions. Use dry red or white wine in any quantity you like. A court bouillon with a high proportion of wine would be too strong for poaching delicate fish such as flounder and turbot, but it would be ideal for strongly flavored fish such as grouper or tuna.

To draw out the flavors of the vegetables and herbs, simmer them in water and wine for 30 to 40 minutes. If you want a mild-tasting court bouillon, add the wine at the beginning; long simmering will evaporate its alcohol and help its flavor blend with those of the vegetables and herbs. For a more assertive wine taste, add the wine halfway through the cooking, as shown here. If you include peppercorns, add them for the last few minutes; they will impart a bitter taste to the liquid if cooked too long.

A vinegar court bouillon *(below, center)* substitutes wine vinegar for wine, but in a smaller proportion to the water, since vinegar has a much stronger taste and higher acidity than wine. The piquancy of a vinegar court bouillon suits such fresh-water fish as carp, trout and pike and its acidity makes it possible to cook them *au bleu (recipe, page 97)*. In this classic preparation, a small, fresh-water fish—usually a trout—is killed, quickly cleaned and plunged immediately into a boiling vinegar court bouillon. The acid in the liquid interacts with the fish's natural coating to turn its skin a delicate shade of blue.

A milk-and-lemon court bouillon *(below, right)* helps keep fish steaks and fillets white. Turbot, cod and smoked haddock are often poached in this mild liquid and emerge with their flavor heightened by the lemon's acidity.

A fish stock, or fumet, is usually prepared with fish trimmings, water and wine, but because a fumet should have an intense flavor (the word means "flavor" in French), it generally contains less water than a court bouillon. Indeed, a fumet can simply be a court bouillon that has been reduced in the process of poaching a fish. The concentrated flavor makes it especially good for mild-tasting fillets.

After the poaching, a fumet can be transformed into a sauce *(pages 34-35)* or reserved for a stew or braise *(pages 42-45 and 48-49)*. And if it is clarified and strengthened with gelatin, it becomes an aspic jelly that can be used to coat cold poached fish *(pages 84-85)*.

To store fumet, place a plastic freezer bag in a small bread pan or other suitably sized container, pour in the cooled fumet, tie up the bag, label it and freeze. It can be stored for up to three months.

A Trio of Court Bouillons

A wine court bouillon. Trim and slice an onion, a carrot and a leek, and dice a rib of celery. Add the vegetables and parsley, thyme, dill and a bay leaf to about 1 quart [1 liter] of salted water. Simmer, uncovered, for 15 minutes, then pour in 2 cups [½ liter] of dry white wine. Cover, and simmer for 15 minutes more, adding a few peppercorns for the last 10 minutes. Strain before using.

A vinegar court bouillon. Combine the same water-and-vegetable mixture used for the wine court bouillon *(left)*, and add white or red wine vinegar to taste; as a rough guide, allow ¼ cup [50 ml.] of wine vinegar to each pint [½ liter] of water. Simmer, uncovered, for 30 to 40 minutes. Strain before using.

A milk-lemon court bouillon. Peel the skin and bitter pith from a lemon. Slice the lemon finely and remove the seeds. Add as many lemon slices as you like to a mixture of 1 part milk to 6 parts salted water. This court bouillon requires no preliminary cooking before the fish is placed in it.

Fumet: An Essence Made with Trimmings

1 Assembling ingredients. Ready vegetables and herbs as for a court bouillon *(opposite page)*. Rinse fish trimmings — here, the heads and the bones of sole and whiting — discarding the gills, which are bitter. Break the skeletons into convenient sizes. Put the ingredients in a pan, cover with cold water, and salt very lightly.

2 Skimming the liquid. Bring the liquid to a boil. Skim the surface scum that forms as the liquid reaches a simmer *(above)*. Reduce the heat and simmer for 15 minutes, uncovered. Add dry white wine — up to 1 part of wine to 1 part of water. Simmer for 15 minutes, but do not overcook, lest the fish bones make the liquid bitter.

3 Straining the fumet. Pour the fumet through a colander set in a deep bowl. Pressing on the solids with a spoon will speed the process but also make the liquid cloudy; do not press them if you need the fumet for a clear sauce or aspic. The strained liquid is now ready for use in poaching.

4 Removing small particles. If you want to make aspic from the fumet, strain the liquid a second time, through a fine sieve lined with damp cheesecloth or muslin *(left)*. Do not press the liquid. Leave the strained fumet in the refrigerator for several hours to allow the fine solids it contains to settle *(above)*. The liquid will then be ready to be decanted and clarified *(page 84)*.

Producing Perfectly Poached Small Fish

Successful poaching calls for meticulous preparation to help the fish retain its shape, and precise timing to preserve the fish's taste and texture. Small fish— from 9 to 12 inches [23 to 30 cm.] long, and up to about 1 inch [2½ cm.] thick— may be poached in cheesecloth wrappers to protect them, as shown here. (Smaller fish—smelt or herring, for example— should never be poached; they should be fried, so their hard-to-remove bones will become soft and edible.) Fish steaks may be poached by the same basic method demonstrated here, but they do not require a cheesecloth wrapping: they can easily be handled with a spatula. Larger whole fish and fillets need a slightly different treatment.

Among the small fish that make good candidates for poaching are such firm ones as trout, ocean perch and catfish. Clean them as shown on pages 18-20, and curl them into rings *(box, below)* if they are too long to fit flat into a pot.

Determine cooking time as described on page 27, and begin timing when the poaching liquid reaches a simmer. Check a whole fish for doneness by inserting a skewer or trussing needle through the cheesecloth into the thick flesh behind the gills. The skewer should slide in easily. Check a fish steak by pricking it with a fork: the flesh should barely flake.

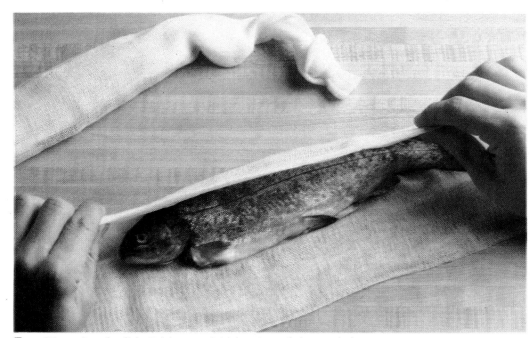

1 **Wrapping the fish.** Fold several thicknesses of cheesecloth into a rectangle at least twice as wide and about 10 inches [25 cm.] longer than the fish. Center the fish — here, a rainbow trout — in the cloth. Fold the long sides of the cloth over the fish. Make knots in the ends of the cloth to hold the package together.

A Neat Fitting Trick

Securing the head. Put the fish — a whiting is shown — on its belly and steady the head. Curl the tail to catch it on the fish's teeth. Poach the fish in cheesecloth; cut off the head and tail to flatten the cooked fish for filleting.

2 **Starting the cooking.** Grasp the knotted ends of the cloth and lower the fish, seam side up, into cold or tepid poaching liquid — a court bouillon is shown. The liquid should cover the fish. Drape the knots over the sides of the pot. Bring the liquid to a simmer. As soon as the liquid trembles, reduce the heat, cover the pot and begin timing.

3 **Unwrapping the fish.** When the fish is done, remove it from the pot, using the knotted ends of the cheesecloth as handles. Hold the wrapped fish over the pot to drain. Put the fish on a warmed serving plate, cut off the knots from the cloth with scissors and unfold it. Gently pull one long edge of the cloth to slide it out from under the fish.

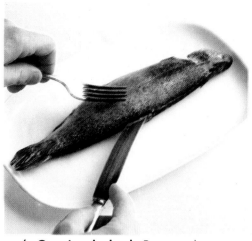

4 **Opening the back.** Pressing the back of a fork lightly against the top of the fish to hold it steady, cut a slit ¼ to ½ inch [6 mm. to 1 cm.] deep along the back of the fish from its head to its tail. The fish's belly, of course, was slit open when the fish was cleaned.

5 **Splitting the fish.** Extend the belly slit through the base of the tail without severing the tail. Slide the fork under the backbone to lift the top half. Run the knife under the bones *(above)* from tail to head, splitting the body. Cut down through the fish, separating the head from the now-filleted bottom half.

6 **Removing the bones.** With the knife under the spine and the fork steadying the top half of the fish, gently flip the top half over. Catch the tail end of the spine in the tines of the fork and lift it up; as you lift, loosen the spinal column with the knife to remove the skeleton and head in one piece.

7 **Serving the fillets.** The boned fillets may be garnished with parsley, slices of lemon and melted butter, as shown here. For an even more elaborate presentation, coat the fillets with one of the sauces described on pages 34-35.

Tactics for Handling Large Fish

A large poached fish makes an impressive centerpiece for a dinner or buffet and, with the proper preparation and equipment, it is not difficult to produce. Depending on your pan, the fish for such a place of honor can be as long as 24 inches [60 cm.]. The candidates include trout, red snapper and striped bass as well as the salmon shown in this demonstration. Here the salmon flesh is quite pale: flesh color varies with the type of fish and with its diet.

Cleaning the fish should be limited to gutting it; leave the scales and fins on to avoid tearing the skin, which helps the fish keep its shape during cooking. A fish gutted through the gills *(page 19)* needs no more preparation; one gutted through the belly, however, should be trussed with cotton string, as shown at right, or sewn up so that the belly does not gape open unattractively.

A large fish requires a large pan—and a rack to support it during cooking (the cheesecloth wrapping used for smaller fish would allow a large fish to sag and possibly break as you lifted it). Although you may improvise with a covered roasting pan and a roasting rack, the most efficient equipment is the fish poacher, an oblong pan fitted with a removable rack.

Once the prepared fish is on its rack, poaching proceeds much as for smaller fish. However, it is essential that a large fish be started in cold or tepid liquid and allowed to warm gradually—otherwise the surface flesh will be cooked before the inside is done. Timing is the same as for smaller fish: 10 minutes per inch [2½ cm.] of thickness, counted from the moment the poaching liquid starts to simmer. The internal temperature of a perfectly done fish is 140° F. [60° C.]; check it by inserting a rapid-response thermometer into the thickest part of the flesh.

As soon as the fish is removed from the poacher, peel off its skin and remove its fins. This is an easy task, provided the fish is hot: as it cools, the protein begins to coagulate and stick.

Large fish, whether they are served hot or cold, usually are presented whole, then filleted as shown opposite. The fillets are cut away from the fish in manageable sections that will remain neat and whole during serving.

1 **Trussing the fish.** Gut and clean the fish but do not remove its fins and scales. Tie up the mouth to keep it from gaping: push a trussing needle, threaded with about 12 inches [30 cm.] of cotton string, through the gills *(above, left)*, then cross the two ends of the string over the snout and tie them under the mouth. If the fish has been gutted through the belly, cut two pieces of string long enough to encircle the fish. Tie them loosely around it *(right)*.

2 **Using a fish poacher.** Place the fish on the poaching rack and lower it into the empty pan *(above, left)*. Cover with cool or tepid strained court bouillon *(page 28)*. Put on the lid *(center)*, set the pan over two burners and heat the court bouillon until it begins to simmer, then cover the poacher and cook the fish, checking frequently to make sure that the water does not boil. The fish is done when a skewer or trussing needle inserted in the thick flesh behind the gills meets almost no resistance. Carefully lift out the rack and slide the fish onto a warmed platter *(right)*.

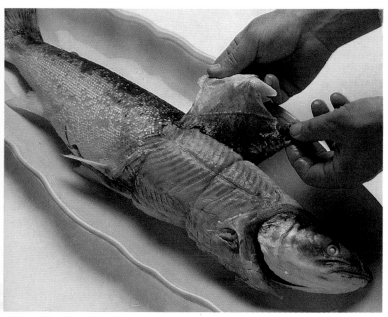

3 **Skinning.** Cut the trussing string and pull it free. With a small knife, cut out the fins. Slit the skin from head to tail along the back and the belly, then use your fingers to pull the skin from the exposed upper side of the fish *(above)*.

4 **Dividing the top fillets.** With a flexible, long-bladed knife, cut down the center of the fish just to the depth of the backbone *(above)*. Then insert the blade in the incision, turning it outward so that it is almost flat. Work down the length of the fish, easing one half of the upper fillet from the bones.

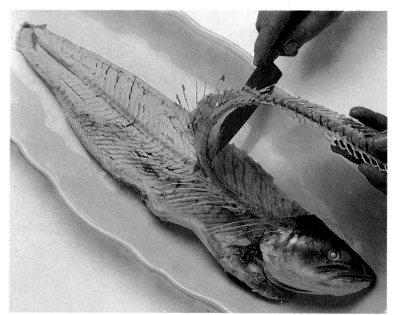

5 **Serving the fish.** When half of the fillet has been freed, divide it into serving portions. Lift the servings onto plates. Detach and serve the second half of the upper fillet in the same manner.

6 **Final division of the fish.** When the entire upper fillet has been removed, pull the tail forward *(above)* to free the attached backbone and head from the lower fillet. Divide the lower fillet also into two segments, and lift these away from the underskin with a fish server.

A Range of Sauces from Mild to Pungent

Two kinds of sauces *(recipes, pages 164-166)* may enhance poached or steamed fish. Mild-flavored sauces add richness while emphasizing the taste of the fish itself. Aromatic or acidic sauces, on the other hand, make the finished dish a study in contrasts.

The mildest of the sauces is a savory sabayon *(right; recipe, page 164),* a close relative of hollandaise. A perfect partner for any hot, poached, white-fleshed lean fish, sabayon is begun by whisking egg yolks into reduced fumet *(page 29).* To keep the heat low and thus prevent the yolks from curdling, cooking is done either over simmering water in a double boiler or, as here, in a bain-marie—a water bath made by setting one pan on a trivet inside another pan that is partly filled with simmering water. At first the mixture of eggs and fumet will be thin, but as it is whisked and heated, the sabayon will thicken and froth. Butter then is whisked into the sauce to give it the consistency of light custard.

Butter sauce, known as *beurre blanc* in France *(below, right; recipe, page 165),* is an aromatic, shallot-flavored combination of butter, wine and vinegar, good with any hot, poached fish. The trick of making the sauce is to use chilled butter, to keep the heat very low, as shown here, and to whisk continuously. This way, the butter forms a smooth emulsion with the liquid instead of separating into oil and butter solids.

Montpellier butter *(opposite, top; recipe, page 161)* is an aromatic purée of spinach, watercress, cornichon pickles, capers, anchovies, shallots, herbs and garlic, all bound together and mellowed —without cooking—by butter, egg yolk and oil. This classic mixture includes parsley, chervil, chives and tarragon, but the herbs can be varied according to taste. Usually served with cold, poached fish, Montpellier butter also will complement broiled or grilled fish.

Aioli *(opposite, below; recipe, page 163)* is mayonnaise with pounded garlic. It is traditionally used in Provence with hot, poached salt cod, but also complements such hearty-flavored hot or cold poached fish as salmon or grouper. This sauce is thickened by olive oil and egg yolk; both must be at room temperature.

Savory Sabayon: A Blend of Egg Yolks and Butter

1 Mixing eggs and fumet. Boil the fumet until it is as thick as syrup. Put the pan in a larger pan of simmering water and whisk in the egg yolks over low heat.

2 Adding the butter. When the mixture froths and thickens, drop in cold butter chunks by handfuls, whisking constantly to incorporate them.

3 Thickening the sauce. Continue adding the butter, whisking constantly, until the sauce is thick enough to coat the sides of the pan.

4 Finishing the sauce. Take the pan off the heat. Whisk for 30 seconds as the sauce cools slightly, then pour it into a warmed serving bowl.

Beurre Blanc: Wine and Shallots Bound with Butter

1 Reducing the liquid. Boil white wine, vinegar and chopped shallots *(left)* until the liquid reduces enough to barely moisten the shallots *(right).*

2 Whisking. Let the mixture cool, then put the pan on a fireproof pad over low heat. Whisk in butter chunks until the sauce is as thick as mayonnaise.

Montpellier Butter: Flavor and Color from Herbs

1 **Blanching.** Parboil herbs—parsley, tarragon and chives are used here—with stemmed spinach and watercress. Drain, and rinse in cold water.

2 **Pounding.** Dry the herbs and put them in a mortar with chopped pickles, chopped and parboiled shallots, anchovies, capers, garlic and salt *(above, left)*. Pound to a paste. Pound in hard-boiled egg yolks *(center)* and butter *(right)*.

3 **Sieving.** When the mixture is well blended, rub it through a fine nylon or stainless-steel sieve onto a plate. Wipe the mortar and put the mixture in it.

4 **Incorporating oil.** Add olive oil by drops, stirring the sauce constantly. To control the flow of oil, pour it through a slit cut in a cork *(above)*.

5 **Finishing the sauce.** Add oil until the sauce looks glossy and has a smooth, creamy texture *(above)*. The sauce is now ready to serve.

Aioli: Garlic-enhanced Mayonnaise

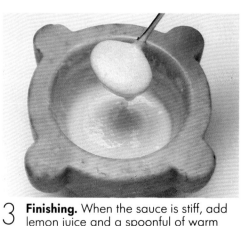

1 **Adding yolks to garlic.** Put peeled garlic cloves and salt in a mortar and pound to a purée. Add the egg yolks and stir until they lighten in color.

2 **Incorporating oil.** Add olive oil by drops, stirring briskly all the while. When the sauce starts to thicken, pour in the oil in a thin, steady stream.

3 **Finishing.** When the sauce is stiff, add lemon juice and a spoonful of warm water. Stir in oil until the sauce reaches a spooning consistency *(above)*.

Fillets Twice Enriched by Their Cooking Medium

Skinned fish fillets form attractive, individual servings—and require no special poaching equipment. Because they have no bones to keep their shape, however, thin fillets such as those of flatfish must be flattened and scored *(box, below)* to keep them from curling as they cook.

In a broad pan, fillets can be poached flat, side by side. To save space, they may be folded *(demonstration, right)* or rolled into cylinders, secured with toothpicks and poached standing upright. To keep them from moving in the liquid, cover them with buttered wax paper *(right)*; the paper also helps concentrate the aromatic steam from the poaching liquid.

Fillets lose some of their flavor because they are cooked off the bone, but a rich-flavored poaching liquid makes up for that. Fumet *(page 29)* is a good choice, and it may be used afterward to make a butter sauce *(Step 4, opposite)* or a velouté sauce *(box, opposite)* for the fillets.

1 Folding the fillets. Prepare the skinned fillets *(box, below)* and lay them scored side up on a work surface. Season them with salt and pepper, and sprinkle them with chopped parsley. Place a sliver of butter on each fillet and fold the fillet to enclose the butter.

2 Preparing the pan. Thickly butter a heavy sauté pan, scatter some chopped parsley or other herbs in it and arrange the fillets close together in the pan. Sprinkle the fillets with more chopped herbs, salt and pepper. Add enough cold or tepid fumet to cover the fillets. Lay buttered wax paper over the fillets and cover the pan.

Keeping Fillets Shapely

1 Rinsing the fillets. Skin and fillet a flatfish — in this case, sole *(pages 19 and 22-23)*. Rinse the fillets thoroughly in cold water. Place the fillets on a napkin or paper towel and press another napkin or towel on them to dry them.

2 Flattening the fillets. With the flat of a wide knife blade, press each fillet firmly along its length *(above)*. The pressure will break down the muscle fibers slightly, which will help prevent the flesh from shrinking and curling.

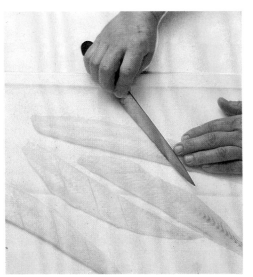

3 Scoring the fillets. When flatfish are skinned, a thin layer of membrane often remains behind. This can contract during cooking, causing the fillets to curl slightly. To prevent curling, score each fillet on the side that formerly bore the skin. With a sharp knife, cut gently through the membrane in three or four places along the length of the fillet.

3 **Cooking.** Place the pan over medium heat until the liquid simmers — lift the lid and paper to check. Replace the paper and lid, reduce the heat and cook the fillets 5 minutes per ½ inch [1 cm.] of thickness. When done, the fillets will be opaque and firm; their flesh will flake with a toothpick. Remove the fillets, drain them and keep them warm.

4 **Making a butter sauce.** Reduce the cooking liquid over high heat to a few syrupy spoonfuls. Take the pan off the heat and whisk cubes of butter — about 2 tablespoons [30 ml.] of butter for each fillet — into the liquid *(above, left)*, adding about 4 tablespoons [60 ml.] at a time and incorporating each batch completely before adding the next. The blended butter and liquid will form a light, rich sauce. Pour it over the fish and serve *(right)*.

A Velvety Sauce Thickened with Flour

1 **Combining ingredients.** Begin the velouté sauce about 30 minutes before poaching the fish. Melt 2 tablespoons [30 ml.] of butter in a saucepan. Stir 2 tablespoons of flour into the butter and cook the mixture for a minute or two without letting it brown. Pour 2 cups [½ liter] of fumet into the pan, whisking as you pour *(above)*.

2 **Reducing the sauce.** Bring the sauce to a boil over high heat, whisking. Reduce the heat so that the liquid simmers, then move the pan half off the heat. A skin will form on the cooler side of the liquid; remove it with a spoon from time to time. Continue cooking the sauce for 45 minutes to reduce its volume and eliminate any floury taste.

3 **Finishing the sauce.** When the velouté has been reduced to half its original volume, stir in poaching liquid that has been reduced to a few spoonfuls *(Step 4, above)*. Taste for salt. Remove the pan from the heat and finish the sauce, if you like, by stirring heavy cream and chunks of butter into it. Pour the sauce over the fillets.

Steaming: A Flavor-retentive Approach

Any fillet, steak or whole fish suitable for poaching may also be suspended over boiling liquid and steamed. The advantage of steaming is that the fish, because it is not immersed, retains more of its natural flavor than when poached.

The essential equipment for steaming is a vessel that can be covered tightly and that incorporates some means of raising the fish above the cooking liquid. You may improvise with a metal colander fitted into a saucepan, or you may use the simple, collapsible metal basket shown opposite, which is adjustable to fit pots of different sizes.

There are, in addition, vessels made exclusively for steaming. One type is a large pot containing a single perforated metal insert. Another type is a Chinese steamer *(box, below)* composed of bamboo or aluminum trays; the trays fit inside one another to form a stack whose height depends on the amount of food you wish to cook. By putting plates of fish, vegetables and rice on different trays, you can cook an entire meal at once. Or you can steam several fish simultaneously, as in the demonstration below *(recipe, page 100)*. Chinese steamers have their own tight-fitting lids and need not be placed in covered pots; any large, open pan will do, although the wok shown here is traditionally used.

Water is the cooking liquid usually used for steaming. If fresh herbs such as fennel and dill are added to water, they perfume the steam—and the fish as it cooks. Chinese steamers lend themselves to another flavoring method: aromatic ingredients are poured onto the fish and the plate it rests on, and during cooking the steam that condenses on the plate dilutes the ingredients into a light sauce.

For the standard method of steaming demonstrated at right, fillets, steaks and whole fish are prepared as they would be for poaching *(pages 30-33 and 36-37)*. If you wish to flavor the fish in the Chinese style, slash its sides to allow sauce to penetrate the flesh.

A steamer basket should be coated with oil or butter so the fish does not stick to its surface. Put the greased basket in the pot and bring the water to a boil before adding the fish.

With a Chinese steamer, the plates of fish are first arranged on trays and then the trays are stacked over boiling water. To allow steam to circulate freely and cook the fish evenly, the plates for a Chinese steamer should be at least 1 inch [2½ cm.] smaller in diameter than the trays. For the same reason, the fish on each plate—or in the steamer basket—should be arranged in a single layer. Timing—10 minutes for each inch of thickness—begins when you cover the pot after adding the fish. Tests for doneness are the same as those for poached fish; you may also check the fish with chopsticks, as shown opposite, below.

The Chinese Steamer

Multitiered cooking. Chinese steamers for fish may be 10 to 14 inches [25 to 35 cm.] in diameter and may be made up of as many as three stacked trays, each one intended to hold a plate on which food is cooked. If you are steaming more than one sort of food, add trays to the steamer according to the cooking time of their contents so that all the food will be ready at once.

A Steaming Method That Yields a Sauce

1 **Scoring the fish.** Clean the fish *(pages 18-19)* — a sea bass is shown. Rub 1 teaspoon [5 ml.] of salt over the skin and inside the fish. With a large chef's knife, cut slits ¼ inch [6 mm.] deep into the flesh at about ½-inch [1-cm.] intervals on both sides of the fish.

2 **Adding sauce ingredients.** Put the fish on a plate deep enough to hold ½ cup [125 ml.] of liquid. Cover the fish with the sauce ingredients — in this case, finely chopped fresh ginger root, scallion strips and a mixture of sugar, soy sauce, oil and dry sherry.

Using an Everyday Pot

1 **Starting the cooking.** Put the greased steamer basket in a pot containing 1 to 2 inches [2½ to 5 cm.] of liquid. Cover the pot and bring the liquid to a boil. In 3 to 5 minutes, when the pot is full of steam, place the fish — salmon steaks here — in the basket.

2 **Steaming.** Immediately cover the pot and begin timing the fish. Keep the water boiling vigorously so that the pot is filled continuously with steam.

3 **Testing for doneness.** When the cooking time is up, remove the pot lid and, with a fork or the tip of a small, sharp knife, gently separate the flesh at its thickest point. If the interior of the flesh is opaque and just beginning to flake, the fish is done.

3 **Filling the trays.** To avoid spilling the sauce, hold the plate level and tilt the steamer tray to slide it under the plate. Gradually raise the tray and lower the plate until the plate rests inside. Add the tray to the stack and cover.

4 **Steaming the fish.** Place the steamer in a wok or a large skillet filled with 1 to 2 inches [2½ to 5 cm.] of boiling water, cover the top tray, and begin timing the fish. Test for doneness by sticking chopsticks into the thickest part of the flesh *(above)*. If the chopsticks enter easily, the fish is done.

5 **Removing the fish.** Lift off the top tray and, protecting your hands from the hot plate with potholders or towels, press your thumb against one edge of the plate so that the other edge tilts up. Slip a pad under the tilted side *(above)* and slide the plate out of the tray. Repeat with the next tray.

2
Braising and Stewing
Assemblages for a Mingling of Flavors

Onions that have been simmered in a mixture of red wine and fumet are poured into a pan containing skinned eel segments, pieces of carp and a bouquet garni. The resulting matelote, traditionally an angler's stew, can be made with any fresh-water fish.

So far as fish are concerned, stewing and braising really are elaborations of the simple poaching techniques described on pages 30-33. As with poaching, both stews and braises use liquid as the cooking medium. But vegetables and herbs are invariably present as well, and the liquid and its aromatic ingredients always are served as part of the finished dish.

A fish stew is by no means identical to a fish braise. Stews are simplicity itself: most contain several kinds of fish and vegetables, which are simmered in copious amounts of liquid and served straight from the pot with no further treatment, so that they retain their individual tastes and textures. The purpose of braising, by contrast, is to produce a concentrated exchange of flavors among the various ingredients. In braises, vegetables serve primarily as flavoring agents, and the braise usually contains only one type of fish, which is cooked in a minimum of liquid. At the end of cooking, the vegetables—often puréed—and liquid are combined with other ingredients to make a sauce for the fish.

Neither the stewing nor the braising of fish is a long cooking process. Fish flesh is delicate and would disintegrate if subjected to the hours of simmering traditionally associated with these methods. For this reason, the vegetables in a fish stew, which take longer to cook than the fish, are cooked almost to completion in the broth before the fish is added, as in the matelote demonstrated on page 44. Similarly, the aromatic vegetables used to flavor a braise are usually sautéed and then cooked in broth to release their flavors before the fish is added for a brief simmering.

For the best flavor and texture in either stews or braises, choose firm-fleshed fish: cod, eel, haddock, catfish and sea bass all are good choices. Avoid very fatty fish such as sablefish or soft fish such as shad; they tend to disintegrate when cooked in liquid. Fish fillets are too delicate for braising, although thick ones may be cut into chunks and briefly stewed. Do not include strong-flavored fish—herring, anchovies, swordfish or tuna, for example—in a mixed fish stew; they will overpower the delicate tastes of the other ingredients. However, tuna and other strong-flavored fish that have oily flesh lend themselves to braising; when they are cooked with layers of moisture-rendering vegetables and minute amounts of liquid (pages 46-47), these fish baste themselves and emerge tender and succulent.

The Fundaments of a Braise

To achieve the concentrated blend of flavors characteristic of a braise, the liquid used for cooking whole fish or steaks with aromatic vegetables is kept to a minimum. And both the vegetables and the cooking liquid are chosen to complement the particular fish being braised.

Delicate-tasting fish are at their best when they are combined with relatively mild aromatics; in this demonstration a striped bass is cooked with carrots, celery and onion (recipe, page 113). Fish with more assertive tastes combine well with the more strongly flavored vegetables; a salmon braise, for instance, might include tomato, green pepper and garlic.

The same principles apply when choosing a braising liquid: water is the mildest, of course, but delicate fish often are braised in a court bouillon, and stronger-tasting fish in an aromatic fumet. Dry wine, too, is often used in braises: a white wine will suit any type of fish; red wine usually is reserved for hearty-flavored fish such as salmon.

Fish are prepared for braising just as they are for poaching (pages 32-33); a whole fish is cleaned, steaks are simply wiped off. Vegetables are finely chopped and often sautéed beforehand to encourage the release of their flavors and to ensure that they will cook through in the same time as the fish. The vegetables and the cooking liquid are then simmered together to begin the merging of flavors, and finally the fish is added to the aromatic mixture. The liquid must be cooled somewhat before the fish is added so that the outside of the fish does not overcook before the inside is done.

The puréeing of the cooked vegetables can be achieved either with a sieve, as shown here, or in a food mill, blender or food processor. The purée of vegetables and cooking liquid may be enriched and thickened in many ways. Simplest of all embellishments is the addition of cream; or you can use a beurre manié, consisting of equal parts of flour and butter that are kneaded together—but not cooked—before being stirred into the purée.

Other enrichments may incorporate additional vegetables or herbs; for example, the cooked flour-and-oil mixture employed in this demonstration includes mushrooms. Instead of mushrooms, you could use small onions or chunks of celeriac; both these vegetables should be parboiled before they are sautéed.

1 **Preparing the vegetables.** Dice the aromatics — here, carrots, onions and celery with sprigs of parsley — then chop them finely by rocking the blade of a heavy chef's knife back and forth over them. In a heavy casserole or saucepan that is large enough to hold the fish, sauté the vegetables in butter or oil for 2 to 3 minutes, until the onions become translucent.

2 **Braising the fish.** Add the cooking liquid — here, white wine and water — to the vegetables and boil the mixture, uncovered, for 5 minutes. Remove the casserole from the heat to cool the mixture. Season the fish inside and out with salt and pepper. Put the fish — striped bass is shown — on top of the vegetables and return the casserole to the stove. The liquid should come halfway up the sides of the fish. If it does not, add more water and wine. Bring the liquid to a gentle simmer and cook the fish, partly covered, for 10 minutes for each inch [2½ cm.] of thickness: start timing when the liquid reaches a simmer. Baste the fish every 5 minutes.

3 **Removing the fish.** While the fish cooks, sauté small whole mushrooms and chopped parsley in oil in a skillet for 5 minutes. Stir in flour and remove the skillet from the heat. When the fish is done, lift it carefully from the pan on two broad metal spatulas to keep it intact, and place it on a warmed platter.

4 **Puréeing the vegetables.** Use a fine sieve — here, a conical sieve called a *chinois* — to purée the aromatics with the braising liquid. Press down firmly on the vegetables with a pestle or wooden spoon to extract all of their juices before discarding the pulp.

5 **Cooking the sauce.** Add the puréed aromatics to the mixture of mushrooms, parsley and flour. Stir thoroughly as you bring the sauce to a boil; then lower the heat and simmer the sauce, uncovered, for 5 minutes to reduce and thicken it.

6 **Serving the fish.** When the sauce reaches the consistency of heavy cream, remove the skillet from the heat and spoon the sauce over the fish. Garnish the platter with parsley and serve.

Setting Off the Rich Taste of Eel

Among the fish suitable for stewing and braising, eel is something of a rarity on American tables, although the waters of the United States teem with it. The neglect is undeserved, for eel has sweet, rich flesh. It goes particularly well with tart, strongly flavored sauces, an affinity that is celebrated in two dishes popular in northern France and Belgium—matelote, a thick version of a mixed fish stew, and *l'anguille au vert,* or "eel cooked with herbs," an egg-enriched braise.

Matelote, in culinary terms, simply means a stew of fresh-water fish; it may be based on carp *(recipe, page 103)* as well as eel, or on the two together. Burbot, perch, pike and catfish can be added in any combination. The fish are cleaned and cut into steaks; but to retain maximum flavor only the eel is skinned, although catfish would also require skinning *(page 20)* if it were included.

As with other fish stews, the preparation of a matelote begins with the cooking of the broth and vegetables: small onions are sautéed, coated with flour and simmered in dry red wine and herbs. After this robust mixture has blended, it is poured over the sliced fish, and a hearty fumet *(page 29)* is added to strengthen the sauce. As the fish cooks in the liquid, the flour disperses throughout the stew to thicken it. When the fish is almost done, the broth is removed to a separate pan and boiled to reduce it, thereby intensifying its flavor and ridding the wine of any lingering taste of alcohol.

Dry white wine, together with layers of herbs and leafy vegetables, adds sharpness to eel in *l'anguille au vert (recipe, page 105),* a dish that epitomizes the mingling of concentrated flavors typical of braises. Traditionally, the dish includes parsley, mint, sage, chervil, tarragon and either spinach or sorrel; the slight astringency of these ingredients balances the richness of the eel flesh and of the eggs used to thicken the sauce.

Eel is prepared the same way for both stewing and braising. It is an oily fish and therefore spoils soon after it is killed. Ideally, it should be bought live and killed just before cooking. The tough, inedible skin can then be peeled off the flesh as if it were a tight stocking *(box, opposite, below).*

Fresh-water Fish Stew Made with Red Wine

1 **Preparing the fish.** Kill and skin the eel *(box, opposite page).* Cut it into 3-inch [7½-cm.] pieces. Clean, scale and slice the other fish — here, a carp — into steaks *(page 21).* Put both fish, including the flavor-giving carp head, into a large skillet with a bouquet garni.

2 **Preparing the onions.** In a separate pan, melt some butter and sauté small, peeled onions over low heat until they are lightly colored. Sprinkle flour over the onions, shaking the pan to coat them. Cook until the flour turns yellow, then pour in wine *(above)* and add salt.

3 **Cooking the fish.** Add warm fumet and simmer, uncovered, for 30 minutes. Pour the mixture over the fish and simmer, covered, for 15 minutes until the fish is tender. Toward the end of cooking, pour most of the sauce into a separate pan and boil to reduce it to half its volume, skimming off the skin that forms as it cooks *(page 37).* Pour the sauce over the fish. Remove the head and bouquet garni. Garnish the dish with croutons and parsley.

A Braise of Eel and Herbs in an Egg-thickened Sauce

1 **Assembling ingredients.** Melt butter in a heavy pan and stir in about half of the chopped, fresh herbs and leaf vegetables. Spinach, used here, is parboiled beforehand; if you add onions, sauté them first. Add the eel pieces *(above)*, then the rest of the greenery. Cook, covered, for about 5 minutes. Pour in white wine to cover.

2 **Thickening the sauce.** Cover the pan and simmer for 10 to 15 minutes, until the eel is tender. Beat the eggs with a little lemon juice — some recipes also call for cream — and pour a little of the cooking liquid into the mixture to warm it. Remove the pan from the heat, and add the warmed egg mixture *(above)*, stirring until the sauce thickens.

3 **Serving.** You can eat the dish warm, served straight from the pan, or cold *(above)*. To chill the eel, arrange the pieces on a serving dish, pour the sauce over them, let the eel cool, and then refrigerate it, covered, for a few hours. Serve it straight from the refrigerator.

How to Kill and Skin an Eel

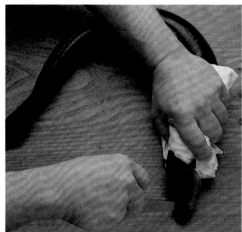

1 **Killing the eel.** Grip the eel below the head and stun it by knocking its head against a hard surface. Holding its slippery body in a cloth, pierce the head with the tip of a small, sharp knife *(above)*. The eel will continue to twitch for several minutes after it is dead.

2 **Skinning.** Grasp the eel's head in a cloth, and cut into the skin behind the gills, circling the body. Separating the skin from the flesh is difficult. To start the process, use pliers to loosen a tab of skin that is large enough to grip with your fingers *(above)*.

3 **Cleaning the eel.** Using cloths to prevent slipping, grasp the tab of skin with one hand and the eel's body with the other. Pull back the skin. Decapitate the eel about 3 inches [7½ cm.] behind the head. Discard the head, which contains the viscera.

A Robust Treatment for Meaty Steaks

Although most types of fish must be half-immersed in liquid to prevent their flesh from drying out and disintegrating when they are braised, there are a few exceptions to the rule. Tuna, swordfish and bonito are oily enough so that, when sliced into thick steaks and cooked in a snug-fitting vessel, they become self-basting and require only a tiny amount of added liquid to keep them moist. This braising process is the same as pot roasting, and it produces especially delectable results if the fish steaks are sandwiched between layers of vegetables; all the flavors will blend into a complex and delicious whole that needs no extra sauce or garnish.

To eliminate any possible rancid taste in these oily fish, many cooks first blanch them briefly in boiling water. Another preliminary—shown here with tuna—is a technique sometimes used to add piquancy: the fish are larded with canned or salt anchovy fillets that have been rinsed in water to remove their excess salt, then patted dry.

The array of vegetables cooked with the fish should be chosen to keep the fish flesh moist and also to flavor it. The rich flesh of tuna, swordfish and bonito is best complemented by tart, acidic vegetables. Here, sorrel, lemon, tomatoes and onions become foils for the distinctive taste of tuna; lettuce leaves are added mainly for the use of their plentiful moisture (recipes, pages 110-111).

The vegetables, cut up or shredded and arranged in layers above and beneath the fish, also provide a shield that prevents the fish's own moisture from escaping. And a little dry white wine poured over the assembly guarantees that the cooked fish will be succulent.

Older recipes that describe this pot-roasting technique sometimes call for cooking times as long as two hours. Fish braised for such a lengthy period, however, will be overdone by contemporary standards. Time the fish as you would for any other cooking method—10 minutes per inch [2½ cm.] of thickness.

1 **Larding with anchovies.** Choose a large steak—in this case, tuna—weighing from 3 to 5 pounds [1½ to 2½ kg.]. Blanch the steak and remove the skin. Then, with the blade of a small knife, pry apart two of the concentric rings of flesh to form a slot just deep enough to slip in a salt anchovy fillet. Place the fillets about 1 inch [2½ cm.] apart on one side of the steak only.

2 **Preparing a vegetable bed.** Use olive oil to coat the inside surfaces of a casserole just large enough to hold the steak. Line the bottom with whole lettuce leaves, overlapping them; then add layers of peeled, seeded and sliced tomatoes and lemons along with rings of sliced onions. Season with salt and chopped herbs, such as parsley, bay leaf and thyme; add a layer of shredded sorrel and put the steak on top (left). Moisten it with olive oil.

3 **Covering the steak with vegetables.** Place another layer of tomatoes, onions and lemons over the steak, season, then cover the vegetables with more sorrel *(above, left)*. Arrange lettuce leaves on top, tucking each leaf down the side of the casserole *(center)*. Pour in a little white wine *(right)* and tightly cover the casserole with its lid or with foil.

4 **Braising the steak.** Set the casserole in a preheated 425° F. [220° C.] oven and cook the steak for 20 to 30 minutes, depending on its thickness. By the end of the cooking time, the upper layer of lettuce leaves will be dry *(above)*, but the fish itself and the vegetables underneath will be moist and tender. Serve the steak directly from the casserole, as shown at right.

Preserving Individual Tastes and Textures

Unlike a braise, a successful fish stew clearly expresses the individuality of its makings: the chunks of fish and vegetable must be cooked just to doneness so that they retain their varied textures and tastes when served in the savory broth. The way to achieve this is to cook the fish and vegetables separately, combining them in the liquid at the last minute for a brief blending of flavors.

A stew may include only one type of fish (recipe, page 102), but its taste will be more interesting if several types are combined. Cod, haddock, black sea bass and Spanish mackerel are used here, but almost any assortment of firm-fleshed fish will do. Strong-tasting fish such as sardines and herring should not be included, however, since they will overpower the other ingredients.

As for the vegetables, the choice is limited only by seasonal availability and personal preference. Potatoes frequently form part of a fish stew because their starch lends natural body to the broth. Stews that do not contain potatoes may be thickened by the addition of rice. Most stews also include some aromatic vegetables—onions, carrots, celery or peppers, for example. The stew demonstrated here combines potatoes with peppers, onions, corn, tomatoes and acorn squash. Green beans, peas, spinach or leeks could be added to the array or used as substitutes.

The broth for a fish stew frequently is plain water, although a court bouillon or fumet (pages 28-29) adds distinction. Wine and other acidic liquids such as tomato juice may be added in order to flavor the cooking liquid and to help the vegetables retain their firmness during cooking. As a general rule, allow about 1 quart [1 liter] of liquid for every pound [½ kg.] of fish and vegetables.

Since the vegetables require longer cooking than the fish, they are prepared first. After any necessary peeling, they should be cut into sizes that will help to minimize the differences in their cooking times. Aromatics often are quickly sautéed in fat or oil, as here, to help seal in their flavors and to perfume the oil or fat, which will be used later to sauté the fish. Then the aromatic and other vegetables are simmered in the liquid just long enough to cook them through. You may find it necessary to add vegetables to the broth at different stages: potatoes and root vegetables, for example, need to cook for as long as 15 to 20 minutes; fragile young peas or green beans require only about 5 minutes' cooking.

The fish—skinned fillets, cut in equal-sized pieces for uniform cooking—usually are quickly sautéed in the oil left from precooking the aromatic vegetables. To add interest, the fillets may be marinated briefly beforehand in lemon or lime juice. They are simmered in the broth just long enough to marry all the flavors.

1 **Advance preparation.** Peel the potatoes, squash and tomatoes, husk the corn, and cut these vegetables into chunks. Peel the garlic and onions, and slice the onions. Seed the peppers and cut them into strips. Cut skinned fish fillets into 2-inch [5-cm.] squares. Put the fish in a bowl and sprinkle with lemon juice. Marinate at room temperature for 10 to 15 minutes.

2 **Sautéing the aromatics.** Heat a thin coat of oil in a large, heavy casserole. Sauté the peppers, onion, garlic and parsley over medium heat for 3 to 5 minutes, or until the onions are translucent. Drain and reserve the vegetables; discard the garlic.

3 **Sautéing the fish.** Add enough fresh oil to film the bottom of the casserole. Dry the marinated fish with paper towels, put it in the casserole and sauté it over low heat for about 5 minutes. Turn the pieces frequently so that they cook through evenly and color lightly on all sides.

4 **Removing the fish.** As soon as the fish loses its translucence, remove the pieces from the casserole with a slotted spoon or wire skimmer, letting the oil and juices drain back into the casserole. Set the fish aside in a bowl.

5 **Simmering the stew.** Add to the casserole the sautéed vegetables and the raw vegetables — here, squash, corn and tomatoes. Cover the vegetables with water and white wine. Bring to a simmer and cook for 15 minutes, or until the vegetables are tender.

6 **Cooking the fish.** Add the chunks of fish. Stir gently to mix the fish into the broth, and add salt and pepper to taste. Simmer the stew for 5 minutes, or until the fish just begins to flake when it is pierced with a fork.

7 **Serving the stew.** Immediately remove the stew from the heat and ladle it into soup plates. Alternatively, the broth may be served as a first course, followed by the fish and vegetables.

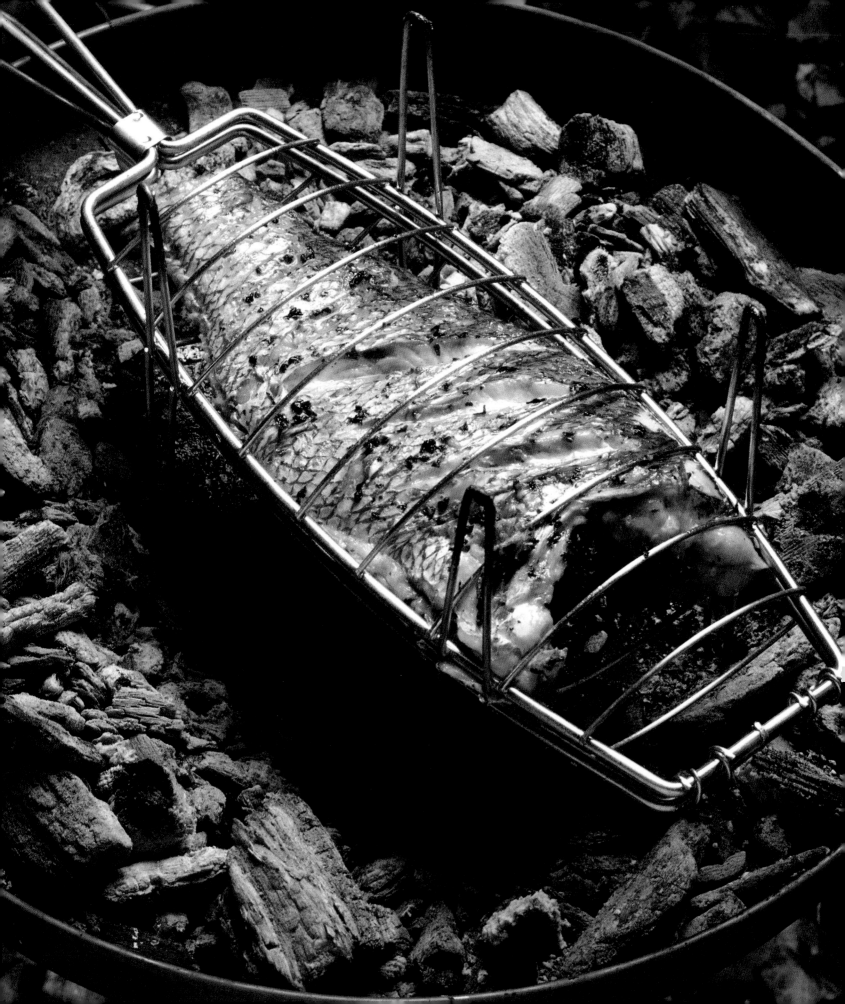

3
Baking, Broiling and Grilling
A Range of Effects from Dry Heat

Whether fish are baked, broiled or grilled over hot coals, the results will be delicious—as long as the cook compensates for the effects of dry-heat cooking. Because fish have little of the internal fat that keeps meats moist during cooking, cooking times must be short and defenses against drying must be stringent.

In baking, one of the best precautions against drying is to cook the fish in a small amount of liquid—melted butter, oil or fumet *(page 29)*—that can be used for basting during cooking and can become the basis for a sauce afterward. Another tactic is to enclose a fish in a wrapping: an envelope of leaves contributes liquid and flavor while conserving the moisture of the fish; alternatively, a foil wrapper *(pages 54-55)* causes the fish to steam in its own juices. For broiling or grilling, fish may be marinated beforehand or basted heavily during cooking—or both.

A fish that emerges unadorned from the grill or broiler, its skin crisp and its flesh succulent, ranks as one of cooking's triumphs of simplicity. A baked fish, on the other hand, invites elaboration. For example, a trout may be boned and generously stuffed *(pages 56-57)* or given a gratin topping *(pages 52-53)*. The inclusion of vegetables in the gratin topping yields a complete and appetizing course in a single dish.

Fatty fish such as mackerel, bluefish and shad are particularly well suited to baking, broiling and grilling; they render enough oil to baste themselves, and need little extra liquid to prevent parching. With proper attention, however, almost any fish can be cooked by these methods. The only exceptions are fish less than 6 inches [15 cm.] long, which should be deep fried to soften their tiny, hard-to-remove bones.

The guidelines for temperatures and cooking times for fish are refreshingly simple, whether the fish is baked or broiled. For baking any fish, preheat the oven to 425 to 450° F. [220 to 230° C.] and allow 10 minutes' cooking time per inch of thickness of the fish. If the fish is stuffed, measure its thickness after stuffing. This general baking rule is altered only when the fish is stuffed with mousseline; then the oven temperature is lowered and the cooking time increased, as described on page 56, to keep the delicate stuffing mixture from toughening. Fish are broiled or grilled 4 to 6 inches [10 to 15 cm.] from the heat source; cooking times are the same as for baking.

Held in a fish-shaped grilling basket, a red snapper cooks to a crisp, smoke-flavored finish over smoldering coals. Metal legs welded to the basket hold the fish above the heat as each side cooks; a space has been cleared in the coals to accommodate the legs.

51

Simple Strategies for Whole Fish

There are two basic ways to keep a fish from drying out as it bakes. The first is to supply extra moisture by basting the fish with butter or oil and flavorings *(right)*. The second is to shield the fish from the dry oven heat by blanketing it with other ingredients—chopped vegetables, for example. When crumbs and butter top this vegetable shield, they form a crisp gratin over the fish *(bottom, far right)*.

Either approach to baking can be used with any type of fish. Lean fish such as flounder and sea bass, however, will require more frequent basting—or moister coatings—than oily ones.

To further lessen the risk of drying, fish baked by the basting method usually are left whole, complete with their heads and tails. For extra flavor and moisture, the belly cavities may be filled with any of a wide variety of stuffings, ranging from simple mixtures of bread crumbs or chopped vegetables to the hearty combination of bread crumbs and aromatics that is shown here.

Fish baked with a gratin coating require somewhat more elaborate preparation. In order to brown evenly, the surface of the gratin must be approximately level; roundfish intended for a gratin have to be filleted *(pages 22-23)* or boned and flattened *(pages 24-25)*. A cleaned flatfish may be cooked whole; however, the rough dark skin on its upper side should be removed. For additional succulence, you may loosen the upper fillets of a flatfish from the backbone *(page 56)* and insert strips of butter under them. By themselves, flatfish fillets usually are too thin for baking in gratins: they will overcook in the time that it takes for the coating to brown.

Supplementary Moisture from Within and Without

Preparing the fish. Wipe a cleaned whole fish inside and out with damp paper towels. Dry the fish thoroughly and sprinkle it inside and out with salt. Brush the belly cavity with melted butter and stuff it loosely; the stuffing mixture used here includes diced, sautéed celery, onions, leeks and scallions.

A Gratin Topping to Protect Delicate Flesh

Layering the ingredients. Mix chopped mushrooms, shallots and parsley, and spread half the mixture in a buttered gratin dish. Season with salt and pepper. Lay a boned, flattened roundfish—a whiting, in this case—or a whole flatfish on the vegetables.

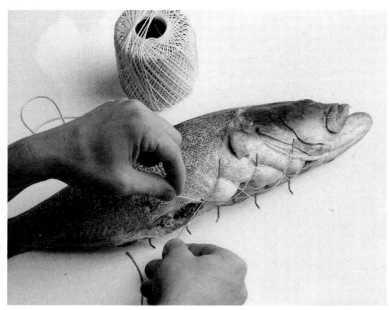

2 **Securing the stuffing.** Pin the fish together over the stuffing by sliding small metal skewers through both belly flaps. At about the midpoint of a 2-foot [60-cm.] length of cotton string, make several turns around each of the skewers closest to the head. Cross the two ends of the string, wind them around the second pair of skewers and continue to lace up the fish in this crisscross fashion.

3 **Baking the fish.** Place the fish in a well-buttered or oiled baking dish and paint it with the basting liquid—here, lemon juice and butter. Bake in a preheated 450° F. [230° C.] oven, basting frequently and allowing 10 minutes per inch [2½ cm.] of thickness—measured after stuffing. The fish is done when a skewer inserted behind the gills meets no resistance. Remove the skewers and string before filleting (page 31) and serving the fish.

2 **Covering with bread crumbs.** Salt and pepper the upper side of the fish, cover it with the rest of the mushroom-and-shallot mixture and season it once more with salt and pepper. Add just enough dry white wine to moisten the ingredients. Scatter fresh bread crumbs evenly over the surface of the dish (above). Spoon a generous quantity of melted butter over the bread crumbs.

3 **Baking the fish.** Bake the fish in a preheated 450° F. [230° C.] oven for 10 minutes per inch [2½ cm.] of thickness or until the bread crumbs have browned. Slice a boned roundfish into serving portions. If you have cooked a whole flatfish, lift off the upper fillets and remove the backbone before serving.

Cooking under Wraps

Rather than covering a fish to shield it from the heat of the oven, you may enclose it in layers of vegetable leaves to keep the flesh succulent during baking. The leaves help retain the fish's moisture and exude their own liquid to baste and flavor the fish. In the demonstration at right *(recipe, page 114)*, lettuce is used to wrap a sea bass, but chard or spinach leaves, if large and tender, could be chosen instead. The leaves, made supple by parboiling, are spread out and applied to the fish in an overlapping pattern. They adhere naturally and need not be tied.

Alternatively, you may wrap the fish in foil *(below, right)*, a modern variation on the traditional method of cooking in buttered parchment paper *(page 86)*. Although the aluminum package must be sealed tightly, it should be large enough to allow the steam to circulate around the fish. Technically, the fish—a trout, in this case—is steamed rather than baked.

A stuffing is a delicious, moisturizing supplement to fish cooked in these two ways. Any white fish is flattered by a mildly astringent mixture of spinach, sorrel and herbs. Other combinations include chard and tomatoes or shallots and mushrooms. If the fish has been boned *(pages 24-25)*—as with this sea bass—the flavors of the stuffing will be able to penetrate the flesh more easily. Boning also simplifies serving and allows fish and stuffing to be scooped up together.

Trout—like any other fish—benefits from the inclusion of aromatics in its body cavity, and the flavors will be more concentrated if the fish has been gutted through the gills *(page 19)*. Chopped fennel is used here to perfume the trout; dill could be substituted with equal success. Additional flavor can be provided for the sea bass or the trout by garnishing it with chopped onions or shallots and by moistening it with dry white wine, supplemented, if you like, by fish fumet.

Either fish may be served with its cooking liquid alone, or with a rich sauce such as the one demonstrated for sea bass. The liquid left in the baking dish or foil package after cooking is reduced by boiling, enriched with cream, reduced again, then thickened with butter.

A Natural Sheathing of Leaves

Wrapping the fish in leaves. Stuff the cavity of the fish. Parboil the leaves of two large Boston or Bibb lettuces for 3 seconds and drain them. Overlap the leaves around the fish, first down its belly, then down its back. Sprinkle a buttered baking dish with chopped shallots and lay the fish on top. Add salt and pepper, and enough dry white wine to generously cover the bottom of the dish. If you like, dribble a little dry vermouth over the fish.

A Foil Package to Keep in Steam

Flavoring from within. Gut the fish through its gills*(page 19)*. Finely chop some fennel — either the bulb, as here, or the leaves. Season the fennel with salt and pepper and, with your fingers, push it into the fish's cavity through the gill openings.

Adding more flavor. Fold a large piece of aluminum foil in a rectangle half again as long as the fish. Finely chop some carrots, onions and fennel leaves. Sauté them briefly, scatter them on the foil, lay the stuffed fish on top and sprinkle the fish with more vegetables.

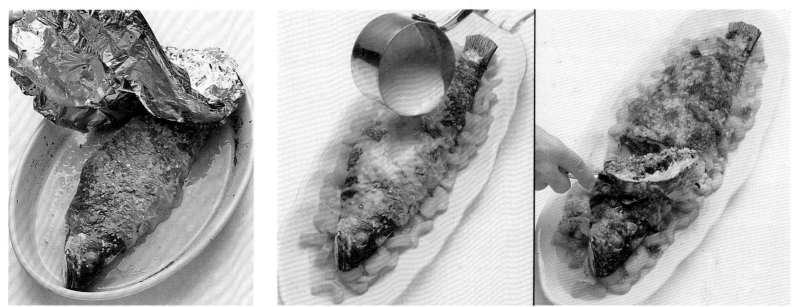

2 **Cooking the fish.** Put butter pieces on the lettuce. Cover the dish and bake in a 450° F. [230° C.] oven, timing the cooking as described on page 51. Baste often during the last 10 minutes of cooking. Transfer the fish to a plate; garnish with sautéed cucumber.

3 **Transforming the juices into a sauce.** Pour the liquid left in the baking dish into a saucepan, and boil rapidly for about 3 to 5 minutes until it reduces to a syrupy consistency. Add heavy cream and boil until the liquid is the consistency of a light white sauce. Take the pan off the heat and whisk in small pieces of cold butter to thicken the sauce. Pour the sauce over the fish *(above, left)*. Cut the boned fish crosswise into steaks for serving *(right)*.

3 **Wrapping the fish.** Lay slices of peeled lemon on top of the fish. Season with salt and pepper. Raise the two long sides of the foil and fold the short ends together so that liquids will not run out. Pour in some olive oil, a little dry vermouth and a little concentrated fish fumet *(above, left)*. Fold the long sides of the foil together. Then fold them again to seal the fish in a loose parcel *(right)*.

4 **Cooking and serving.** Place the fish in a preheated 450° F. [230° C.] oven and cook, allowing 10 minutes per inch of thickness. When the fish is done, transfer the parcel to a platter and unwrap it. To serve, skin the fish *(page 33)* and halve each fillet by cutting down the center line, then lift the fish onto a plate *(above)*.

Capacious Pouches for Stuffing

When you bone a whole fish through its back, you can bake it lying on its belly— and create an open pouch or pocket on top that can be heaped with more stuffing than the confines of the body cavity ordinarily would hold. The baking procedure, once the fish is stuffed, is essentially the same as the basic method demonstrated on pages 52-53, but the final presentation is particularly attractive.

The technique of boning through the back differs according to the fish's shape. A roundfish is boned through cuts along the dorsal fins on each side of the backbone, a flatfish along its backbone on the dark, upper side *(diagrams, page 17)*.

Obviously, if a roundfish has already been gutted through the belly, it will split in half when you cut open the back. A roundfish should therefore be bought whole, and its viscera removed with its backbone and ribs. Fortunately, a number of roundfish—trout *(above, right)*, whiting and small sea bass, for example—are usually sold intact, in serving-sized portions. Flatfish such as sole or flounder, which are gutted through a slit behind their gills, may be bought cleaned and then boned through their backs at home, as demonstrated here with a sole.

Because the stuffing is a visible feature of the finished dish, it should contribute to the appearance as well as the flavor and moisture of the fish. You may use vegetables alone, or combine them with chopped fish, shellfish or fish roe.

In the demonstration above at right *(recipe, page 129)*, the trout is stuffed with a mixture of spinach, butter and chopped onions, then garnished with raw salmon and cooked on a bed of onions moistened with white wine. But the richest stuffing of all—used with the sole at right—is a mousseline *(pages 78-79; recipe, page 166):* a purée of fish, bound with egg white and heavy cream.

The cooking time for most stuffed fish is the standard 10 minutes per inch of thickness; measure the thickness from the top of the mound of stuffing to the bottom of the fish. A fish stuffed with mousseline, however, must be cooked at a lower temperature than usual and for 15 minutes per inch of thickness rather than 10, so that the delicate mixture of egg white and cream will cook properly.

Boning Roundfish through the Back

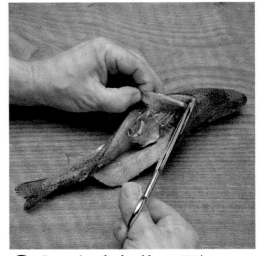

1 **Freeing the backbone.** Place the roundfish—here, a trout, yellow-fleshed from a diet of crustaceans—on its belly. Using a small, sharp knife, cut past each side of the dorsal fin and along the backbone to free the two fillets *(above)*. Do not pierce the belly. Work the backbone and ribs free, from the head to 1 inch [2½ cm.] from the tail.

2 **Removing the backbone.** With a pair of kitchen scissors, sever the backbone at the head *(above)* and tail. Pull out the backbone. Some of the fish's viscera will probably come out with the backbone; scrape out the rest of them with your fingers.

A Boning Variation for Flatfish

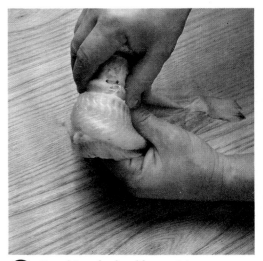

1 **Separating the fillets.** Skin the dark, upper side of the flatfish *(page 19)* — here, a sole. Using a sharp, flexible knife, slice through the flesh down to the backbone along its length. Turn the knife toward one side of the fish; with the blade almost flat against the bones, cut away one fillet to the edge of the fish. Repeat with the other fillet, then fold back both fillets to expose the ribs on both sides of the backbone.

2 **Breaking the backbone.** It is easier to remove the backbone in sections than to remove it in one piece. Bend the middle section of the fish until the backbone snaps in the middle. Change your hold on the fish and bend the backbone once more to break it in a different place. Repeat this procedure two or three times.

3 **Removing the gills.** Pull back the fish's head so that you can insert your thumb and forefinger into the gill opening on one side, and grasp the gill. Carefully pull out the gill. Repeat on the other side. Rinse and dry the fish.

4 **Stuffing the fish.** Stuff the empty space, pushing in the stuffing as far as the head. Arrange the fish on a bed of chopped shallots or onions in a buttered baking dish. Place pieces of raw salmon and slivers of butter on top of the fish and pour a little white wine over all.

5 **Cooking the fish.** Cover the dish with buttered parchment paper or aluminum foil. Bake in a preheated 425° F. [220° C.] oven for about 15 minutes or until the flesh at the edge of the pocket begins to flake. If you like, pour a tablespoon [15 ml.] of heated heavy cream over the fish before serving.

3 **Removing the bones.** Pull out all the broken sections of backbone, together with the ribs attached to them (above). Leave the fins on each side in place to support the fish.

4 **Stuffing the fish.** Salt and pepper the pocket between the two folded-back fillets. Fill the pouch with the stuffing — in this case, a mousseline. Pour a little fish fumet into a shallow baking dish, place the stuffed fish in the dish and cover it loosely with buttered parchment paper, wax paper or aluminum foil.

5 **Serving the fish.** Bake the fish in a preheated 350° F. [180° C.] oven for about 15 minutes per inch of thickness. During cooking, the mousseline will swell. With a broad spatula, transfer the fish to a warmed platter. If you like, garnish the fish with vegetables — here, sautéed mushrooms and grilled tomato halves.

The Challenge of a Broiler's Drying Heat

Keeping Steaks Juicy

Properly done, broiling is unsurpassed as a way of bringing out the flavor of fresh fish. Because of the intense, dry heat involved, the process demands a critical eye and undivided attention if overcooking is to be avoided.

Any fish, fat or lean, may be broiled in any form—whole, cut into steaks, cubed to make kebabs or filleted. As a general rule, the fish must be at least ¾ inch [2 cm.] thick so that it broils slowly enough for you to control the process—by lowering the broiler rack if the fish is drying out or browning too fast. Long, thin fillets also can be broiled if handled by a special technique: they are pushed onto skewers and turned sideways to present a cross section of ¾ inch or more to the heat, as shown opposite.

If you are broiling a whole lean fish—snapper or trout—leave the head and tail on; this will minimize the loss of natural juices that protect against drying. Whether whole or cut up, lean fish require frequent basting with oil, clarified butter *(page 65)* or an oil-based marinade. Fattier fish—tuna, swordfish, sablefish—require only occasional basting because of their abundant natural oil.

Any fish destined for broiling gains a generous bonus of flavor if it is first steeped in a marinade for an hour or two in the refrigerator. Most marinades combine oil and an acidic element—dry wine, lemon juice or vinegar—plus herbs or spices. Marinades for very fatty fish, however, should contain only a small amount of oil or none at all.

The actual broiling procedure varies very little from fish to fish and cut to cut. Before you begin, remove the broiler rack and its pan and preheat the broiler for at least 15 minutes. To prevent sticking, oil the rack—unless you are making kebabs over a pan *(opposite, top)*. Adjust the broiler pan and rack under the broiler so that the top of the fish will be 4 to 6 inches [10 to 15 cm.] from the heat—the thicker the fish, the greater the distance. This ensures that the outside flesh will not overcook before the inside is done.

Plan on broiling the fish for 10 minutes per inch [2½ cm.] of thickness, but lower the pan and rack at the first sign that the fish is browning too fast.

1 Marinating the steaks. Place the steaks—here, sablefish—in a shallow dish and marinate. In this case the marinade is lemon juice, oregano, minced garlic and snipped fresh dill. Marinate the steaks for 1 hour in the refrigerator, turning them once.

2 Preparing to broil. Remove the broiler pan with its rack. Preheat the broiler at the highest setting for about 15 minutes. Oil the rack before placing the marinated steaks on it. Reserve the marinade for basting.

3 Broiling the fish. Slide the rack, still in its pan, under the broiler. Since these steaks are about 1 inch [2½ cm.] thick, they are positioned about 4 inches [10 cm.] below the heat source. Broil the steaks for about 10 minutes, turning them with a spatula halfway through the timing period. Baste the steaks occasionally with the marinade.

4 Testing for doneness. When the surfaces of the steaks are lightly browned *(above),* they should be ready to serve. Test for doneness by slipping a small knife or skewer between the backbone and the flesh; if the fish is sufficiently cooked, the flesh will separate easily from the bone.

Combining Fish Chunks with Vegetables

1 **Preparing ingredients.** Choose a steak about 1½ inches [4 cm.] thick, cut from a large, firm-fleshed fish such as this tuna. Cut the steak into cubes *(above)*. Prepare the vegetables; in this picture cucumbers have been peeled, halved, seeded and cut into segments that are about 1 inch [2½ cm.] thick.

2 **Marinating and skewering.** Put the fish and vegetables in a dish and pour a marinade over them — here, a mixture of white wine, soy sauce and melted butter. Turn the pieces, then let them steep in the refrigerator. After 1 hour, skewer the pieces *(above)*, alternating fish and vegetables. Balance the skewers across a shallow pan.

3 **Broiling the brochettes.** Place the pan under a preheated broiler on a shelf set about 6 inches [15 cm.] below the heat source. Cook for 15 minutes, turning the skewers occasionally and basting the fish frequently with the marinade. Serve from the skewers, pushing the pieces free with the back of a fork.

Skewering Fillet Strips

1 **Marinating the fillets.** Skin the fillets *(page 23)* and wipe them with a damp cloth. Marinate the fillets; flounder fillets are shown being steeped in vinegar and oil mixed with paprika, scallions and red pepper. Just before broiling, remove the fillets from the marinade and cut them into 1-inch [2½-cm.] strips *(above)*. Reserve the marinade.

2 **Broiling the strips.** Thread each skewer through a fillet at 2- to 3-inch [5- to 8-cm.] intervals along its length, adding a second fillet if there is room. Place the skewered fillets on their narrow edges on an oiled broiler rack. Broil 4 inches [10 cm.] from the heat for 10 minutes, basting with marinade and turning the fillets after 5 minutes.

3 **Serving the fillets.** When the fish is golden brown, remove the skewers from the broiler. Rest the tip of each one on a warmed platter, steady the fillet with the back of a fork and pull out the skewer.

The Ways and Means of Barbecuing

A Basket Designed for Flat Portions

Any whole fish, fillet or steak that can be broiled in an oven can be barbecued outdoors over hot coals. Fish with assertive flavors—mackerel or bluefish, for example—are good choices for this method, as their tastes are especially complemented by the distinctive, smoky flavor barbecuing gives the flesh.

The fish should be whole or thickly cut, just as they are for broiling. And, as in broiling, oily fish require only a little basting during cooking since their natural oils help keep the flesh moist. Lean fish should be marinated beforehand and liberally basted during cooking.

The major difference between barbecuing and broiling is the equipment. It is possible, but difficult, to turn fish on the rack of an outdoor grill without breaking up their fragile flesh. A simple solution is to clamp the fish into hinged, basket-like metal grills that can be turned over, fish and all, to cook both sides of the flesh.

Steaks and fillets can be barbecued in a flat, rectangular grilling basket such as the one shown at right; the cook balances it on the edges of the grill during cooking. Large, plump fish, however, would be mashed in such a basket; they require a fish-shaped grilling basket that has legs on both sides to hold the fish about 4 inches [10 cm.] above the coals (opposite). Whole fish are best cooked complete with their heads and tails, but you may have to cut them off, as shown, to fit the fish into the grilling basket.

Barbecue grills must, of course, be preheated. Turn on outdoor electric or gas grills 15 minutes before cooking time, but light charcoal 30 to 40 minutes in advance to give it time to develop the even film of white ash that indicates it has reached the correct temperature.

No matter what type of grill you have, place the fish 4 inches above the heat source, where the cooking temperature will be a moderate 350° F. [180° C.]. As a general rule, barbecue fish for about 10 minutes per inch of thickness. Watch the fish carefully, however, and begin testing for doneness (pages 53 and 58) well before the cooking time is up; humidity, wind, even air currents can affect the grill's heat—and the fish's cooking time.

1 **Preparing the grill.** Spread the hot coals in one even layer. Oil the grill basket, baste the fish — here, halibut steaks are coated with melted butter, white wine, lemon juice and herbs — and place them on the basket. Position it 4 inches [10 cm.] above the coals.

2 **Barbecuing the steaks.** As the fish steaks cook in the closed grill basket, brush them repeatedly with the basting mixture. Halfway through the cooking time, carefully turn over the basket. Continue basting the steaks.

3 **Boning the steaks.** When both sides are lightly browned, place the steaks on a cutting board. At the center of each steak, stick the tine of a large fork into the backbone, lifting it — and all attached bones — away from the flesh. Then serve the steaks.

A Free-standing Container for Whole Fish

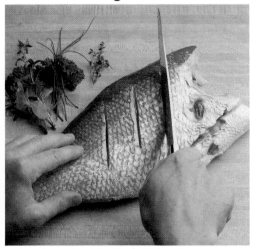

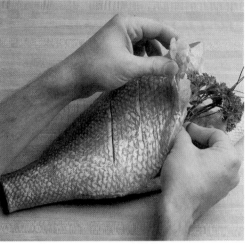

1 **Preparing the fish.** Clean the fish — this is a red snapper — and cut off its head and tail if necessary to make it fit the grilling basket. Cut three shallow diagonal slashes about 4 inches [10 cm.] long and 2 inches [5 cm.] apart into each side of the fish so that the marinade can penetrate into the flesh.

2 **Flavoring from within.** Stuff the cavity of the fish with sprigs of fresh herbs — in this case, parsley, thyme, basil, winter savory and chives. Do not truss the fish: the basket will hold it closed during cooking.

3 **Marinating the fish.** Place the fish in a deep dish and pour marinade over it. The marinade used here is a mixture of olive oil and seeded, puréed tomatoes with chopped basil, garlic and parsley. Rub some of the marinade over the top of the fish. Cover the dish and let the fish marinate for 2 hours in the refrigerator, turning the fish over once.

4 **Preparing to cook.** Remove the fish from the marinade and place it in the grilling basket; close the grill and clasp the handles securely together. The grilling basket need not be oiled: the marinade left on the fish will prevent sticking. Clear a space in the center of the hot coals so that you can stand the basket in the bottom of the grill.

5 **Barbecuing.** For even cooking, bank extra coals around the space at the thick end of the fish. Baste the fish through the basket with marinade. Halfway through the cooking time, turn the basket over. When the fish is browned, test for doneness and remove it to a platter. Fillet the fish for serving (page 31).

4

Frying
Sealing in Succulence

When fish are fried, their flesh is exposed to temperatures that range as high as 375° F. [190° C.]—more than twice the temperature involved in poaching. Such heat causes the protein in the skin or surface flesh to coagulate and form a seal that preserves the flavor of the fish. The cooking—whether by deep frying, pan frying or stir frying—then proceeds so rapidly that a minute or two may make the difference between a perfectly cooked fish and a dry one. For this reason, the cook should be ready to remove the fish from the pan the moment it is done; to avoid distractions, any accompanying sauces should be made beforehand.

The best fish for frying are lean, firm-fleshed types; oily fish such as shad or salmon are not ordinarily fried, as they produce overrich results. Pan frying or sautéing—cooking in a shallow layer of oil or fat—is an excellent method for whole small- to medium-sized fish, fillets and steaks. It is the gentlest form of frying, ideal for easily broken fish roe *(pages 66-67)* and fish cakes *(pages 74-75)*.

Chinese stir frying is a briefer version of pan frying, and deep frying calls for immersion in a deep layer of oil or fat. The high heat used in both of these methods limits the size of the fish that can be cooked; large fish and thick fillets dry and scorch on the outside before they are done within. Small fish and thin fillets are therefore the most suitable candidates for deep frying; small pieces of fillet are most easily tossed in the hot pan used for stir frying.

Among the frying mediums, butter can be used only for pan frying, and even then it should be clarified *(page 65)* or mixed with oil, since plain butter smokes and burns at 248° F. [120° C.]. For deep frying or stir frying, corn or peanut oils are the best choices: these oils can be heated safely to 518° F. [270° C.] and they both have neutral flavors that will not mask the taste of the fish. Some cooks, preferring its distinctive flavor, use lard, which can be heated as high as 392° F. [200° C.].

However they are fried, fish are almost always given a preliminary coating that shields their flesh from the searing heat. In pan frying, fish may be dusted with flour or cornmeal only; in deep frying, fish need more protection and should be enveloped in batter or eggs and crumbs, which also give them a delicious, crisp crust. For stir frying, Chinese cooks use a coating of egg white and cornstarch to produce a satiny finish.

A batter-coated cod fillet is lifted from hot oil while a second piece cooks in the pan. The batter holds in the fish's natural juices and protects its flesh from drying at the high temperature required for deep frying. It also forms a crisp crust for the tender fish within.

A Straightforward Sauté

French by name but universally adopted for fish, cooking *à la meunière*—literally, "in the style of the miller's wife"—is the most straightforward form of frying: the fish is coated with flour, sautéed and served with a sauce of hot butter. In the pan, the flour forms a thin golden crust around the flesh, sealing in the juices and keeping the fish moist and tender.

Cooking *à la meunière* is closely associated with sole, shown here; however, any firm, white-fleshed fish—flounder, trout or perch, for example—is suitable. If you are frying a whole flatfish, first remove the tough dark skin on the upper side; this simplifies the task of filleting the fish after it is cooked *(page 31)*. Round-fish can be cooked either whole and unskinned or in fillets.

Fry the fish in a mild vegetable oil, in a half-and-half combination of oil and butter, or—shown here—in clarified butter *(box, opposite)*. Do not use plain butter; it will blacken and burn at the high temperature required for cooking *à la meunière*. Choose a skillet that holds the fish snugly; the more the oil or fat is covered by the fish, the less chance that it will burn. An oval skillet is ideal for flatfish.

For best results, fry fish less than ½ inch thick [1 cm.] over a high heat; by the time the coating has turned crisp and brown, the fish will be done. Start larger fish and thick fillets, which take longer to cook through, over high heat to set the coating; then reduce the heat to prevent drying as you pan fry them to doneness.

When the fish is done, remove it from the pan, and prepare the extra butter used for saucing *(Step 4, opposite)*. Pour the sauce over the fish just before serving: if the sauced fish stands for more than a few seconds, the butter will soak into the crust and turn it soggy. The finished dish may be garnished with parsley and slices of lemon or toasted almonds; more elaborate garnishes would detract from the finely balanced flavors of the fish and the butter.

1 **Coating the fish with flour.** Dampen the flesh of the fish — this is a sole — with milk or water so that the flour will adhere to it. Season the fish with salt and pepper. Spread out the flour on a plate, then dip each side of the fish in the flour *(above)*. Lay the coated fish on a wire rack for a moment to set the coating.

2 **Heating the butter.** Heat a ⅛-inch [3-mm.] layer of clarified butter in a skillet until a bread cube dropped into it sizzles and immediately begins to brown. Gently lay the fish (marked in this case by the grid of the rack) in the pan.

3 **Frying the fish.** Cook the fish until the underside turns golden brown—from 3 to 5 minutes for a whole sole. Carefully turn over the fish *(above)*, and fry it for about the same length of time. Lift the fish onto a hot serving dish. Garnish with lemon and parsley.

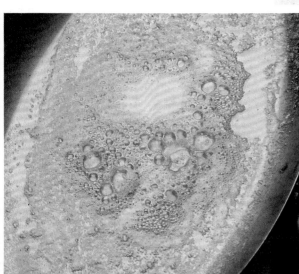

4 **Preparing the sauce.** Pour the butter out of the skillet. Put a generous knob of plain butter in the pan and heat it until it begins to froth *(above)* and turn golden. Pour the butter sauce over the fish *(right)* and serve.

Ridding Butter of Burnable Solids

To keep butter from burning during pan frying, you must clarify it by cooking off the water it contains and then removing the so-called milk solids—particles of protein and minerals—which smoke at fairly low temperatures. The end product is pure fat that may be heated up to 375° F. [190° C.]—high enough to crisp the coatings on fish or other delicate, pan-fried foods.

Clarifying butter is just about as simple as melting it. The butter is warmed slowly over low heat until the fat liquifies, some watery froth rises to the surface and the proteins and minerals sink to the bottom of the pan. The froth is then skimmed off and the liquid fat is decanted. The solids may be added to soups or sauces to give them extra flavor and food value. The clarified butter may be used immediately or it can be stored, covered, in the refrigerator for as long as three weeks.

1 **Skimming the foam.** Cut butter into small pieces, allowing one third more butter than you need for the recipe. Melt the pieces — do not brown them — over low heat. When the butter melts, turn off the heat and let the liquid cool for a few minutes. Skim off any foam with a spoon or a wire-mesh skimmer.

2 **Decanting the liquid fat.** Set the butter aside for 20 to 30 minutes to let the sediment settle to the bottom of the pan. Gently pour the transparent fat into a bowl or pitcher *(above)*, leaving the solids behind. If solids remain in the liquid, strain it through two layers of dampened cheesecloth.

A Simple Treatment for a Seasonal Luxury

Early each year—from January through May, depending on the species—most female fish produce a delicious bonus of eggs, or roe. Around the world, the roe of various fish—the Russian beluga sturgeon is the paragon among donors—are salted to make caviar. Roe is also eaten fresh, baked, broiled or—most delectably—pan fried in butter or bacon fat.

The most famous of American roes is that of the shad, shown here; this delicacy is widely available in markets along the Atlantic Coast; West Coast cooks must depend on angler friends for shad roe. Herring roe, too, is sometimes available commercially, especially in the New England states and Maritime Provinces. But fishermen can reserve and eat the roe of almost any fish they hook: yellow perch, walleyed pike, mullet, salmon, flounder, tuna and halibut among them. The only exceptions are the roe of gar, great barracuda, puffer and trunkfish, which are toxic.

The eggs of a fish are clustered inside a pair of oval sacs or lobes, connected at one end by a thick blood vessel. Each lobe is covered by a paper-thin, transparent inner membrane, which is edible, and a thicker, loose-fitting outer membrane, which is not. Freshness is of paramount importance. Do not buy roe that looks dried out or clouded—it will be soft and mushy and smell of rotten fish—and do not store roe for longer than a day.

Wash roe just before cooking it, handling the lobes carefully to avoid tearing the fragile inner membrane, which holds the eggs together and retains their juiciness during frying. Use the same care when separating the pair of lobes from the blood vessel between them.

The cooking itself should be kept simple; extravagant sauces and embellishments are out of place with fresh roe. Some cooks insist on frying roe in clarified butter, as here, for its delicate flavor; others consider bacon fat a proper complement to the faintly fishy taste of roe, and they serve the crisp bacon with the roe (recipes, pages 94 and 151). In either case, the roe should first be coated with flour, which helps protect against drying or breaking, and forms a thin, crisp crust on the surfaces of the lobes to provide a subtle contrast to the soft roe within.

1 Washing the roe. Dip the roe gently in a bowl of cold water: the force of running tap water might tear the surface membrane that holds the eggs together. Drain the roe on several layers of paper towels, turning the roe over carefully to dry it on all sides.

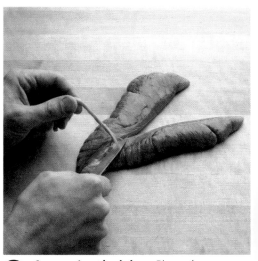

2 Separating the lobes. Place the roe on a cutting board and lift the free end of the thick, gristle-like membrane that joins the lobes. Hold this up with one hand and slice it away from the lobes.

6 Turning the roe. Slide a wide spatula under one lobe and brace the top of the lobe with another spatula so that you can turn over the roe gently. Repeat with the other lobes. Cook the second sides for 5 to 7 minutes. To test for doneness, make a small slit through the membranes to reveal the eggs within. If they are opaque and brown, the roe is done.

3 **Cutting the lobes apart.** A thick vein joins the lobes at one end. With a sharp knife, slice down through the vein to separate the lobes. With the tip of a needle, prick the membrane covering each lobe in several places so that it will not burst as it cooks.

4 **Coating with flour.** Put flour onto a plate. Gently turn each lobe of roe in the flour to coat it thoroughly. Put the roe on a clean plate, cover it with wax paper and let it rest for 15 minutes.

5 **Frying the roe.** Melt a thin layer of clarified butter in a skillet over moderate heat. When the butter develops a light haze, lower the heat and gently place the lobes of roe in the pan. Baste the tops of the lobes with some of the butter and cook until the roe is brown on the bottom — about 5 minutes.

7 **Serving the roe.** Season the lobes of roe with salt and pepper and sprinkle them with lemon juice. Transfer them to a heated platter. The pan juices may be made into a light sauce by adding lemon juice, chopped parsley and other chopped fresh herbs such as dill or tarragon. Pour the sauce over the roe.

Two Stages for a Perfect Stir Fry

Stir-fried fish pieces emerge from the pan with what Chinese cooks call a "velvet" surface—a smooth, soft finish quite unlike the crisp crust usually associated with frying. Another integral part of the dish is a distinctive light sauce that is quickly formed during the final seconds of cooking. Success with both the surface of the fish pieces and the sauce depends on proper preparation and cooking methods unique to this form of frying.

Choose firm-textured fish such as sea bass or the sole used in this demonstration *(recipe, page 147);* soft-textured fish such as shad tend to fall apart during the rapid tossing that gives the technique its name. To ensure that the fish cook as quickly as possible, they are first filleted, then cut into thin slices.

Before cooking the fish pieces, steep them in a mixture of egg white and cornstarch. During the steeping, the natural moisture of the fish binds the coating to the flesh. A brief preliminary cooking—in oil for a firm coating, in water for a softer one—seals the cornstarch mixture so that when the pieces are stir fried they actually steam inside their coating.

Stir frying itself requires no special equipment. The traditional vessel is a wok, whose sloping sides allow the fish to be tossed easily; however, you may use any large skillet made of a metal, such as aluminum, that conducts heat well.

Vegetable oil is always used for stir frying, and it should be a lightly flavored type that will not overwhelm the other ingredients. A peanut oil is the usual choice. As you heat the oil before frying, you may enhance its flavor by sautéing in it seasonings such as garlic, ginger and red peppers; the oil will absorb the flavors and transfer them to the fish. During the final moments of frying, the oil is turned into a sauce thickened with cornstarch and enlivened by such ingredients as rice wine or sherry, soy sauce, dark sesame-seed oil or white vinegar.

Because stir frying must be completed in moments once the actual frying begins, the cook should have all ingredients organized near the stove ahead of time. Follow the timing instructions given in this demonstration for all fish.

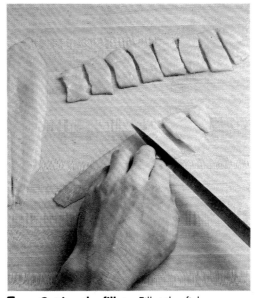

1 Cutting the fillets. Fillet the fish *(pages 22-23)* — petrale sole is used here — and wipe the fillets with a damp paper towel. Halve the fillets lengthwise, then cut each half crosswise into narrow strips.

2 Coating the fish. Beat the egg white to just break it up; do not allow it to become frothy, lest it puff up during cooking. Stir in the cornstarch and a pinch of salt. Turn the fish pieces in the mixture to coat them, then remove them and refrigerate for 30 minutes.

5 Stir frying. Chop the seasonings that will flavor the oil — garlic, ginger root and sweet red peppers are used here. Heat the wok over high heat until a drop of water sizzles upon contact. Return 2 tablespoons [30 ml.] of the reserved oil to the wok. After 30 seconds, lower the heat to medium, add the ginger root and stir for 5 seconds *(left)*. Add the garlic and red peppers. Stir for another 5 seconds. Raise the heat to medium high and add the fish.

3 **Cooking the fish pieces.** Heat 1 cup [¼ liter] of oil in the wok over medium heat until the oil reaches 275° F. [140° C.] on a deep-frying thermometer or until a bread crumb thrown in the wok sizzles slowly while browning. Immediately add the coated fish pieces. Stir the pieces to separate them, then turn them in the oil for 30 to 45 seconds until the coating turns white.

4 **Draining the fish.** Remove the fish pieces and drain them through a strainer set over a bowl. Strain and reserve the cooking oil. Mix the sauce ingredients — in this case, cornstarch and water flavored with sugar, sherry, vinegar, sesame-seed oil and soy sauce.

6 **Adding the sauce.** Toss the fish in the oil for 10 seconds, then pour the well-mixed sauce ingredients over the fish and continue tossing for about 1 minute. As the sauce reaches a boil, it will form a thick glaze. Turn the fish quickly in the glaze *(left)* to coat all the pieces. Remove the fish from the wok and serve immediately on a warmed platter.

Crisp Coatings for Texture and Flavor

A simple tactic that yields munificent dividends in pan frying is to first moisten the fish, then coat it with a dry, starchy ingredient. During cooking, the coating keeps the flesh from drying out; at the same time, the protective envelope is transformed into a crisp crust that provides the finished dish with contrasting tastes and textures.

Any lean, small whole fish, steak or fillet may be fried this way. If the fish is not purchased in cut-up form, its head and tail ideally should be left on to help the flesh retain moisture. Catfish heads must be cut off *(above, right)* because they bear spiky fins; the tail of a pan-fried catfish, however, is appetizingly crunchy. Tough, leathery catfish skin must be peeled off before the fish is fried. Skin other fish or not, as you choose; an intact skin will give a sharper flavor to the finished dish.

Fillets and steaks usually are fried whole. Fillets may also be cut into strips known as *goujonnettes*. This attractive treatment—shown below with sole—derives its name from a European fish, the gudgeon, which is customarily fried with a bread-crumb coating.

Coatings often consist of alternate layers of liquid and dry ingredients. The liquids may be milk, beaten eggs or melted butter. The choice in dry ingredients includes flour, cornmeal, cracker-, cereal- or bread crumbs, or any combination of these. As shown here in the demonstration with catfish *(recipe, page 148)*, whole fish usually are given a thick coating composed of four or more liquid and dry layers that will protect the flesh during the relatively long cooking. Steaks or fillets cook so briefly that they can be safely fried in thinner, two-layer coatings.

The coated fish is pan fried in no more than ¼ inch [6 mm.] of oil or fat—enough to prevent sticking. Vegetable oils, which stand high temperatures for long periods without burning, usually are used for whole fish. Quick-cooking fillets may be fried in oil, clarified butter *(page 65)* or half oil and half plain butter.

The oil or fat must be hot but not smoking when the fish goes into the pan. If the oil or fat is too cool, the coating will become heavy and soggy; if it is too hot, the coating will burn before the fish cooks.

Cornmeal: An American Tradition

1 **Coating the fish.** Dip the fish in milk, then roll them in flour to coat them lightly but thoroughly. Shake off any excess flour and dip the fish into beaten eggs. Then roll the fish in cornmeal. Place the fish on a wire rack set on a baking sheet or wax paper; leave them for 15 minutes or until the coating dries.

2 **Frying the fish.** Choose a skillet just large enough to hold the fish side by side. Pour oil into the skillet about ¼ inch [6 mm.] deep and warm over medium heat until a bread crumb dropped into it sizzles. Lay the fish in the pan without letting them touch one another.

Buttery Bread Crumbs: A French Favorite

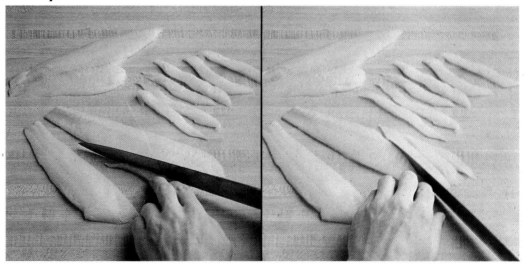

1 **Preparing the fillets.** Halve each whole sole fillet. Slice off any tiny bones that cling to the cut edge of each fillet half *(left)*. Trim off the bony outer edges and pluck out any tiny bones that remain in the flesh. Then slice the fillet halves diagonally *(right)* to produce strips about ½ inch [1 cm.] wide.

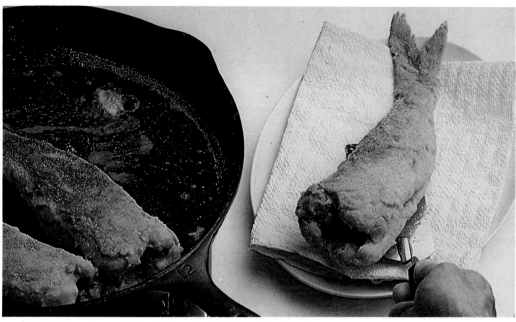

3 **Turning the fish.** Allow 10 minutes' cooking time for each inch [2½ cm.] of thickness. When half the time is up, and the bottom surfaces are crisp and brown, turn the fish, using two spatulas to avoid breaking the crusts.

4 **Finishing the cooking.** When the fish have fried on the second side, test them for doneness by gently separating the flesh near the backbone; a wooden pick or skewer can be used. If the flesh is white and opaque rather than translucent, the fish are done. Remove them from the pan and drain them on paper towels.

2 **Coating the strips.** Dip the strips one at a time into melted butter and shake off the excess. Immediately roll each strip in fresh, dry bread crumbs to coat it lightly on all sides.

3 **Securing the coating.** Press each strip firmly with your hand, making sure the crumbs adhere to the flesh. Set the strips aside on wax paper or a plate for 15 to 20 minutes to firm the coating.

4 **Frying the fish.** Melt clarified butter in a skillet over medium heat. When the butter forms a light haze, add the fish strips; do not crowd them. Cook for 2 or 3 minutes, until the bottoms brown, then turn the strips and cook them for 2 minutes more. When the second sides brown, remove the strips, drain on paper towels and serve.

Deep Frying Small Fish

The heat involved in deep frying is so high that every precaution must be taken against overcooking fish. Fish or fish pieces thicker than 1½ inches [4 cm.] are not suitable for deep frying: they will overcook on the outsides before the insides are done. The fish may be small pieces cut from steaks and fillets, thin whole fillets or tiny whole fish no longer than 5 to 6 inches [13 to 15 cm.]—such as smelt or the whitebait shown at right. Deep frying has a special advantage for tiny fish: it softens their hard-to-remove bones and makes them edible.

A deep-fried fish needs some kind of coating to help the flesh retain its moisture. Batter provides an effective shield and yields a flavorful crust *(opposite)*. However, small whole fish are partially protected by their skins and may be given a simpler coating of flour or bread crumbs, which will develop into thin, crisp crusts when fried.

For deep frying, the correct vessel is a heavy metal pan. Choose one that is deep enough for the fish to be immersed in oil or fat when the pan is no more than half full. Deep-frying pans should never be filled beyond that point because of the danger that the hot fat may bubble over when the fish are added.

The oil must be preheated for the fish coating to seal crisply. The ideal cooking temperature is 375° F. [190° C.]. If the oil is hotter, the coating may brown too rapidly and burn; if it is cooler, the coating will absorb too much fat, with soggy rather than crisp results. Test the oil temperature with a deep-frying thermometer, or throw a small cube of bread into the oil; at the correct temperature, the bread will brown in about 30 seconds.

Remember that the temperature of the oil will drop when food is placed in it. To minimize the cooling effect, cook the fish in small batches. Keep each batch warm in a 200° F. [100° C.] oven until all the fish are fried and ready to serve.

1 **Flouring the fish.** Fill the bottom of a paper bag with flour seasoned with salt, pepper and cayenne pepper. A handful at a time, shake the whitebait in the bag to coat them with flour.

2 **Removing excess flour.** Toss the coated fish gently in a sieve to shake off excess flour. Let them rest 10 minutes to set the coating, then flour and toss again.

3 **Deep frying.** Drop the fish by small handfuls into the pan of hot oil — or into a deep-frying basket *(opposite)*. Cook for about 1 minute, until the fish are lightly browned. Remove the fish; drain them.

4 **Frying parsley.** After cooking the fish, skim the oil to remove bits of batter, and drop in a handful of rinsed and dried parsley. Cook the parsley for a few seconds, then lift it out and drain it.

5 **Serving the dish.** Garnish the finished dish with the fried parsley and some lemon halves or wedges. Traditionally, whitebait are served on a white cloth napkin, which helps to absorb any remaining oil.

Extra Protection from an Egg-based Batter

Fish pieces to be batter fried should be cut to approximately the same size so that they cook in the same amount of time. Dry each piece thoroughly to ensure that the batter adheres to the flesh.

Batter mixtures are made of seasoned flour, beaten eggs and a liquid—either water, milk or beer; the use of beer produces a very crunchy crust with a faintly bitter tang that sets off the flavor of the fish. Batter that contains beaten egg whites will be exceptionally light and airy, and the addition of baking powder will cause a batter to puff up.

Whatever batter you choose, make it thick enough to provide an even covering—it should have the consistency of lightly whipped cream. Beat the mixture only long enough to eliminate lumps, then let it rest at room temperature for 1 hour before using it. During this period, the flour will absorb the liquid and will cling better to the fish.

1 **Cutting chunks.** Cut the fish — here, halibut steaks — into 1½-inch [4-cm.] chunks. Cut crosses about ⅓ inch [1 cm.] deep in the bottom and top of each chunk *(above)* so that its inside will be cooked when the batter is golden.

2 **Coating the fish.** Dry the chunks with paper towels. Whisk the prepared batter to make sure it is thoroughly mixed and dip the chunks of fish into it, coating each piece completely.

3 **Frying the fish.** Lift the fish chunks from the batter and allow excess batter to drain off. Then drop a few chunks — one by one, to keep them from sticking together — into a deep-frying pan half filled with hot oil; the pan used here is fitted with a deep-frying basket for easy removal and draining of the fish.

4 **Draining the fish.** Fry the fish 5 to 6 minutes, turning them to brown all sides. When the batter coating is crisp and golden brown, the fish are done; lift out the frying basket and let the fish pieces drain for a few seconds over the pan. Transfer them to paper towels on a pan inside a warm oven while you fry the rest of the fish.

Cakes Fashioned from Cooked Fish

Like whole fish or fish portions, cakes made with flakes of cooked fish profit from frying. Brief contact with hot fat or oil crisps the surfaces of the cakes—or such shape variants as balls or sticks—and cooks them through without drying them out. For pan frying, cakes or sticks should be no more than ½ inch [1 cm.] thick; because of this size limit, balls are a less suitable shape. To withstand the high temperatures and the immersion of deep frying, cakes, sticks or balls should be about 1 inch [2½ cm.] thick.

Any fresh- or salt-water fish can provide the flakes. The fish can be cooked especially for this purpose, or it can be a leftover, provided it has no rich sauce or coating or marinade to interfere with the taste and texture of the cakes.

In the demonstration of pan frying fish cakes at right *(recipe, page 149)*, the fish is salt cod, which possesses a pleasantly firm, almost chewy quality. A legacy from the days of sailing ships, when fish had to be salt-cured to survive the long journey from fishing grounds to market, salt cod hardens and dries during the preserving process.

To prepare it for use in cakes—and in a broad array of other dishes, ranging from the baked salt cod with tomatoes and peppers *(recipe, page 117)* to the Sicilian cod fish stew *(recipe, page 104)*—soak the cod in cold water overnight to restore its tenderness and to remove its saltiness *(Step 2, bottom right)*. Then poach it, remove the skin and bones and separate the flesh into large flakes that will keep their identity when they are mixed with other ingredients.

The fish mixture for cakes always includes starch to supply body—bread or cracker crumbs, cooked oatmeal or, as shown here, a combination of crumbs and boiled, mashed potatoes. Eggs bind the cakes together and flavor them. The eggs may be added whole, or the whites may be beaten stiff and added to the mixture just before frying to give the cakes lightness. Including grated cheese, grated onion, minced garlic, chopped celery, parsley or fresh herbs enhances both the taste and the texture of the cakes.

1 Flaking the fish. Dry the flesh of the cooked fish on paper towels to rid it of any excess moisture. Put the flesh in a bowl and break it into large flakes about ¼ to ½ inch [6 mm. to 1 cm.] thick by pulling it apart with two forks.

2 Adding seasonings and eggs. Add flavoring ingredients—freshly grated Parmesan cheese, minced garlic and chopped parsley are used here—to the bowl of fish. Stir in eggs to help bind together the finished cakes.

Reconstituting Salt Cod

1 Cutting up salt cod. Gutted and opened out before preserving, whole cod has a triangular shape. If you buy it whole rather than in pieces, slice the fish *(above)* into sections that will fit into the bowl you plan to use for soaking.

2 Soaking the cod. Put the cod in the bowl and cover it with cold water. Refrigerate the bowl and let the cod soak for at least 12 hours, pouring off and replacing the water at least three times. The fish will be ready for cooking when it has roughly doubled in volume, but you can leave it soaking for up to 48 hours if you want a fish with only a mildly briny taste.

3 **Filling out the mixture.** Add mashed potatoes and bread crumbs and mix the ingredients lightly with your fingers. The mixture should be firm enough to form into cakes. If it is not, add more potatoes or bread crumbs.

4 **Forming the cakes.** Pat the fish mixture into cakes ½ inch [1 cm.] thick and about 3 inches [8 cm.] in diameter. Heat a ⅛- to ¼-inch [3- to 6-mm.] layer half of butter and half of vegetable oil in a heavy skillet over medium-high heat.

5 **Frying the cakes.** When the oil mixture is hot enough to sizzle a crumb of bread on contact, put the cakes in the pan. Keep the heat medium high to prevent the cakes from soaking up oil. After 2 to 3 minutes, when the cake bottoms are golden brown, turn the cakes. When the second sides are golden brown, drain the cakes.

3 **Poaching the cod.** Transfer the cod to a pan full of fresh, cold water. Add a sprig of thyme and a bay leaf. Heat the water gently until it just simmers, ladle off the scum that forms on the surface *(above)*, then reduce the heat until the surface of the water barely trembles.

4 **Removing skin and bones.** Continue poaching the fish until the thickest part of the flesh flakes apart easily when it is probed with a knife — about 10 minutes. Drain the fish and discard the poaching water unless your recipe calls for it. Peel off the fish's fatty skin *(above, left)*. Separate the fish into large flakes *(right)*. Remove the exposed bones with your fingers.

Special Presentations
Tempting Textures and Combinations

By adding a few refinements to familiar cooking methods, you can transform any fish into the most dramatic of dishes. Making an envelope of parchment paper called a papillote or forming a fish-shaped pastry crust provides decorative packaging for whole fish or fillets. Applying an aspic coating gives a whole, cold, cooked fish a glittering surface. And puréeing raw fish with egg whites and cream produces a mousseline, a versatile amalgam that is one of the glories of French cuisine.

Most cooks nowadays prepare a mousseline with an electric food processor or food mill. Although the results are entirely creditable, the old-fashioned method of pounding the fish in a large, heavy mortar *(pages 78-79)* will produce the silkiest texture of all. Because of the presence of egg whites, the mousseline will become lighter still when it is cooked—by any one of a number of methods. Shaped into the dumplings called quenelles, it can be poached and then graced with a velouté sauce *(page 80)*. Packed into a mold lined with fish fillets, mousseline may be steamed to make a ring—often called a turban—such as the one shown opposite. Mousseline also can serve as an ineffably delicate stuffing for a wide range of fish dishes: it makes a handsome presentation when it is used to fill a whole baked fish *(page 57)*, but it is equally effective—and delicious—when wrapped in fish fillets and poached.

By comparison with mousselines, fish packages are simple contrivances. The most straightforward is the papillote *(page 86)*, which requires only dexterous folding and pinching; when precooked fish and aromatic ingredients are briefly heated in the papillote, the wrapper concentrates their flavors, and when the papillote is opened at the table their combined fragrance is released in an aromatic puff of steam. Somewhat more artistry is required in fashioning a pastry-dough package that resembles a fish *(page 83)*. In much the same way as a papillote, pastry seals in the flavor of its contents, but it also adds crusty layers of taste and texture to the finished dish.

Creating an aspic cloak for a fish *(pages 84-85)* requires patience and close attention from the cook, but the techniques that ensure an aspic of crystal clarity and of the right consistency are not at all difficult to master. The rewards, moreover, are outsized: in its satiny aspic sheath, a whole cooked fish is every bit as bewitching to the eye as to the palate.

The first slice is lifted from a ring of airy, pistachio-studded mousseline enclosed by overlapping salmon and sole fillets. Cooked in a mold, the turban was allowed to settle for a few minutes so that it retained its perfect form when turned out for serving.

Making a Basic Mousseline

The magical transformation of raw fish fillets into the smooth, light, rich mixture called a mousseline *(recipe, page 166)* is accomplished by puréeing the fish flesh and then patiently incorporating egg whites and heavy cream. The mixture—perhaps flavored by chopped, cooked shrimp or mushrooms, peeled pistachios or other ingredients—may then be used to make stuffings or the delicate dumplings called quenelles *(page 80)*.

For the best results, the fish fillets for the purée base of a mousseline should be firm, lean, white-fleshed and mild in flavor—pike, flounder and halibut all are good choices. Some cooks use salmon for its pink color and distinctive flavor; this slightly oily fish can make the mousseline heavy, however. To lighten a salmon mousseline, use a mixture of one third salmon and two thirds lean white fish. Do not use very oily fish such as mackerel for a mousseline: the flesh will not absorb the liquid ingredients properly.

The traditional way of puréeing the fillets is to pound them in a mortar *(below)*, sieving them afterward to remove tiny bits of membrane and cartilage. This method produces the smoothest possible texture in the finished mousseline.

You may, however, prefer quicker puréeing methods. The fillets can be puréed through a food mill fitted with the finest blade, then sieved. Although an electric blender is not suitable for the job—the flesh sticks in the blades at the base of the narrow container—an electric food processor will purée the fillets in less than a minute. The purée must be sieved afterward, but the food processor will shorten your working time considerably. Because the processor chops rather than crushes the flesh, however, the purée will not be quite as luxuriant in texture as one made by hand.

The amounts of egg whites and cream added to the fish purée must be precisely controlled. Egg whites bind the mixture into a mass, but too many will make it rubbery. Cream contributes lightness—

especially if part of the cream is whipped beforehand—but too much will make the mousseline runny. Recipes for quenelle mixtures call for more egg whites and less cream than those for mousselines used as stuffings because the quenelles must be bound tightly enough to hold their shape when poached. Quenelle recipes, therefore, produce a slightly heavier mousseline than stuffing recipes, although the quenelles will be perfectly satisfactory. If you wish to make quenelles of unparalleled lightness, you can experiment with a soft mousseline stuffing mixture *(box, opposite, below)*.

For the fish purée to absorb the cream, it must be very firm in texture, and the cream must be incorporated a little at a time. Before you start adding the cream, firm up the mixture by chilling it. In addition, use very cold cream to prevent it from warming and softening the purée, and chill the purée after each addition of cream to firm it up again.

1 **Pounding the flesh.** Remove any trace of skin or bone from the fillets and scrape a knife across the flesh to remove as much membrane and connective tissue as possible. Chop the fillets—pike, in this case—then pound them in a mortar until smooth.

2 **Adding egg whites.** Season the purée with pepper and any other flavorings your recipe specifies—except for salt. Add the egg whites to the purée little by little, pounding the fish after each addition to make sure the egg whites are thoroughly absorbed.

3 **Smoothing the purée.** Continue pounding the purée until the fish has been pulverized into a creamy paste *(above)*. The more the fish is pounded at this stage, the finer the texture of the finished mousseline will be.

4 **Sieving the purée.** Rub small batches of the purée through a fine-meshed sieve, discarding any cartilage left on the mesh after each batch. Pack the purée into a bowl and cover it tightly with plastic wrap. Put the bowl inside another, ice-filled bowl and refrigerate the purée for 1 hour.

5 **Adding cream.** Remove the stiffened purée from the refrigerator and replenish the ice in the large bowl to keep the purée chilled. Add a few tablespoons of cold heavy cream.

6 **Incorporating the cream.** Work the cream thoroughly into the purée with a wooden spoon; a metal spoon would conduct heat from your hand and soften the purée. Then return the mixture to the refrigerator for 15 minutes. Repeat the process until half of the cream has been incorporated.

7 **Folding in whipped cream.** Vigorously beat the mixture — now softened by the cream — and season it with salt to taste. Return it to the refrigerator to chill for 5 to 10 minutes. Whip the remaining cream until it forms soft peaks; add it to the purée and fold it into the mixture with a spatula. Refrigerate the mousseline, covered with plastic wrap, until you are ready to use it.

The Water Test

For the lightest possible quenelles, make a soft mousseline and test it for firmness as shown below. If it fails the test, add a few teaspoons of egg white and test again. Repeat these steps until the mousseline is the right consistency.

Checking for consistency. Simmer water in a small pan. Dip a spoon in hot water to prevent sticking, scoop up a little mousseline, and with another spoon, push it into the pan. If the mixture is right, it will hold its shape.

Two Mousseline Classics

Quenelles: The Airiest Dumplings

Whether a mousseline is to be used as a stuffing or for making quenelles, it presents the cook with attractive options at every step of the cooking process.

If you are making quenelles, for example, you can shape the mousseline mixture for poaching in any number of ways. You can fill a pastry bag with mousseline and, using a plain tube, pipe quenelles into their poaching vessel. You can mold the mousseline in well-buttered tartlet tins and poach it; as the quenelles finish cooking they will unmold themselves by floating out of the tins. You can roll the mousseline into a cylinder and cut it into 3-inch [8-cm.] quenelles. And, simplest of all, you can shape the mixture with the aid of two identically sized spoons—repeatedly dipped in hot water to prevent the mousseline from sticking to them.

All quenelles are poached in salted water or fumet *(page 29)* that is never heated above a simmer; if the liquid boils, the delicate dumplings will crack and fall apart. When the quenelles rise to the surface of the liquid, they are done, ready to be drained on paper towels. If they are to be served by themselves, the quenelles usually are bathed in a rich sauce: a velouté is used here *(recipe, page 164)*; another possibility would be a hollandaise sauce *(recipe, page 165)*. Briefly broiling the quenelles in sauce develops a rich, brown crust on their surface.

If you decide to use mousseline as a stuffing, you are offered a similarly wide field of alternatives. You may use it to stuff a whole, baked fish *(page 57)*, but you can also roll fish fillets around it and poach them or sandwich the mixture between fillets, then wrap the fillets in pastry and bake them *(pages 82-83)*.

One particularly impressive stuffing treatment is the turban of fish shown opposite: a mold is lined with fish fillets, then filled with mousseline. The mold is covered with buttered wax paper to prevent drying and is baked gently with the aid of a bain-marie. The unmolded turban will present handsome variations in both color and texture—especially when it is sliced to reveal a pistachio-studded mousseline within.

1 Molding with spoons. Set a bowl of mousseline into another, ice-filled bowl. Dip two spoons in hot water. With one spoon, scoop up mousseline; with the other, smooth the mixture into an egg shape. Push each quenelle into a buttered sauté pan; do not crowd them.

2 Poaching the quenelles. Gently pour just enough simmering water or fumet into the pan to cover the quenelles. Simmer the quenelles, covered, for 10 to 15 minutes: when they float, they are cooked. Remove the quenelles and drain them.

3 Finishing in the oven. Arrange the quenelles in a buttered, ovenproof dish. Cover them with a sauce—here, a velouté enriched with cream. Sprinkle with cheese, and bake in a preheated 400° F. [200° C.] oven for 15 to 20 minutes, until the cheese browns *(right)*. Serve immediately.

A Turban: The Peerless Mold

1 **Lining the mold.** Lay equal-sized fish fillets, prepared as for poaching (*page 36*), across a buttered ring mold; let their ends hang over the rim. In this demonstration, sole and salmon fillets alternate. Spoon chilled, pistachio-flavored mousseline into the mold (*left*). Next, fold the ends of the fillets over the mousseline (*above*).

2 **Cooking.** Lay a circle of buttered wax paper — perforated in the center to allow steam to escape — over the surface of the filling. Set the mold on a rack in an ovenproof pan; add hot water to come halfway up the sides of the mold. Cook in a preheated 325° F. [160° C.] oven for 35 to 40 minutes, until the filling is springy to the touch. Remove from the pan *(above)*.

3 **Draining the mold.** Leave the mold to settle for 10 minutes. Remove the paper, place the wire rack over the mold and turn both over quickly so that the ring rests on the rack but is still enclosed by the mold (*above*). This will enable any liquid that may have accumulated in the mold to drain. When the liquid has drained, turn the mold over again so that the mousseline ring is once more resting in it.

4 **Unmolding the turban.** Place a serving plate over the mold and invert plate and mold together to release the mousseline. Soak up any water on the plate with paper towels. Brush the top of the turban with melted butter to make it glisten. Serve the turban hot with a separate sauce, such as a velouté (*recipe, page 164*); or serve it cold — as it is or covered in aspic (*pages 84-85*).

A Pastry That Presages the Delights Within

Because fish baked inside a pastry crust is protected from the drying oven heat— the fish is actually steamed rather than baked—it emerges particularly succulent. The cooked crust provides a crisp contrast to the soft flesh within and, if the crust is cut into the shape of a fish as shown here, the dish gains extra appeal.

Although this decorative package may contain a whole fish, a pair of fillets stacked on top of one another is a better choice. The sandwich of fillets can enclose additional flavoring elements such as herbs and aromatic vegetables or a stuffing like the one described on pages 52-53 or an elegant mousseline, used in this demonstration. The fillets should be of equal size and shape, and they must be ¼ to ½ inch [6 mm. to 1 cm.] thick so that they will cook in the same time as the pastry. Any firm, lean fish will do; striped bass fillets are used here.

To enclose the fish, you can use simple short-crust pastry dough. Or, with a bit of extra rolling, turn the dough into rough puff pastry, which becomes especially light when baked (recipe, page 167, but increase the quantity according to the size of the fish).

For a crisp and tender result, keep the pastry dough cold and firm while you work with it. When the fish is sealed, chill it in the refrigerator until the dough has firmed up again. Then transfer the fish to an oiled baking sheet, apply the final decorative touches (Steps 6 and 7), and bake it immediately.

Cooking times for fish in pastry vary slightly from those for other preparations. The assembly is baked at a high temperature until the pastry is set— about 15 minutes. Then the temperature is reduced to prevent the fish from overcooking. For this second stage, allow 10 minutes per inch [2½ cm.] of thickness of a whole fish or the fillet-and-stuffing sandwich. The fish is done when a rapid-response thermometer inserted through the crust into the flesh registers 140° F. [60° C.]—or a metal skewer inserted for a few seconds feels hot at the tip.

1 Cutting the pastry bottom. Roll the pastry dough, here rough puff pastry (recipe, page 167), ⅓ inch [1 cm.] thick and divide it into two rectangles at least 2½ inches [6 cm.] wider and longer than your fillets. Cover and refrigerate one rectangle. Center a thoroughly dried-off fillet on the other rectangle. With a pastry wheel or sharp knife, cut the pastry to form a fish shape at least ½ inch [1 cm.] wider than the fillet on all sides.

2 Spreading the stuffing. Remove the scraps of pastry from around the fish shape, wrap them in plastic and chill them. Transfer the fish-shaped pastry and the fillet to a lightly floured baking sheet. Spread a stuffing—in this case, mousseline—on top of the fillet.

6 Decorating the pastry. Remove the pastry scraps from the refrigerator and roll them out ⅓ inch [1 cm.] thick. With a pastry wheel or sharp knife, cut out pieces to represent fins, an eye and a gill opening. Brush the edges of these decorative pieces with water and press them into place on the fish. Use a plain pastry tube or a soupspoon to press half circles into the pastry to resemble scales. Score decorative lines on the tail and fins with a knife.

7 Glazing the pastry. Brush the pastry with a light glaze of beaten egg yolks (above) to ensure that it browns to a golden finish. Place the assembly in an oven that has been preheated to 425° F. [220° C.]. After 15 minutes, reduce the heat to 350° F. [180° C.].

3 **Adding the second fillet.** Place the second fillet on top of the stuffing *(above)*. If a fillet varies in thickness, adjust the depth of the stuffing layer so that the sandwich is the same thickness throughout. This will ensure even cooking. Measure the thickness of the fillet-and-stuffing sandwich to determine the cooking time.

4 **Cutting the pastry top.** Drape the second rectangle of pastry over the stacked fillets. Using the outline of the bottom fish-shaped pastry as a guide — it will show as a ridge under the pastry rectangle — cut a second pastry fish ½ inch [1 cm.] larger than the first. Remove the excess pastry and chill.

5 **Sealing the pastry.** Brush a light film of water under the edges of the top piece of pastry to make it slightly sticky. Then tuck the edges of the top pastry under those of the bottom all around and pinch them to make sure they are sealed. Place the assembly, on the floured baking sheet, in the refrigerator and chill it for about 15 minutes. When firm, transfer the assembly to an oiled baking sheet.

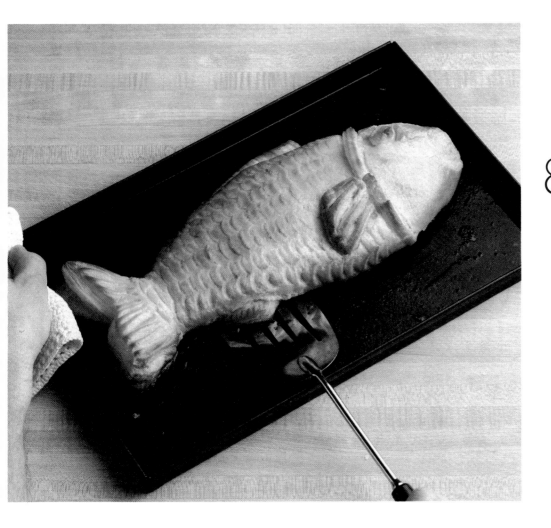

8 **Cooking the fish.** Cook the fish at the reduced heat for 10 minutes per inch [2½ cm.] of thickness, until the pastry is puffy and golden brown. Test for doneness and remove the fish from the oven. Loosen the pastry from the pan by gently sliding a spatula underneath all the edges *(above)*. Using two spatulas, carefully transfer the pastry-wrapped fish to a platter and garnish it with parsley. Cut the assembly into crosswise slices at the table.

Jellied Fumet: A Shimmering Cloak

A limpid aspic jelly, decorated with a pattern of herbs or vegetable slices, turns a whole poached fish into a handsome dish for a cold buffet. The aspic is made from fumet *(page 29)* and may be flavored with a fortified wine such as Madeira *(recipe, page 164)*. In addition to contributing its own flavor to the dish, the aspic helps to keep the fish from drying out.

On these pages, aspic is used to coat skinned trout decorated with tarragon leaves, which lend a subtle anise flavor. Other cold whole fish—or molded dishes, such as the one demonstrated on page 81—can be presented in a similar way, and decorations can range from slices of parboiled carrot or hard-boiled egg to whole, peeled, cooked shrimp. How much aspic you need depends on the size of the fish or the mold; glazing the six trout here required 1 quart [1 liter] of aspic. To make an aspic firm enough to glaze the fish evenly and hold decorations, you must add commercial gelatin to the fumet. Unlike meat and poultry stock, fumet contains little natural gelatin.

To make the aspic crystal clear, all solid fragments must be removed from the fumet. The larger particles will form a sediment if the fumet is left overnight in a bowl, and they can be separated from the liquid by decanting *(page 29)*. But small particles will remain in suspension; the only way to extract them is to add an absorbing agent that will bond with the fumet fragments, thus enlarging their size and making it possible to strain them out of the liquid. Egg whites and broken egg shells serve as this agent. After they are added, the fumet must be boiled to coagulate the egg whites. The boiling liquid drives the tiny particles against the solid egg whites, where they adhere. Straining the liquid through layers of dampened cheesecloth removes the whites, shells and all impurities.

Once it is clarified, the aspic must be chilled until close to its jelling point before it will stick to the well-chilled fish. Since only a thin film of liquid will cling to the fish with each application, the aspic coating should be built up in layers, with a period of refrigeration after each layer is applied to allow the aspic to set. Decorations are suspended in the jelly by adding them after the first layer.

1 Mixing in the gelatin. Pour the fumet into a large saucepan and set it over medium heat. Soften gelatin for a few minutes in a little cold water. Add some of the heated fumet to the gelatin, and stir until the gelatin dissolves. Then whisk the gelatin-fumet mixture into the fumet in the saucepan.

2 Adding egg whites. Test to make sure that the fumet will jell by refrigerating a spoonful of it. It should set within 10 minutes; if it does not, add more dissolved gelatin to the fumet. Beat egg whites to soft peaks. Add the whites and broken egg shell to the fumet. Place the pan on a high heat and whisk the fumet until it boils.

3 Clarifying the fumet. As the fumet comes to a boil, the egg whites will rise and coagulate. After the fumet bubbles up through the egg whites, remove the pan from the heat for 10 minutes to allow the foam to settle and form a bond with the particles. Bring the fumet to a boil twice more, letting it stand for 10 minutes after each boil.

4 Straining the fumet. Place four layers of dampened, wrung-out cheesecloth in a fine sieve over a deep bowl and slowly pour in the fumet. Allow the fumet to drip through the cloth—do not squeeze the cloth, as you may force impurities through it. Let the strained liquid cool to room temperature.

5 **Preparing the fish.** Skin the poached fish while still warm *(page 33)*, cover them with a damp towel and refrigerate them for at least an hour. Remove the fish and place them on a rack over a plate or platter. Taste the cooled aspic for salt; add a little Madeira or other fortified wine. Pour some of the aspic into a bowl embedded in crushed ice. Stir the aspic, removing it from the ice as soon as it begins to thicken.

6 **Coating the fish.** Working fast before the aspic sets, spoon a thin layer of it over each of the fish and add decorations. Here, tarragon leaves — dipped in boiling water to make them greener and drained — are dipped in aspic, then arranged on the fish.

7 **Completing the dish.** Refrigerate the fish for 10 minutes before adding another layer of aspic. Apply two or three more coatings in this way, then transfer the fish to a large, chilled platter. Decorate the platter; here, strips of skinned sweet red pepper are used. Cover the entire dish with several more layers of aspic. Refrigerate the dish until you are ready to serve it.

A Parchment Package Filled with Scented Steam

Any steamed or poached fish can be finished with flair by sealing it with flavorings in a paper package and baking it briefly. As the package heats, the flavors of its contents mingle. Steam inflates the paper like a balloon and, when the package is opened at the table, the steam escapes in an aromatic puff.

Butcher's paper or foil will serve, but the parchment paper shown here makes the most attractive casing. Although the paper can be cut and folded into a rectangle or oval, the classic method is to cut a heart shape and fold it, as demonstrated, into a papillote—a name that derives from *papillon*, French for "butterfly." Some cooks will brush the edges of the paper with beaten egg yolk to make certain they seal firmly when they are folded together.

For cooking *en papillote*, use a pair of skinless fillets—slightly underdone so they do not dry out with reheating. Between the fillets spread a thick sauce such as a velouté or, as shown here, substitute aromatic vegetables. All ingredients must be precooked, since the papillote is baked only until it puffs and browns—about 5 minutes.

1 **Preparing the fish.** For each serving, poach *(page 30)* or steam *(page 39)* a 1-pound [½-kg.] fish—a pompano is shown *(recipe, page 159)*. Allow 8 minutes' cooking per inch of thickness so that the fish will be slightly underdone. Peel the skin off the hot fish *(above)* and then fillet it *(page 31)*.

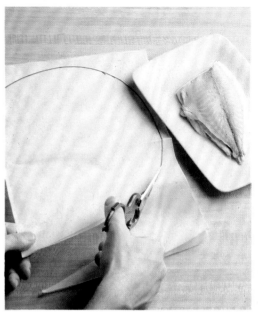

2 **Cutting the papillote.** Fold a sheet of parchment paper in half. As if you were making a valentine, start at the fold and draw a half-heart shape that is at least twice as wide as the fillets. Cut along the line through both layers of paper and unfold the heart.

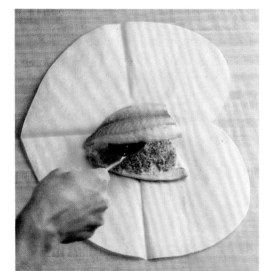

3 **Adding the fish.** Place a fillet on the paper near the fold, its narrow end nearest the point of the heart shape. Spread on the fillet a thin layer of stuffing—here, a mixture of sautéed mushrooms, shallots, chives, green pepper, parsley and seasonings moistened with sherry and fumet. Cover the stuffing with the other fillet.

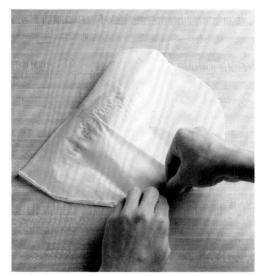

4 **Sealing the papillotes.** Refold the paper over the fish so that the cut edges meet. Starting from one end of the papillote, fold a short length of the paper edges together, then fold again. Hold this section down *(above)* as you fold the next section partly over it to strengthen the seal. Continue folding until the cut edges are completely sealed.

5 **Presenting the papillote.** Transfer the papillote to a baking sheet and place it in a preheated 450° F. [230° C.] oven. After about 5 minutes, when the papillote is brown and puffed up, remove it from the oven, transfer it to a plate and serve it. At the table, each diner tears open his papillote with his fingers.

Anthology of Recipes

Drawing upon the cooking traditions and literature of more than 30 countries, the Editors and consultants for this volume have selected 200 published fish recipes for the Anthology that follows. The selections range from the simple to the unusual—from fried catfish and codfish cakes to poached stuffed sole with truffles and shad stuffed with stuffed dates.

The Anthology spans nearly 2,000 years. Many of the recipes were written by world-renowned exponents of the culinary art, but the Anthology also includes selections from now rare and out-of-print books and from works that have never been published in English. Whatever the sources, the emphasis always is on authentic dishes meticulously prepared with fresh, natural ingredients that blend harmoniously.

Since many early recipe writers did not specify amounts of ingredients, the missing information has been judiciously added. Where appropriate, clarifying introductory notes have also been supplied; they are printed in italics. Modern terms have been substituted for archaic language and some instructions have been expanded; but to preserve the character of the original recipes, and to create a true anthology, the authors' texts have been changed as little as possible. For this reason, cooking times, especially in older recipes, may seem overlong by today's standards—and you may want to shorten them.

For ease of use, the recipes are organized by cooking method. Since the Anthology is international in scope and includes recipes for types of fish that may not be available in all markets, each recipe includes—wherever possible—a list of suitable options that will produce similar results when substituted for the specified fish. Recipes for standard preparations—court bouillon, batter for deep frying, fumet, pastry and basic sauces—appear at the end of the Anthology.

All recipe ingredients are listed in order of use, with both the customary U.S. measurements and the new metric measurements provided in separate columns. The metric quantities supplied here reflect the American practice of measuring such solid ingredients as flour and sugar by volume rather than by weighing them, as European cooks do.

To make the quantities simpler to measure, many of the figures have been rounded off to correspond to the gradations that are now standard on metric spoons and cups. (One cup, for example, equals 237 milliliters; wherever practicable in these recipes, however, a cup appears as a more readily measurable 250 milliliters.) Similarly, weight, temperature and linear metric equivalents are rounded off slightly. For these reasons, the American and metric figures are not equivalent, but using one set or the other will produce equally good results.

Poaching and Steaming

Poached Bass with Almond Curry Sauce

(Options: corvina, drum, flounder, sole)

To serve 3 or 4

3 or 4	bass fillets, skinned	3 or 4
	Poaching liquid	
½ cup	water	125 ml.
⅓ cup	dry white wine	75 ml.
¾ tsp.	salt	4 ml.
2 tsp.	butter	10 ml.
1	bay leaf, broken in half	1
¼ tsp.	thyme	1 ml.
3	whole white peppercorns	3
1 tsp.	finely chopped orange peel	5 ml.
¼ tsp.	fennel seed, pulverized	1 ml.
	Almond curry sauce	
3 tbsp.	butter	45 ml.
1 cup	chopped onions	¼ liter
2 cups	canned peeled tomatoes, drained and mashed	½ liter
⅛ tsp.	ground coriander	½ ml.
½ tsp.	ground turmeric	2 ml.
⅛ tsp.	ground cumin	½ ml.
¼ tsp.	chili powder	1 ml.
⅛ tsp.	ground cloves	½ ml.
⅛ tsp.	ground cinnamon	½ ml.
¹⁄₁₆ tsp.	ground ginger	⅔ ml.
⅛ tsp.	dry mustard	½ ml.
⅛ tsp.	cayenne pepper	½ ml.
1 cup	water	¼ liter
¾ cup	slivered, blanched almonds, coarsely pulverized	175 ml.
½ tsp.	salt	2 ml.
¼ tsp.	freshly ground black pepper	1 ml.
¾ tsp.	sugar	4 ml.

Place the fish fillets in a large heavy skillet along with all the ingredients for the poaching liquid. Bring to a boil over high heat, then reduce the heat sufficiently to keep just a low simmer going. Cook at a low simmer for 8 to 9 minutes, then remove the fillets from the liquid with a large slotted spatula, allowing the liquid to drain back into the pan. Place the fillets on a large platter or on four serving plates, cover loosely with aluminum foil and set in a 175° F. [85° C.] oven to keep warm while you prepare the sauce. Strain the poaching liquid and refrigerate it, covered, for use as a fish stock. (If you plan to keep it longer than two days, freeze it.)

To prepare the sauce, melt the butter over medium heat in a large sauté pan or skillet. Add the onions and sauté until quite soft but not browned. Add the mashed tomatoes and stir thoroughly. Continue cooking over low heat. Add the remaining ingredients in the order given, stirring to mix well after each addition. Raise the heat to medium and cook, stirring frequently, for 8 to 10 minutes, until the sauce is completely mixed and even in color and the consistency is thick and pleasantly lumpy, similar to that of cooked tapioca. Taste to check for a thorough integration of seasonings. If any of the elements seems to stand out distinctly from the others, reduce the heat a bit and cook for 3 or 4 minutes longer, stirring gently but constantly. To serve, place the fillets on heated plates and spoon generous quantities of the sauce over each one.

RIMA AND RICHARD COLLIN
THE PLEASURES OF SEAFOOD

Carp with Saffron

Carpe au Safran

(Options: muskellunge, pike)

To serve 6

1	whole carp (4 lb. [2 kg.]), cleaned and cut crosswise into ½-inch [1-cm.] slices	1
3	medium-sized onions, very finely chopped	3
4	garlic cloves, very finely chopped	4
2 tbsp.	oil	30 ml.
1 quart	water	1 liter
2 cups	dry white wine	½ liter
	salt	
½ tsp.	ground saffron	2 ml.

Lightly brown the onions and garlic in the oil. Add the water and wine, and season with salt. Add the saffron and boil for 30 minutes. Reduce the heat to a simmer, put the carp portions into this court bouillon and cook them for 30 minutes. Remove the fish and arrange the slices in a deep platter.

Reduce the court bouillon by two thirds, then strain it and pour it over the fish. Allow the court bouillon to cool and jell before serving.

ÉDOUARD DE POMIANE
CUISINE JUIVE GHETTOS MODERNES

Poached Carp with Raisins and Almonds

Carpe à la Juive

(Options: muskellunge, pike)

This recipe from Lorraine uses Malaga raisins, which are made from Muscat grapes, and are much larger and sweeter than ordinary raisins. Malaga raisins are obtainable from European specialty stores.

To serve 6

1	whole carp (5 lb. [2½ kg.]), cleaned and left whole or cut into large pieces	1
1 cup	oil	¼ liter
5	boiling onions (about ½ lb. [¼ kg.])	5
2 tbsp.	flour	30 ml.
1 tbsp.	sugar	15 ml.
1 tbsp.	vinegar	15 ml.
1 cup	Malaga raisins	¼ liter
¾ cup	slivered blanched almonds (4 oz. [125 g.])	175 ml.
	salt	

Heat the oil in a saucepan (or in a fish poacher, if you want to cook the fish whole). Put in the onions and cook them until partially softened. Add the flour and half of the sugar and cook, stirring, without letting the mixture brown. Add the vinegar, the remaining sugar, the raisins and almonds, and enough water to just cover the fish. Bring to a boil, add salt and reduce the heat. Put in the fish and simmer for 10 to 15 minutes if cut into slices, or up to 45 minutes for a whole fish.

When the fish is cooked, place it in a deep serving platter and pour the sauce over it, arranging the onions, raisins and almonds around the fish. Allow to cool. Serve the fish cold when the sauce jells.

E. AURICOSTE DE LAZARQUE
CUISINE MESSINE

Cod, Potatoes and Eggs

Estofinade à la Rouergatte

(Options: salted haddock, salted halibut, salted pollock)

Stockfish, which is air-dried cod, was originally used for this preparation, but it requires at least three days' more soaking than salt cod. The cod should be poached and the potatoes and eggs boiled so that all are still hot when assembled.

To serve 4

1½ lb.	salt cod, soaked in water overnight and drained	¾ kg.
1	bay leaf	1
1	sprig thyme	1
6 to 8	medium-sized, firm-fleshed potatoes (about 2 lb. [1 kg.]), unpeeled	6 to 8
4	eggs	4
2 or 3	garlic cloves, pounded to a purée in a mortar	2 or 3
¼ cup	chopped fresh parsley	50 ml.
1 cup	olive oil	¼ liter
	pepper	
	salt (optional)	

Place the cod in a saucepan and cover generously with cold water. Add the bay leaf and thyme. Bring slowly to a boil, and remove any scum that forms on the surface. Reduce the heat and poach in the hot, but not simmering, water for about 10 minutes, depending on the thickness of the fish. When the flesh at its thickest point shows little resistance to the tip of a sharp knife, the cod is ready. Remove the skin and bones, and flake the flesh into large pieces.

Meanwhile, boil the potatoes in their skins and hard-boil the eggs. Then peel and thickly slice the potatoes. Shell the eggs and cut them into pieces.

Mix the garlic purée and parsley together well, add the egg pieces and stir gently with half of the olive oil. In a saucepan over medium heat, add the potatoes to the remaining oil, toss with the flaked cod and gently stir in the egg-and-parsley mixture, peppering generously. Taste and add salt if needed; the cod may be salty enough. Turn out onto a heated platter and serve.

RICHARD OLNEY
SIMPLE FRENCH FOOD

Brandade Home-Style

Brandade de Morue à la Ménagère

(Options: salted haddock, salted halibut, salted pollock)

To serve 6 to 8

1 lb.	very white salt cod, soaked in several changes of cold water for 24 hours and drained	½ kg.
1 to 1½ cups	olive oil	250 to 325 ml.
1	garlic clove, crushed	1
½ cup	light cream or milk	125 ml.
½ cup	potato, boiled or steamed, and mashed	125 ml.
	freshly ground white pepper	
	salt (optional)	
2 to 3 tbsp.	lemon juice	30 to 45 ml.
	tiny bread croutons, fried until golden in oil or butter	

Cut the cod into several pieces and place them in a saucepan with 4 quarts [4 liters] of water. Bring to a boil. As soon as the water boils, turn the heat as low as possible and poach the fish for 10 to 12 minutes.

Drain the pieces of cod. Remove the black and white skin, and the bones. Break the flesh into fine flakes.

In a heavy saucepan, heat ½ cup [125 ml.] of the olive oil. Add the cod and the crushed garlic. Work the mixture quickly with a spatula or a wooden spoon until the fish is reduced to a fine paste. Lower the heat. Beat the paste without stopping, adding the rest of the oil and the cream or milk.

Add the mashed potato and mix thoroughly. Season with white pepper and, if necessary, add a little salt. Finally, mix in the lemon juice well. When finished, the *brandade* should be a smooth paste, light and very white.

Serve the *brandade* on a platter in the shape of a dome. Surround with tiny croutons.

PAUL BOCUSE
PAUL BOCUSE'S FRENCH COOKING

Curried Haddock Fillets

Schelvisfillets met Kerrie

(Options: cod, shark, swordfish, wolf fish)

This recipe is one of many that show the influence of the East Indies on Dutch cookery. But the Dutch adapted rather than

adopted, applying Oriental themes to their own fish, as here. The best curry powders to use for spicy effect are those made in, or in the style of, Madras, India.

To serve 4

2 to 2½ lb.	fresh haddock fillets divided into 4 equal pieces	1 kg.
3 tbsp.	soy sauce	45 ml.
1 tbsp.	fresh lemon juice	15 ml.
2 cups	water	½ liter
	salt	
5	peppercorns	5
1	bay leaf	1
5 tbsp.	butter	75 ml.
2	apples, peeled, cored and sliced	2
3	onions, sliced and separated into rings	3
2 tbsp.	flour	30 ml.
1 tbsp.	curry powder	15 ml.
½ tsp.	ground thyme	2 ml.

Wash the fish fillets carefully and set them beside each other in a shallow dish. Sprinkle the soy sauce and lemon juice over them, cover the dish with aluminum foil or a lid and leave them for 30 minutes.

Heat the water in a shallow saucepan. Add salt, the peppercorns and the bay leaf. Leave this mixture over low heat for 10 minutes. Then place the fish fillets carefully in the water and poach them, with the water barely simmering, for 10 to 15 minutes.

Meanwhile, melt half of the butter in a skillet and cook the apple slices until golden brown. Remove them to a plate. Add the onion rings to the butter remaining in the pan. Cook them until golden brown, then transfer them to a plate. Keep the apples and onions warm.

Once the fish fillets are cooked, lift them carefully from their pan, set them beside each other in a warmed serving dish and keep them hot. Strain and reserve the liquid in which the fish was cooked.

Melt the rest of the butter in a saucepan and add the flour and the curry powder, stirring well. As soon as the mixture is smooth, gradually stir in about ½ cup [125 ml.] of the strained liquid. Add salt to taste and the thyme. Let the sauce continue to simmer for 4 or 5 minutes, then pour it over the fish fillets. Garnish the dish with the apple slices and onion rings before serving.

TON VAN ES
HET VOLKOMEN VISBOEK

Haddock Strachur

(Options: smoked cod, smoked halibut, smoked pollock)

The term finnan haddie is the colloquial form of Findon haddock—split, smoked haddock named after the Scottish fishing village of Findon (or Findhorn).

A rich and satisfying dish from Strachur in Argyllshire, Scotland. Fingers of buttered toast can be served with it.

To serve 6 to 8		
2 lb.	smoked finnan haddie	1 kg.
2 cups	heavy cream	½ liter
	freshly ground black pepper	

Poach the haddock in gently boiling water for 4 minutes. Drain and flake the fish, taking care to remove all the bones. Arrange the fish in a buttered baking dish; pour the cream over the fish until it is completely covered. Season with pepper; put under a hot broiler until brown. Serve at once.

LIZZIE BOYD (EDITOR)
BRITISH COOKERY

Hake in the Basque (or San Sebastian) Style

Merluza a la Koskera o a la Donostiarra

(Options: angler, bluefish, cod, haddock, whiting)

To serve 3 or 4		
1½ lb.	hake, cut into 4 slices	¾ kg.
4 to 6 tbsp.	olive oil	60 to 90 ml.
3	garlic cloves	3
½	bay leaf	½
1 tbsp.	flour	15 ml.
2	sprigs parsley, chopped	2
½ to 1 cup	fish fumet *(recipe, page 164)* or water	125 to 250 ml.
1 cup	cooked peas	¼ liter
12	asparagus tips, parboiled	12
	salt (optional)	
3 or 4	eggs	3 or 4

Heat the oil with the garlic cloves in a fireproof earthenware casserole. Toss in the bay leaf, flour and parsley. Stir it all

well and add the fish fumet (or, less preferable, plain water). Add the slices of hake, the peas and the asparagus tips.

When the fish is cooked (after about 10 minutes, depending on the thickness of the slices) remove the bay leaf. Taste the cooking liquid, and season with salt if needed. Break the eggs over the casserole. As soon as the eggs are cooked, the dish is ready to serve.

ANA MARIA CALERA
LA COCINA VASCA

Mackerel in Port with Leeks

Maquereaux aux Poireaux

(Options: cod, herring, mullet, whiting)

To serve 8		
8	whole mackerel, cleaned, heads and tails removed and reserved, and each fish cut crosswise into 3 pieces	8
3 tbsp.	butter	45 ml.
1	carrot, sliced	1
1	large onion, coarsely chopped	1
1	bouquet garni	1
	salt and pepper	
1 cup	port	¼ liter
1½ cups	water	375 ml.
5	leeks, white parts only, sliced crosswise	5
1 tbsp.	flour	15 ml.

Melt 1 tablespoon [15 ml.] of the butter in a large saucepan and sauté the heads and tails of the mackerel for 5 minutes. Add the carrot, onion, bouquet garni, salt and pepper, port and water. Cover and cook over medium heat for 15 minutes. Strain the stock, return it to the cleaned pan, and leave to simmer over low heat.

Meanwhile, in another pan, sauté the leeks in 1 tablespoon more of the butter for 2 to 3 minutes. Add the leeks and the pieces of mackerel to the simmering stock, and let them simmer very gently, covered, for 10 minutes. With a slotted spoon, remove the fish and leeks to a warmed serving dish. Blend the remaining butter with the flour and stir this *beurre manié* into the stock. Cook for a minute or two until lightly thickened, pour this sauce over the fish, and serve.

ROBERT COURTINE
MON BOUQUET DE RECETTES

Mullet with Tomato Sauce

Triglie alla Livornese

(Options: bluegill, perch, sea robin, smelt)

The original version of this recipe calls for the red mullet of the Mediterranean.

	To serve 6	
12	whole small mullet, cleaned	12
¼ cup	olive oil	50 ml.
1	garlic clove, thinly sliced	1
3 tbsp.	coarsely chopped fresh parsley	45 ml.
	salt and pepper	
4 or 5	medium-sized tomatoes (about 1½ lb. [¾ kg.]), peeled, seeded and chopped	4 or 5

Put the oil in a skillet with the garlic, parsley, a pinch each of salt and pepper, and the tomatoes. Simmer, uncovered, for about 10 minutes to cook the tomatoes, then increase the heat to reduce the sauce and cook for a further 10 to 15 minutes. Add the mullet and cook briefly (8 to 10 minutes) until the mullet are done.

FLAVIO COLUTTA
CUCINA E VINI DELLA TOSCANA

Perch in Waterfish Sauce

Waterfish de Perches

(Options: burbot, pike, trout)

"Waterfish" or, more correctly, "waterfisch," is a Dutch word adopted by the French to describe a sauce served with fresh-water fish, particularly perch. The technique of scoring whole fish is demonstrated on page 38.

	To serve 6	
2	whole perch (1½ lb. [¾ kg.] each), cleaned, trimmed and the flesh scored at regular intervals	2
1	large onion, thinly sliced	1
1 cup	celeriac, cut into julienne	¼ liter
2 cups	dry white wine	½ liter
2	whole cloves	2
	salt	
2	fresh chilies, stemmed and seeded	2
1 tbsp.	flour	15 ml.
2 tbsp.	butter	30 ml.
1 tbsp.	chopped fresh parsley	15 ml.

Line a large pan or a heavy oval casserole with the onion and celeriac, and arrange the fish on top. Pour in the wine and add the cloves, salt and chilies. Bring to a boil, then cover and simmer for 10 minutes. Transfer the fish to a warmed platter. Continue to cook the vegetables if necessary. When done, drain the onion and celeriac and keep warm with the fish; discard the cloves and chilies.

Reduce the cooking liquid to one third of its original quantity. Make a *beurre manié* with the flour and half of the butter; whisk this into the reduced liquid to make a thin, light sauce. Add the parsley, remove the sauce from the heat and whisk in the remaining butter. Pour over the fish and vegetables and serve.

URBAIN DUBOIS
ÉCOLE DES CUISINIÈRES

Pike with Horseradish and Sour-Cream Sauce

Hecht mit Saurer Sahne und Meerrettich

(Options: bass, bluefish, carp)

	To serve 4	
1	whole pike (2 lb. [1 kg.]), cleaned	1
Lemon court bouillon		
2 quarts	water	2 liters
	salt	
¼ cup	fresh lemon juice	50 ml.
1	rib celery, sliced	1
1	carrot, sliced	1
1	leek, including 1 inch [2½ cm.] of the green leaves, sliced	1
1	parsley root or small parsnip, sliced	1
Horseradish sauce		
2 tbsp.	grated horseradish	30 ml.
1 tbsp.	flour	15 ml.
1½ cups	sour cream	375 ml.
2 tbsp.	butter	30 ml.

Put the court-bouillon ingredients into a large pan and cook over low heat for 10 to 15 minutes. Add the pike and poach for 25 to 30 minutes.

Meanwhile, put the horseradish in a saucepan, sprinkle the flour over it and add the sour cream. Bring to a boil, stirring. Then whisk in the butter and 1 tablespoon [15 ml.] of the fish broth.

Drain the fish, place it on a warmed platter and pour the sauce over it. Serve immediately.

ELEK MAGYAR
KOCHBUCH FÜR FEINSCHMECKER

Salmon Cooked in Red Wine

Saumon au Vin Rouge

(Options: arctic char, trout)

	To serve 2	
2	salmon steaks (about ½ lb. [¼ kg.] each)	2
1	medium-sized onion, finely chopped	1
6 tbsp.	butter	90 ml.
	salt and pepper	
1½ cups	dry red wine	375 ml.
1	bouquet of 2 parsley sprigs, 1 bay leaf and 1 garlic clove	1
2 tsp.	flour	10 ml.

Put the onion into a sauté pan with 4 tablespoons [60 ml.] of the butter. Lightly brown the onion, then add the salmon and season with salt and pepper. Pour in enough red wine to cover the salmon completely. Add the bouquet of herbs and garlic, cover the pan and simmer for 15 to 18 minutes, depending on the thickness of the salmon steaks.

When the salmon is cooked, remove it to a very hot platter. Discard the bouquet, bind the sauce by mixing the remaining butter with the flour and adding the mixture, little by little, to the cooking juices, blending well. Check the seasoning, pour the sauce over the salmon, and serve at once.

You can vary this dish by lightly frying some thinly sliced mushrooms at the same time as the onion. The salmon steaks can also be served on slices of bread fried in butter. Dry white wine may be used instead of red wine.

I should also point out that this very simple recipe, intended for household cooking, can be refined: the sauce can be strained and the fish can be garnished with little onions glazed in butter and with mushroom caps. Carp's roe and crayfish tails may also be used as garnish.

AUGUSTE ESCOFFIER
LE CARNET D'ÉPICURE

Sardine Rolls in Squash Blossoms

Sardines à la Niçoise

(Options: anchovies, chub, herring, smelts)

When squash blossoms are not available, tender Bibb or Boston lettuce leaves may be substituted.

	To serve 4 to 6	
12	fresh sardines, filleted	12
24	squash blossoms	24
4 tbsp.	butter	60 ml.
½ cup	fish fumet (recipe, page 164)	125 ml.
	salt and pepper	
1 tbsp.	flour	15 ml.
4	anchovy fillets, soaked in water for 10 minutes, patted dry and pounded or sieved to a purée	4
	Duxelles stuffing	
1 tbsp.	butter	15 ml.
1	onion, finely chopped	1
2 cups	fresh mushrooms, finely chopped	½ liter
	salt	
	grated nutmeg	
1 tbsp.	chopped fresh parsley	15 ml.
1 tbsp.	fresh lemon juice	15 ml.

To make the *duxelles* stuffing, melt the butter in a skillet and sauté the onion until soft but not brown. Increase the heat, add the mushrooms. Season with salt and nutmeg, and cook, stirring occasionally, until the mushroom liquid has evaporated. Stir in the parsley and lemon juice, remove from the heat and let the stuffing cool.

Spread the sardine fillets with the stuffing and roll them up. Put a sardine roll into each squash blossom, folding over the tops of the petals to make closed bundles. Melt 2 tablespoons [30 ml.] of the butter in a sauté pan and put in the squash-blossom rolls. Sweat, covered, for a few minutes, turning the rolls once or twice. Pour on the fish fumet, season with salt and pepper, and cook, covered, over low heat for about 15 minutes. Remove the squash-blossom rolls and arrange them on a warmed platter.

Make a paste with the remaining butter, the flour and the anchovy purée, and whisk the paste into the cooking liquid remaining in the sauté pan. Heat until thickened, and pour this sauce over the rolls. Serve immediately.

A. CAILLAT
150 MANIÈRES D'ACCOMMODER LES SARDINES

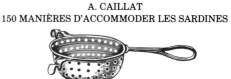

Shad Roe Poached in Butter

(No options)

To serve 6

3	large pairs shad roe	3
16 tbsp.	butter (½ lb. [¼ kg.])	240 ml.
	flour for dredging	
½ cup	finely chopped fresh parsley	125 ml.
	salt and freshly ground pepper	
1 to 1½ tbsp.	fresh lemon juice	15 to 22 ml.
	watercress	
	lemon wedges	

Rinse the roe in cold water, pat them dry and separate the lobes by gently removing the membrane between them.

Melt the butter in a skillet over low heat. Roll each roe gently in flour and place it in the skillet. Turn the roe so that all sides are coated with the butter. Cover the skillet and cook over very low heat for 10 minutes. Turn the roe, sprinkle with the parsley, cover and poach for 10 minutes longer.

Sprinkle the roe with salt and freshly ground pepper and the lemon juice, and transfer them to a warmed serving platter. Pour the pan juices over the roe and garnish with watercress and lemon wedges.

ANN SERANNE
ANN SERANNE'S GOOD FOOD & HOW TO COOK IT

Skate (or Ray) with Capers

Rog met Kappertjes

(No options)

The wings are the best part of the skate. Their flavor and texture are improved if, after washing, they are covered with salted water and left for several days in the refrigerator. Once cooked and skinned, the wings can be returned to their cooking liquor until ready to use; if refrigerated, the liquor will jell and the wings can be stored for several days.

To serve 4

1½ lb.	skate or ray wings	¾ kg.
2 tbsp.	wine vinegar	30 ml.
	salt	
	freshly ground white pepper	
3 tbsp.	capers, rinsed and drained	45 ml.
5 tbsp.	butter	75 ml.

Cut the skate or ray wings into four or eight equal-sized pieces. Put enough water to cover them into an enameled or stainless-steel pan, add 1 tablespoon [15 ml.] of the vinegar and some salt, and bring the water to a boil. Lower the heat, add the pieces of fish and poach them over very gentle heat for about 15 minutes, until done. Remove and drain the fish and transfer to a warmed serving dish. If you wish, take off the skin and cut away the cartilage that runs along the inner side of each wing.

Pepper the fish and sprinkle capers over them. Heat the butter in a pan until it is a light golden brown, then pour it over the fish and capers. Heat the remaining vinegar in the same pan and sprinkle it over the fish.

WINA BORN
HET GROOT VISBOEK

Skate with Black Butter

Raie au Beurre Noir

(Option: ray)

To serve 4

4	skate wings	4
1	medium-sized onion, grated	1
1	sprig parsley	1
1	small bay leaf	1
2	sprigs thyme	2
	salt	
5 tbsp.	wine vinegar	75 ml.
	pepper	
2 tbsp.	chopped fresh parsley	30 ml.
2 tbsp.	capers	30 ml.
1 tbsp.	fresh lemon juice	15 ml.
4 tbsp.	butter	60 ml.

Put the skate wings in a saucepan, cover with about 1 quart [1 liter] of water and add the onion, parsley sprig, bay leaf, thyme, half a tablespoon [7 ml.] of salt and 4 tablespoons [60 ml.] of the vinegar. Bring to a boil and simmer, covered, for 20 to 25 minutes. Drain the wings and place on a towel. Remove the skin from both sides and take off the edges, which should slip off with the skin.

Place the wings in a warmed serving dish and sprinkle with salt and pepper, the chopped parsley, capers, the remaining vinegar and the lemon juice. Cover the dish to keep the wings hot. Melt the butter over low heat and continue cooking it until very brown—almost black, but not burned. Then pour the butter over the fish. Serve very hot.

LOUIS DIAT
FRENCH COOKING FOR AMERICANS

Poached Red Snapper

(Options: bass, dolphin, snook, trout)

To serve 4 to 6

1	whole red snapper (4 to 5 lb. [2 to 2½ kg.]), cleaned	1
¼ cup	chopped shallots	50 ml.
1	rib celery with the leaves, cut up	1
1	carrot, cut up	1
1	bunch parsley	1
1 tbsp.	salt	15 ml.
1 quart	water	1 liter
2½ cups	dry rosé wine	625 ml.
2	lemons, cut into wedges	2

Combine the shallots, celery, carrot, four sprigs of parsley, salt and water in a saucepan. Bring to a boil, reduce the heat and simmer uncovered for 20 minutes. Strain through a double thickness of cheesecloth and discard the vegetables. Pour this stock, or court bouillon, into a fish poacher or large roasting pan. Add the rosé.

Wash the fish inside and out with cold running water. Place the fish on a rack and put it into the pan. If you're using a roasting pan and have no rack, wrap cheesecloth around the fish first, leaving long ends to act as tabs to help with lifting it. If the fish is not at least half-covered by the bouillon—and this varies with the size of pan you use—add up to 1 cup [¼ liter] extra water. Bring the bouillon just to a boil, cover and poach the fish over the lowest heat for 45 minutes or just until the fish flakes easily with a fork. Carefully lift the rack with the fish on it from the pan. Drain the fish well.

Place the fish on a platter and garnish it with lemon wedges and the rest of the parsley. Serve it with Hollandaise sauce *(recipe, page 165)* and with small new potatoes boiled in their jackets.

ELEANOR GRAVES
GREAT DINNERS FROM LIFE

Poached Stuffed Sole with Truffles

La Sole Fourrée au Fumet de Meursault

(Options: flounder, fluke, turbot)

To conform to the original title, both the fish fumet and the velouté sauce called for in this recipe should be made with Meursault, a white Burgundy wine, but any good white wine will serve. The technique of stuffing sole is demonstrated on pages 56-57, and the technique of making a mousseline is shown on pages 78-79.

To serve 4

4	whole sole (10 oz. [300 g.]), skinned and cleaned	4
2 cups	fish fumet *(recipe, page 164)*	½ liter
	thin slices truffle	
1 cup	velouté sauce *(recipe, page 164)*	¼ liter
½ cup	heavy cream	125 ml.
1	egg yolk	1
1 tsp.	fresh lemon juice	5 ml.
1 tbsp.	butter	15 ml.

Sole mousseline stuffing

10 oz.	sole fillets	300 g.
	salt and pepper	
1½ cups	fresh mushrooms (about 4 oz. [125 g.]), finely chopped	375 ml.
1 tbsp.	butter	15 ml.
1	small truffle, finely chopped	1
1	egg white	1
1 cup	heavy cream	¼ liter

First make the mousseline stuffing. Season the chopped mushrooms and sauté them in the butter. When the mushrooms' liquid has evaporated, stir in the chopped truffle and set aside to cool. Pound the sole fillets thoroughly in a mortar; pass the fish through a fine sieve and return it to the mortar. Pound in the egg white and season with salt and pepper. Turn the mixture into a bowl and refrigerate over crushed ice for 1 hour. With a spatula, work the cream into the mixture, a little at a time, refrigerating between each addition. Finally, mix the sautéed mushrooms and truffle into the chilled fish mixture.

Cut each of the sole along the length of the backbone and lift the fillets without detaching them completely. Fill the resulting pockets between each pair of fillets with the prepared mousseline stuffing.

Arrange the fish in a large buttered sauté pan or oven-proof dish. Pour over the fumet, place a sheet of buttered wax paper over the surface and cook in a preheated 350° F. [180° C.] oven for 15 to 20 minutes, or until the mousseline is firm to the touch. Remove the fish, arrange it on a warmed serving platter and garnish it with truffle slices.

Reduce the cooking liquor over brisk heat and add it to the simmering velouté sauce. Bind the sauce with the cream mixed with the egg yolk. Remove the sauce from the heat, whisk in the lemon juice and the butter. Pour the sauce over the fish and serve.

CURNONSKY
BONS PLATS, BONS VINS

Poached Fillets of Sole with Grapes

Filets de Soles Veronique

(Options: flounder, halibut, turbot)

To serve 4

4	sole or flounder fillets	4
2 tbsp.	butter	30 ml.
2	firm white mushrooms, sliced	2
	salt	
	freshly cracked white pepper	
½ cup	dry white wine	125 ml.
¼ cup	dry sherry	50 ml.
¼ cup	water	50 ml.

Veronique sauce

4 tbsp.	butter	60 ml.
4 tbsp.	flour	60 ml.
	salt	
	cayenne pepper	
	strained fish stock (from the sole)	
⅔ cup	light cream	150 ml.
2	egg yolks	2
1 tbsp.	brandy	15 ml.
1 tbsp.	tarragon vinegar	15 ml.
2 tbsp.	heavy cream	30 ml.
6 tbsp.	frozen unsalted butter	90 ml.

Grape garnish

1 tbsp.	butter	15 ml.
¾ cup	skinned and seeded fresh white grapes	175 ml.
1 tsp.	chopped fresh parsley	5 ml.
1 tsp.	brandy	5 ml.
	salt	
	freshly cracked white pepper	

Preheat the oven to 350° F. [180° C.]. Wash the fillets in water and a little lemon juice. Dry them well and fold them lengthwise with their white, bone sides out. Place them in a buttered baking dish.

To make a court bouillon, first melt the butter in a sauté pan and add the mushrooms. Cook over brisk heat with ½ teaspoon [2 ml.] lemon juice, salt and a little pepper. Add the wine, sherry and water. Bring slowly to a boil. Spoon this court bouillon over the fillets. Cover with buttered wax pa-

per and poach in the oven for 15 minutes. Remove from the oven and arrange the fish on a warmed serving platter. Strain the stock and reserve it.

To make the sauce, first melt the butter in a saucepan. Off the heat, stir in the flour. Season with salt and a few grains of cayenne pepper. Add the reserved strained stock. Stir over low heat until the sauce comes to a boil. Add the cream and simmer gently for 10 minutes.

Put the egg yolks in a medium-sized bowl. With a wire whisk, mix in the brandy, vinegar, salt and a little cayenne pepper. Mix in the heavy cream. Stand the bowl in a shallow pan of hot water over low heat. Beat until the yolk mixture is as thick as you want it. Cut the frozen butter into little pieces and beat these into the yolk mixture piece by piece. Mix this egg sauce (which is a hollandaise) into the white wine sauce and set it aside.

In another little pan melt the butter for the grape garnish. Add the grapes, parsley and brandy. Season with salt and a little white pepper. Heat gently over low heat.

To serve, scatter the grapes over the fillets. Spoon the sauce over the fish and brown them under a hot broiler.

DIONE LUCAS AND MARION GORMAN
THE DIONE LUCAS BOOK OF FRENCH COOKING

Sole Fillets with Fines Herbes

Filets de Sole aux Fines Herbes

(Options: flounder, halibut, turbot)

This recipe calls for a variation on the basic poaching technique: the liquid is brought just to a boil, then the cooking vessel is removed from the stove and the cooking completed off the heat. The technique of preparing fillets for poaching is demonstrated on pages 36-37.

To serve 8

4	whole sole (about 1 to 1½ lb. [½ to ¾ kg.] each), filleted and soaked in cold water, carcasses and trimmings reserved	4
	salt and pepper	
20 tbsp.	unsalted butter (10 oz. [300 g.])	300 ml.
1 tbsp.	chopped fresh parsley	15 ml.
1 tbsp.	chopped fresh chervil	15 ml.
1 tsp.	chopped tarragon	5 ml.
2 cups	fish fumet made from sole carcasses and trimmings *(recipe, page 164)*	½ liter

Spread the fillets out, skin side up, on paper towels and place more towels over them, pressing well to sponge them dry. Slit the surface membrane of each fillet three or four times diagonally. Sprinkle the fillets with salt and pepper and place a thin sliver of butter—cut half the length of a fillet—on the wider half of each fillet. Cut the remaining butter into small pieces and set aside to soften. Fold over the narrower half of each fillet and press gently.

Butter the bottom and sides of a tin-lined copper sauté pan or a low, wide, fireproof earthenware or enameled cast-iron casserole just large enough to hold the fillets without squeezing them in. Sprinkle the bottom with half of the chopped herbs and place the folded fillets side by side on this bed. Pour in enough fumet barely to cover the fillets, and sprinkle the surface lightly with salt and pepper (remembering that the fumet will be radically reduced, concentrating its saltiness) and the remaining chopped herbs. Press a piece of generously buttered wax paper—cut to cover the top of the cooking utensil—over the fillets, buttered side down. Everything up to this point, assuming the fumet to be cold, may be done an hour or so ahead of time if desired.

Place the casserole, covered, over medium to high heat (by placing earthenware over an asbestos pad, the stove heat may be turned to maximum). As the liquid heats, check it regularly by lifting the edge of the buttered paper; it is important that the fish not boil. The instant the boiling point is reached, remove the fish from the heat and set aside, tightly covered, to poach for 7 to 8 minutes.

Lift out the fillets, one by one, allowing them to drain well, and place them on a warmed platter. Put a heated plate over them to keep them warm while finishing the sauce.

Transfer the liquid to a small saucepan. Reduce the sauce over high heat, stirring constantly. The cooking liquid should be reduced to the consistency of a light syrup and removed immediately from the heat. With a small whisk, whip in the softened butter in three batches, adding more as the preceding batch is absorbed.

Pour the sauce over the fillets and serve immediately. The sauce will be consistent and creamy in texture without feeling "thick." If wished, garnish with cucumbers.

RICHARD OLNEY
THE FRENCH MENU COOKBOOK

Swordfish Sailor-Style

(Options: bass, bonito, tuna)

To serve 4

2 lb.	swordfish steaks	1 kg.
⅓ cup	chopped onion	75 ml.
2 tbsp.	olive oil	30 ml.
3½ cups	canned whole tomatoes	875 ml.
1 tsp.	salt	5 ml.
¼ tsp.	black pepper	1 ml.
4	fresh basil leaves, or 1 tsp. [5 ml.] dried basil	4
⅓ cup	capers, rinsed and drained	75 ml.

In a large skillet, sauté the onions in hot oil for 3 minutes. Stir in the tomatoes, salt, pepper, basil and capers. Cover the pan and simmer the mixture for 15 minutes. Correct the seasoning if necessary.

Place the swordfish in the sauce and poach until the fish flakes at the touch of a fork and looks opaque—about 5 minutes on each side. Place the swordfish on a warmed platter and spoon the sauce over it.

ANNA MUFFOLETTO
THE ART OF SICILIAN COOKING

Blue Trout

Truite au Bleu

(No options)

It is important to use freshly killed trout for this recipe. Live trout can be kept for several hours in a plastic bag or bucket filled with water. The technique of gutting fish through the gills is demonstrated on page 19.

	To serve 8	
8	live trout (about ½ lb. [¼ kg.] each)	8
2 quarts	vinegar court bouillon (recipe, page 163), made with 2 cups [½ liter] vinegar	2 liters
6 tbsp.	vinegar	90 ml.
4	lemons, halved	4
6 to 8	sprigs parsley	6 to 8

First prepare the court bouillon. Ten minutes before serving time, take the trout out of water, kill each of them by a blow on the head on the edge of a table, and quickly gut them through the gills. Sprinkle the vinegar over the trout and drop them into the boiling court bouillon. Cook for 7 to 8 minutes, making sure that the liquid is just simmering, not boiling. The trout will turn blue and curl up as they cook.

Drain the fish and arrange them on a heated serving dish. Garnish with the lemon halves and parsley. Serve boiled potatoes and melted butter separately. If desired, some of the cooking liquor may be served in a gravy boat.

ACADÉMIE CULINAIRE DE FRANCE
CUISINE FRANÇAISE

Steelhead Trout in Red Wine

Truite Saumonée au Vin Rouge

(Option: salmon)

The original version of this recipe specifies salmon trout, an Atlantic trout that is similar to steelhead trout in America. To prepare the anchovy essence called for here, dilute about ½ tablespoon [7 ml.] of anchovy paste with 1 or 2 teaspoons [5 or 10 ml.] of the red wine fumet, and mix well.

	To serve 10	
1	whole steelhead trout (4 lb. [2 kg.]), cleaned	1
6 tbsp.	butter	90 ml.
1 tbsp.	anchovy essence	15 ml.
	beurre manié, made from 2 tbsp. [30 ml.] flour, kneaded with 2 tbsp. butter	
	Red wine fumet	
1 quart	dry red wine	1 liter
2 tbsp.	butter	30 ml.
1	small carrot, thinly sliced	1
1	onion, thinly sliced	1
2 cups	water	½ liter
1	bouquet garni	1
	salt and pepper	

To prepare the fumet, melt the butter in a saucepan. Add the vegetables, stirring briskly over low heat, then leave to simmer for a few minutes. Add the wine, water and bouquet garni, and season with salt and pepper. Bring to a boil, cover the pan and simmer gently for 30 minutes. Set the fumet aside to cool.

Put the prepared trout on the rack of a fish poacher. Strain the cooled fumet through a fine sieve over the fish. Put the fish poacher on the stove; bring to a boil, cover and simmer over very low heat for about 40 minutes. Remove the trout, still on the rack, and slide it gently onto a very hot serving platter. Keep the fish hot.

To make the sauce, strain the cooking liquor through a fine sieve into a saucepan; bring it to a boil over high heat and continue boiling until its volume is reduced by a third. Remove the pan from the heat and whisk the *beurre manié* into the sauce. Correct the seasoning and add the rest of the butter, cut into small pieces, and the anchovy essence.

Remove the skin from the top of the trout, coat the fish with the hot sauce and serve.

ODETTE KAHN
LA PETITE ET LA GRANDE CUISINE

Poached Fish with Horseradish and Apples

Leshch, Varenii s Khrenom i Yablokami

(Options: bass, carp, perch)

The parsley root called for here is a hardy variety of parsley, often called Hamburg parsley, grown for its fleshy parsnip-shaped root. If unavailable, use a small parsnip.

The original version of this recipe from the classic pre-Revolution Russian cookbook calls for bream, a common European fish.

	To serve 6 to 8	
1	whole fish (3 to 4 lb. [1½ to 2 kg.]), cleaned, rubbed inside and out with salt and cut into 6 or 8 pieces	1
1 to 1¼ cups	cider vinegar	250 to 300 ml.
1	parsley root, cut into pieces	1
1	celery heart, cut into pieces	1
1	leek, sliced	1
2	medium-sized onions, sliced	2
3 cups	water	¾ liter
	salt	
12 to 15	peppercorns	12 to 15
2 or 3	bay leaves	2 or 3
½	lemon, thinly sliced	½
	Horseradish and apple sauce	
3 to 4 tbsp.	freshly grated horseradish	45 to 60 ml.
4 to 6	cooking apples, peeled, cored and grated	4 to 6
2 to 3 tsp.	cider vinegar	10 to 15 ml.
	sugar	

Place the pieces of fish in a dish. Bring the cider vinegar to a boil and pour it over the fish. After a few minutes, remove the fish and transfer it to a fireproof casserole.

In a large saucepan, put the vegetables to boil in the water with the salt, peppercorns and bay leaves. After about 15 to 20 minutes, when the vegetables are well cooked, strain off the cooking liquid and pour it over the fish. Discard the vegetables and seasonings. Set the fish to cook over a fairly high heat for about 15 minutes.

To prepare the sauce, mix together the horseradish, apple, cider vinegar and sugar to taste, and add about 5 tablespoons [75 ml.] of the fish cooking liquid, strained.

Transfer the fish pieces to a warmed serving platter and garnish with the lemon slices. Serve the sauce separately.

ELENA MOLOKHOVETS
PODAROK MOLODYM KHOZYAIKAM

Steamed Fish with Golden Needles

Jing Yü

(Options: rockfish, turbot)

The technique of steaming fish is demonstrated on pages 38-39. The golden needles called for in this recipe are dried tiger-lily buds. These, together with dried Chinese dates and mushrooms, are obtainable wherever Chinese foods are sold.

To serve 2 or 3

1	whole medium-sized sole or dab (1½ lb. [¾ kg.]), cleaned	1
½ tsp.	salt	2 ml.
¼ tsp.	pepper	1 ml.
½ tsp.	sugar	2 ml.
2 tsp.	cornstarch	10 ml.
2 tbsp.	soy sauce	30 ml.
2 tbsp.	oil	30 ml.
2	dried Chinese mushrooms, soaked in hot water for 1 hour and drained	2
2	dried Chinese dates, soaked in hot water for 1 hour and drained	2
12	golden needles, soaked in warm water for 15 minutes, or until soft	12
2	slices fresh ginger, cut into fine slivers	2
1	scallion, chopped	1
1	thin slice smoked Smithfield-type ham, cut into julienne	1

Mix together the salt, pepper, sugar, cornstarch, soy sauce and oil. Place the fish in a dish that will fit into your steamer, and rub half of the seasoning mixture into the fish.

Slice the mushrooms and dates finely. Cut the golden needles into halves. Combine the remaining seasoning mixture with the mushrooms, dates, golden needles, ginger, scallion and ham. Spread this mixture over the fish. Place the fish in a steamer, and steam for about 20 minutes.

DOREEN YEN HUNG FENG
THE JOY OF CHINESE COOKING

Gefilte Fish

Kimsta Zuvis

(Options: carp, pike)

This famous Jewish dish originated in Lithuania. If desired, instead of slicing the fish, remove the skin in one piece; then stuff the skin and shape it to give the appearance of a whole fish. Tie the stuffed fish in a cloth before cooking. The technique of gutting a fish through the gills—required here—is demonstrated on page 19. The fish flesh can be pounded in a mortar or puréed with the onion in a food processor.

To serve 6

1	whole fish (2 lb. [1 kg.]), head and tail removed, gutted without breaking the skin and cut into 6 slices	1
	salt	
2	large onions, sliced	2
2	eggs	2
¼ cup	matzo meal or cracker crumbs	50 ml.
	pepper	
1 to 2 tbsp.	cold water	15 to 30 ml.
1	rib celery, diced	1
1	large carrot, sliced	1
2 or 3 tbsp.	chopped fresh parsley (optional)	30 or 45 ml.

Carefully remove the flesh and bones from the fish without breaking the skin. Sprinkle the skin, head and bones with salt and place them, covered, in the refrigerator while preparing the filling.

Put the fish flesh and one of the onions through a food grinder, place the mixture in a wooden chopping bowl and chop until smooth. Add the eggs and matzo meal or cracker crumbs, and season with salt and pepper. Add enough cold water to make a light, soft mixture, then blend well.

Wet your hands with cold water and form the mixture into six oval cakes that will fit into the bands of fishskin. Fit these cakes into the skin. Rinse the fish head and bones and place them in the bottom of a deep, heavy kettle or saucepan. Add the remaining onion, the celery, carrot, fish cakes and just enough cold water to cover.

Cover the kettle and bring to a quick boil, then remove the lid and reduce the heat. Simmer very slowly for 1½ to 2 hours, by which time the liquid should be reduced by half.

Serve the fish cakes warm, garnished with the cooked carrot and the chopped parsley. Or refrigerate the cakes and the strained cooking liquid separately, and serve the cakes chilled with the jellied cooking liquid as a garnish.

JOSEPHINE J. DAUZVARDIS
POPULAR LITHUANIAN RECIPES

Fish Curry

(Options: mackerel, sturgeon, tuna)

The original version of this recipe calls for hilsa, one of the best-known fish in India. Hilsa is related to the North American and European shad. Masala is an Indian spice mixture.

To serve 4 to 6

1	whole shad (2 lb. [1 kg.]), cleaned	1
2 tsp.	salt	10 ml.
1 tsp.	ground turmeric	5 ml.
½ tsp.	cayenne pepper	2 ml.
1 cup	vinegar	¼ liter
¾ cup	vegetable oil	175 ml.
Ginger-root Masala		
3	medium-sized onions	3
½-inch	cube fresh ginger root	1-cm.
12	garlic cloves	12
2 or 3	fresh green chilies, seeded, deribbed and sliced	2 or 3
2 cups	water	½ liter

Keeping the fish whole, cut slashes ½ inch [1 cm.] deep and 1 inch [2½ cm.] apart diagonally along the entire length of the fish on both sides. Rub the salt, turmeric and cayenne pepper into the fish. Lay the fish in a dish, pour over the vinegar and keep in a cool place for several hours.

Crush together the onions, ginger and garlic to make a *masala*. Heat the oil in a large skillet. Add the *masala* and chilies and fry for 2 to 3 minutes. Add the fish and cover with about 2 cups [½ liter] of water. Bring to a boil and simmer, uncovered, over low heat for about 2 hours, or until all the water has evaporated and the oil is floating on the top of the *masala*. It is important that the curry should not boil. Cooked in this way the fish bones become soft enough to eat.

RACHEL C. MUTHACHEN
INDIAN REGIONAL RECIPES (FOR NEWLY-WEDS)

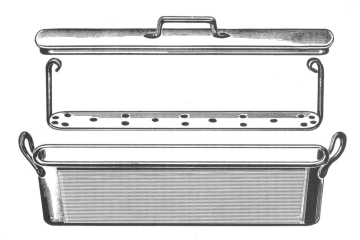

Fish Poached in Milk

(Options: smoked cod, smoked haddock, smoked halibut)

In this recipe, the fish can be poached in milk on top of the stove, or baked in a covered container at 350° F. [180° C.]. Allow 10 minutes per 1 inch [2½ cm.] thickness of fish if cooked on the stove top, 15 minutes if cooked in the oven.

To serve 6 to 8

2 lb.	smoked fish fillets	1 kg.
1 cup	milk	¼ liter
1 tbsp.	butter	15 ml.
	pepper	
	beurre manié, made by working 1 tbsp. [15 ml.] flour with 1 tbsp. soft butter (optional)	

In a covered pan, simmer the fish fillets in the milk until the flesh flakes easily when tested with a fork. Remove the fish to a warmed platter. Dot with the butter and season with pepper. Serve with the milk poured over the fish. Alternatively, stir the *beurre manié* into the milk, simmer until thickened, and pour over the fish.

GOVERNMENT OF CANADA, FISHERIES AND OCEANS
CANADIAN FISH AND SHELLFISH COOKBOOK SERIES

Steamed Fish

Quingzhen Yu

(Options: bass, carp, rockfish, trout)

The technique of using Chinese steamer trays is demonstrated on pages 38-39.

To serve 2 or 3

1	whole fish (½ lb. [¾ kg.]), cleaned, with the head left on	1
1½ tsp.	salt	7 ml.
2-inch	piece of fresh ginger root	5-cm.
4	scallions	4
1 tbsp.	soy sauce	15 ml.
1 tsp.	sesame seed oil	5 ml.
3 tbsp.	Chinese rice wine or dry sherry	45 ml.

Cut deep gashes into the sides of the fish, about ¾ inch [2 cm.] apart; it does not matter if the gashes hit the bone. Rub the salt all over the fish, inside the cavity as well as on the skin outside, then put the fish on a plate or in a shallow bowl.

Peel the ginger, then cut it into slivers about ⅛ inch [3 mm.] wide, the width of a wooden matchstick. Clean the scallions, then smash each one, both green part and white, with the side of your cleaver and cut them into 1-inch [2½-cm.] lengths. Put about half of the scallions, along with half of the ginger, into the cavity of the fish. Carefully sprinkle the soy sauce and sesame oil over the fish. Then spread the rest of the ginger and scallions on top. Set the fish aside to marinate at room temperature for 15 to 20 minutes.

Pour 1 or 2 inches [2½ or 5 cm.] of water into a wok. Put the plate or shallow bowl containing the fish in a steamer tray and set the tray over the water. Sprinkle the wine or sherry over the fish. Bring the water to a boil over a high flame, then cover the steamer and steam the fish for 20 minutes. Remove the plate from the steamer carefully and serve the fish immediately.

ELLEN SCHRECKER WITH JOHN SCHRECKER
MRS. CHIANG'S SZECHWAN COOKBOOK

Fish Hotpot

Fischlabskaus

(Options: bass, cod, whiting)

	To serve 4	
1½ lb.	fish fillets	¾ kg.
	salt	
8	medium-sized potatoes, boiled, peeled and mashed	8
6 tbsp.	butter	90 ml.
1	large onion, chopped	1
	pepper	
2	anchovy fillets, soaked in water for 10 minutes, patted dry and pounded to a paste	2
2½ tsp.	German-style prepared mustard, such as Düsseldorf	12 ml.
1	sour pickle, thinly sliced	1

Poach the fillets in a little salted water for 7 or 8 minutes, or until tender but firm. Drain the fillets, flake them and mix them with the hot mashed potato. Meanwhile, melt the butter in a skillet and cook the onion over low heat until it is golden. Add the pepper, anchovy paste and mustard to make an onion sauce. Put the potato-and-fish mixture on a warmed platter, spread the onion sauce over it and garnish with the pickle slices.

HANS KARL ADAM
GERMAN COOKERY

Fish with Walnut Sauce

Satsivi iz ryby

(Options: burbot, grouper, pollock)

Satsivi is a famous Soviet-Georgian sauce served with meat or chicken as well as fish. Fresh pomegranates are available in the United States in September and October. Halve them and squeeze them to extract the juice, then strain out the seeds.

	To serve 4	
1	whole fish (2 lb. [1 kg.]), cleaned	1
2	bay leaves	2
8	peppercorns	8
	lightly salted water	
1 cup	shelled walnuts	¼ liter
2 to 4	garlic cloves	2 to 4
	Hungarian paprika	
	salt	
1 tsp.	ground coriander seeds	5 ml.
3 to 4	small onions, finely chopped	3 to 4
1 tsp.	ground cinnamon	5 ml.
1 tsp.	ground cloves	5 ml.
	freshly ground black pepper	
⅓ cup	vinegar, or pomegranate juice	90 ml.

Cut the fish into portion-sized pieces. Put the fish pieces into a pan with the bay leaves, peppercorns and just enough salted water to cover. Simmer the fish for 12 to 15 minutes. Remove the fish from the pan, put it on a serving dish and let it cool. Reserve the cooking liquid.

In a mortar, pound the walnuts together with the garlic, paprika and salt to taste. Add the ground coriander and mix well. Dilute the mixture to the consistency of light cream by adding some of the reserved cooking liquid. Pour this sauce into a pan, add the onions and simmer, uncovered, for 10 minutes. Mix the cinnamon, cloves and pepper with the vinegar or pomegranate juice, and add this mixture to the sauce. Continue to cook for 10 minutes more.

Pour the hot sauce over the fish. Leave to cool, then serve, decorated if desired with walnut halves, sprigs of fresh coriander and scallion stems.

N. PAKHURIDZE (EDITOR)
BLYUDA GRUZINSKOĬ KUKHNI

Braising and Stewing

Portuguese Fisherman Stew

(Options: corvina, cusk, grouper, monkfish, tilefish)

To serve 6

2 lb.	striped bass fillets, skinned and cut into 1-inch [2½-cm.] cubes	1 kg.
1 tbsp.	butter	15 ml.
1 cup	chopped onion	¼ liter
1	garlic clove, crushed	1
2 lb.	canned tomatoes, undrained and chopped	1 kg.
3 cups	water	¾ liter
1 tsp.	basil	5 ml.
1 tsp.	thyme	5 ml.
¼ tsp.	crushed red pepper	1 ml.
1 tsp.	salt	5 ml.
4 cups	pumpkin or winter squash (about 1½ lb. [¾ kg.]), cut into 1-inch [2½-cm.] cubes	1 liter
2	ears corn, cut crosswise into 1-inch [2½-cm.] pieces	2

In a large saucepan, melt the butter. Add the onion and garlic, and cook until the vegetables are tender. Add the tomatoes, water, basil, thyme, red pepper, salt, pumpkin and corn. Cover and bring to a boil; simmer for 10 to 15 minutes or until the pumpkin and corn are done. Add the fish and continue to cook for 5 to 10 minutes or until the fish flakes when tested with a fork.

U.S. DEPARTMENT OF COMMERCE
A SEAFOOD HERITAGE

Bonito with Partridge Sauce

Bonito en Salsa Perdiz

(Options: sturgeon, swordfish, tuna)

The bonito is a very popular fish in the north of Spain. The sauce in this recipe is similar to one used for partridge and calls for a little chocolate. Spaniards are the only Europeans who regularly add chocolate to fish dishes, perhaps because chocolate was first introduced to Europe in Spain.

To serve 4

1¼ lb.	bonito steak	⅔ kg.
1 tbsp.	olive oil	15 ml.
4 tbsp.	rendered pork fat or lard	60 ml.
½ cup	dry white wine	125 ml.
3	medium-sized onions, quartered	3
2	garlic cloves, chopped	2
1 tbsp.	fine dry bread crumbs	15 ml.
½ to 1 tbsp.	grated unsweetened chocolate	7 to 15 ml.
1 cup	meat stock	¼ liter
4	slices French bread, fried in olive oil	4

Put the bonito steak, either whole or cut in half, in a fireproof earthenware cooking pot with the olive oil. Add the pork fat or lard, white wine, onions and garlic. Cook over medium heat for 5 minutes, then turn the fish and cook for 5 minutes more, until the fish is golden all over. Cover the pot and cook over low heat for 2 hours.

Transfer the fish to a warmed earthenware casserole and add the bread crumbs, chocolate and stock to the remaining contents of the pot. Mix well together, then strain the sauce through a fine sieve over the fish. Serve the fish garnished with the slices of fried bread.

ANA MARIA CALERA
LA COCINA VASCA

Carp Budapest-Style

Karpfen auf Budapester Art

(Options: catfish, ocean catfish, pike, rockfish)

To serve 4

1	whole carp (2 lb. [1 kg.]), cleaned and cut into serving pieces	1
2 tbsp.	butter	30 ml.
2	carrots, cut into julienne	2
2	ribs celery, cut into julienne	2
1	parsley root, cut into julienne	1
1	kohlrabi or turnip, cut into julienne	1
1	small onion, thinly sliced	1
	salt	
1 quart	dry white wine	1 liter

Melt the butter in a large saucepan and sauté the vegetables over low heat. When they are softened, add the carp. Season with salt. Pour the wine into the saucepan and bring to a boil, then simmer for 15 minutes, or until the carp is cooked. Remove the carp to a heated serving dish. Boil the contents of the pan until the liquid has been reduced by about half. Pour the cooking liquid and vegetables over the fish, and serve with toasted bread slices.

ELEK MAGYAR
KOCHBUCH FÜR FEINSCHMECKER

Fresh-Water Fish Stew

Carpe en Matelotte

(Options: catfish, perch, pike)

To serve 6

1	whole carp (2 to 2½ lb. [1 kg.]), cut into thick slices	1
1½ lb.	fresh-water fish (not carp), prepared according to type and cut into pieces	¾ kg.
4 tbsp.	butter	60 ml.
2 tbsp.	flour	30 ml.
12	small white onions (or substitute 3 large onions, quartered)	12
1½ cups	dry red wine	375 ml.
1½ cups	fish fumet (recipe, page 164)	375 ml.
	salt and pepper	
1	bouquet garni	1
	croutons (recipe, page 167)	

Make a roux in a saucepan with half the butter and all the flour. When it has turned golden brown, add the onions and cook them gently for about 10 minutes, adding the remaining butter. Then add the red wine and the fish fumet, bring the sauce to a boil and simmer for about 30 minutes.

Put the prepared fish in a large saucepan. Pour the sauce over the fish, season with salt and pepper and the bouquet garni, then cook, uncovered, over high heat for 30 minutes. When you are ready to serve the dish, remove the bouquet garni and scatter the croutons over the stew.

MENON
LA CUISINIÈRE BOURGEOISE

Smothered Catfish

Catfish Étouffée

(Options: cod, grouper, haddock, pollock)

To make the brown roux called for in this recipe, combine in a large skillet 8 tablespoons [120 ml.] of unsifted, all-purpose flour with 8 tablespoons of vegetable oil to make a smooth paste. Place the skillet over the lowest possible heat and, stirring constantly with a large metal spatula, simmer the roux for 45 minutes to an hour. The roux will foam for 5 or 10 minutes, and will darken after about half an hour. Continue to cook the roux until it is a dark, rich brown, guarding carefully against burning in the last few minutes of cooking. Let the roux cool to room temperature before using.

To serve 4

2 lb.	catfish fillets, skinned and cut into 1-inch [2½-cm.] chunks	1 kg.
2 cups	fish fumet (recipe, page 164)	½ liter
4 tbsp.	brown roux	60 ml.
1 cup	finely chopped onions	¼ liter
1 cup	finely chopped scallions, including 3 inches [8 cm.] of the green tops	¼ liter
½ cup	finely chopped celery	125 ml.
½ cup	finely chopped green pepper	125 ml.
1 tsp.	finely chopped garlic	5 ml.
2 cups	canned tomatoes, drained and coarsely chopped	½ liter
2	lemon slices cut ¼ inch [6 mm.] thick	2
1 tbsp.	Worcestershire sauce	15 ml.
1	small bay leaf, crumbled	1
¼ tsp.	crumbled dried thyme	1 ml.
¼ tsp.	cayenne pepper	1 ml.
1 tsp.	freshly ground black pepper	5 ml.
2 tsp.	salt	10 ml.
½ cup	finely chopped fresh parsley, preferably the flat-leafed Italian variety	125 ml.
4 cups	freshly cooked white rice	1 liter

In a small saucepan, bring the fish fumet to a boil over high heat. Remove the pan from the heat and cover it.

Warm the brown roux in a heavy 4- to 5-quart [4- to 5-liter] casserole set over low heat, stirring all the while. Add the onions, scallions, celery, green pepper and garlic and, stirring frequently, cook for about 5 minutes, or until they are soft but not brown.

Stirring constantly, pour in the hot fumet in a slow, thin stream. Add the tomatoes, lemon, Worcestershire sauce, bay leaf, thyme, red and black pepper, and salt. Reduce the heat to low and simmer, partly covered, for 30 minutes.

Add the chunks of catfish and the parsley, and stir gently to moisten the fish evenly with the simmering sauce. Cover the casserole partially again and, without stirring, simmer for 10 minutes longer, or until the catfish flakes easily when prodded gently with a fork.

Taste for seasoning and serve the catfish *étouffée* at once, directly from the casserole or arranged attractively on a deep heated platter. Present the rice in a separate bowl.

FOODS OF THE WORLD
AMERICAN COOKING: CREOLE AND ACADIAN

Cod with Saffron Sauce
Cabillaud Fraîche à la Sauce Jaune

(Options: burbot, cusk)

To serve 4

2 to 2½ lb.	fresh cod, thickly sliced	1 kg.
¼ cup	olive oil	50 ml.
	salt	
2 tbsp.	finely chopped fresh parsley	30 ml.
2	garlic cloves, finely chopped	2
½ tsp.	ground saffron	2 ml.
2 tsp.	flour	10 ml.
2 tbsp.	fresh lemon juice	30 ml.
1 cup	hot water	¼ liter

Put the oil, salt, parsley, garlic, saffron, flour and lemon juice into a pan broad enough to hold the fish slices side by side. Cook, stirring, over low heat for 2 to 3 minutes. Add the fish slices, turning them to coat both sides with the seasoning mixture. Cover the pan and cook gently. When the surfaces of the fish slices turn white, after about 10 minutes, turn over the slices and moisten them with the hot water. Bring to a boil, and serve immediately.

L. E. AUDOT
LA CUISINIÈRE DE LA CAMPAGNE ET DE LA VILLE

Codfish Stew

(Options: salted haddock, salted pollock)

To serve 6 to 8

2½ lb.	dried salt cod, soaked in several changes of water for 48 hours, drained and boned	1¼ kg.
	flour	
¼ cup	olive oil	50 ml.
2	large onions, chopped	2
½ lb.	Italian black olives	¼ kg.
Tomato sauce		
1 tbsp.	olive oil	15 ml.
7 oz.	tomato paste	225 g.
1 tbsp.	oregano	15 ml.
½ tsp.	salt	2 ml.
½ tsp.	black pepper	2 ml.
3 cups	water	¾ liter

Cover the cod with warm water and bring to a boil. Simmer until the fish is tender but firm—about 1 hour. Drain well

and dry with absorbent paper. Dredge the fish in flour; salt and pepper lightly. Brown lightly in 2 tablespoons [30 ml.] of hot olive oil. Remove to a heated platter and keep warm.

To make the sauce, heat the olive oil in a saucepan; stir in the tomato paste, oregano, salt and pepper. Stir and sauté for 3 minutes. Add the water; stir and simmer for 10 minutes.

Heat the remaining 2 tablespoons of olive oil and brown the onions and olives for 5 minutes. Pour in the tomato sauce; add the fish and cover. Simmer until all of the flavors are blended and the fish is fork-tender—about 30 minutes.

ANNA MUFFOLETTO
THE ART OF SICILIAN COOKING

Chilean Conger Eel in Casserole
Congrio en Fuente a la Chilena

(No options)

The chef at the Hotel Crillon in Santiago, who supplied this recipe, says conger eel is the best-liked fish dish in all Chile. These marine monsters, sometimes as long as 8 feet [2½ meters], are fine in flavor and very meaty. Even if you don't care for fresh-water eels, you should go for fat congers.

To serve 6

2½ lb.	conger eel, cut into 6 pieces	1¼ kg.
3 tbsp.	oil or butter	45 ml.
	salt and pepper	
2 tbsp.	butter	30 ml.
2 tbsp.	lard	30 ml.
2	medium-sized onions, chopped	2
2	garlic cloves, crushed	2
½ tsp.	dried marjoram	2 ml.
¼ tsp.	ground cumin	1 ml.
4	tomatoes, peeled and thinly sliced	4
4	medium-sized potatoes, peeled and sliced	4
1 cup	fresh corn kernels, cut from 2 large ears	¼ liter
1 cup	freshly shelled peas or lima beans, boiled (optional)	¼ liter
	croutons (recipe, page 167)	
6	sprigs parsley	6

Heat the oil in a skillet. Season the eel with salt and pepper, brown lightly in the oil, then remove from the skillet and drain on paper towels. Heat the butter and lard in a saucepan; add the onions, garlic, marjoram and cumin. Fry gently until the onions are soft, then add the tomatoes, potatoes and corn kernels. Stir and cover. Cook over low heat for about 20 minutes or until the potatoes are tender, then season to taste. At this point the cooked peas or lima beans may be added to make the casserole a fuller one-dish meal.

Place half of this vegetable mixture in a buttered or oiled casserole. Lay the fish over it and cover with the remaining vegetable mixture. Cover the casserole, put it in a preheated 300° F. [150° C.] oven and cook for 40 minutes, or until the fish is done. Garnish the dish with bread croutons and sprigs of parsley, and serve hot.

CORA, ROSE AND BOB BROWN
THE SOUTH AMERICAN COOK BOOK

Conger Eel Stew, Bragança-Style

Congro Ensopado a Moda de Bragança

(No options)

To serve 4

1 lb.	conger eel (center cut), cleaned and cut into 4 slices	½ kg.
½ cup	olive oil	125 ml.
1	medium-sized onion, chopped	1
	pepper	
1	bay leaf	1
	salt	
1 tbsp.	vinegar	15 ml.
½ cup	water	125 ml.
4	thick slices of day-old French or Italian bread	4
3	egg yolks	3
1 tbsp.	chopped fresh parsley	15 ml.

Heat the oil in a saucepan, and add the onion, pepper and bay leaf. Cook until the onion is golden, then put the slices of fish on top, adding salt to taste and the vinegar and water. Simmer, covered, for 10 to 15 minutes, until the fish is done, then remove from the heat.

Place the slices of bread on a warmed platter and put the slices of cooked fish on top of them. Beat the egg yolks with the parsley and pour this mixture into the liquid in which the fish was cooked. Mix well and heat gently until the sauce thickens. Pour this sauce over the fish and serve at once.

MARIA ODETTE CORTES VALENTE
COZINHA REGIONAL PORTUGUESA

Eel Cooked with Herbs

L'Anguille au Vert

(No options)

	To serve 6	
4	whole eel (1 lb. [½ kg.] each), 1 inch [2½ cm.] thick, skinned, heads cut off, cut into sections 2 inches [5 cm.] long	4
8 tbsp.	butter	120 ml.
2	large onions, chopped	2
	salt and pepper	
2 cups	dry white wine	½ liter
½ cup	heavy cream	125 ml.
2	eggs, beaten	2
5 tbsp.	fresh lemon juice	75 ml.
	Herbs	
¼ lb.	sorrel, stems removed	125 g.
¼ lb.	watercress, large stems removed	125 g.
2 oz.	white nettle leaves, stems removed (optional)	75 g.
4 tbsp.	fresh tarragon leaves (optional)	60 ml.
2 tbsp.	fresh parsley	30 ml.
2 tbsp.	fresh chervil	30 ml.
1	sprig mint, stem removed	1
1	sprig sage, stem removed	1
1	sprig savory or rosemary, stem removed	1
1	rib celery	1
2 or 3	shallots, chopped and pounded	2 or 3
	zest of 2 lemons (optional)	

In a large skillet heat the butter until it is foaming, then toss in the pieces of eel and the onions. Meanwhile, finely chop the herbs. This must be done at the very last moment; otherwise they will lose their freshness.

Add the herbs to the eels and leave to sweat, covered, for 5 minutes. Season with salt and pepper. Pour in enough white wine to cover the contents of the pan, adding a little water if necessary, and simmer, covered, for 10 minutes.

Mix the cream with the eggs, lemon juice, salt and pepper. Remove the skillet from the heat and pour in the cream mixture; blend it gradually with the herbs, rotating the pan. Transfer to a serving dish and serve either hot or cold.

CLAUDIAN
À TABLE

Cornish Conger Eel in Cider

(No options)

To serve 6 to 8

3 lb.	conger eel, skinned and cut into 2 or 3 pieces	1½ kg.
4 tbsp.	butter	60 ml.
2	medium-sized onions, chopped (about 1½ cups [375 ml.])	2
½ cup	flour	125 ml.
1 quart	hard cider	1 liter
	salt and pepper	

Melt the butter in a heavy casserole and fry the onions until golden. Add the eel pieces and brown lightly. Stir in the flour and cook until brown. Gradually stir in the cider, season with salt and pepper, and cover the casserole.

Bake in a preheated 350° F. [180° C.] oven for 1 hour. Serve the fish in the sauce.

LIZZIE BOYD (EDITOR)
BRITISH COOKERY

A Ragout of Eels

Catigot d'Anguilles à la Gardiane

(No options)

The technique of skinning an eel is demonstrated on page 45.

To serve 4

8	small whole eel, skinned and cut into 2- or 3-inch [5- or 8-cm.] pieces	8
4 tbsp.	olive oil	60 ml.
12	garlic cloves, crushed	12
1	bay leaf	1
1	sprig thyme or ¼ oz. [12 g.] dried thyme	1
1	piece orange peel	1
1	red chili	1
	salt	
½ cup	dry red wine	125 ml.

In a heavy saucepan, combine the oil, garlic, bay leaf, thyme, orange peel and a tiny piece of chili.

Salt the eel pieces lightly. Put them in the saucepan, sprinkle the wine over them and add just enough water to cover. Cook, uncovered, over moderate heat, for 20 to 30 minutes, depending on their thickness. Serve on hot plates.

JEAN-NOËL ESCUDIER AND PETA J. FULLER
THE WONDERFUL FOOD OF PROVENCE

Eel Stew with Prunes

Matelote d'Anguille aux Pruneaux

(No options)

The technique of skinning an eel is demonstrated on page 45. The marc called for in this recipe is a pungent brandy, distilled from the grapeskins and seeds left over after wine is made. If marc is unavailable, substitute brandy.

To serve 4

1	whole eel (1½ lb. [¾ kg.]), skinned, head removed, and cut into pieces 2½ inches [6 cm.] long	1
4 tbsp.	butter	60 ml.
12	small boiling onions	12
2 cups	red wine	½ liter
¼ cup	marc	50 ml.
1	sugar lump	1
1	garlic clove, crushed	1
1	bouquet garni	1
12	dried prunes, soaked in tea for 3 hours and drained	12

Melt the butter in a heavy pan, and lightly sauté the eel pieces and the onions. Add the wine and the marc, then the sugar, garlic and bouquet garni. Cover the pan and bring the liquid to a boil. Then ignite the liquid as you would if making a punch. When the flames die, cover the pan and simmer the eel very gently for 2 hours over the lowest possible heat. Add the prunes, cover and cook for 1 hour longer.

ROBERT COURTINE
MON BOUQUET DE RECETTES

Muskellunge Fillets in Cream

(Options: dolphin, pike, snook)

To serve 4

4	muskellunge fillets (about ½ lb. [¼ kg.] each)	4
4 tbsp.	butter	60 ml.
1½ cups	chopped onions	375 ml.
¼ tsp.	salt	1 ml.
2 cups	dry white wine	½ liter
3 cups	light cream	¾ liter
	paprika	

Melt 3 tablespoons [45 ml.] of the butter in a heavy skillet and sauté the onions until they become transparent. Dust the fillets lightly on both sides with the salt, and lay them on the onions. Pour the wine over the fillets and simmer for 3 to 4 minutes, then slowly add the cream. Cover the pan and cook the fillets over low heat for 10 to 12 minutes. Just before serving, dot the tops of the fillets with the remaining butter and dust them with paprika.

MEL MARSHALL
COOKING OVER COALS

Braised Pike

Brochet à l'Étuvée

(Options: burbot, carp, grouper, muskellunge)

To serve 4

1	whole pike (2 lb. [1 kg.]), cleaned and cut into steaks 1 inch [2½ cm.] thick	1
4 tbsp.	butter	60 ml.
2 tbsp.	flour	30 ml.
2 cups	dry red wine	½ liter
1	bouquet garni, including tarragon	1
3 or 4	whole cloves	3 or 4
12	small boiling onions, parboiled for 5 minutes	12
1½ cups	button mushrooms (about ¼ lb. [125 g.])	375 ml.
4	artichoke bottoms, parboiled for 10 minutes and quartered	4
	salt and freshly ground pepper	
4	anchovy fillets, soaked in cold water for 10 minutes, patted dry and finely chopped	4
1 tbsp.	capers, rinsed and drained	15 ml.
	croutons *(recipe, page 167)*	

In a large enameled or stainless-steel saucepan set over low heat, make a roux with half of the butter and the flour. Whisk in the wine, bring to a boil, then add the bouquet garni, cloves, onions, mushrooms and artichoke bottoms. Season with salt and pepper. Add the fish steaks, cover, and simmer gently for about 15 minutes.

Transfer the fish steaks, onions, mushrooms and artichoke bottoms to a warmed platter and cover to keep them hot. Discard the bouquet garni and cloves, then remove the pan from the heat and whisk the remaining butter into the sauce. Add the anchovies and capers. Garnish the fish steaks and vegetables with croutons, and pour the sauce over them.

OFFRAY AINÉ
LE CUISINIER MÉRIDIONAL

Braised Shad with Sorrel

Alose à l'Avignonnaise

(Options: bonito, mackerel, sturgeon)

To serve 3 or 4

1	whole shad (about 2 lb. [1 kg.]), cleaned, scraped and trimmed	1
1½ lb.	sorrel, chopped	¾ kg.
½ cup	olive oil	125 ml.
1	large onion, finely chopped	1
3 or 4	tomatoes, peeled, seeded and roughly chopped	3 or 4
1	garlic clove, crushed	1
	salt and pepper	
2 tbsp.	chopped fresh parsley	30 ml.
½ cup	fresh bread crumbs	125 ml.

Lightly sauté the sorrel in 3 tablespoons [45 ml.] of the oil with the onion, tomatoes and garlic for about 10 minutes. Season with salt and pepper, then add the parsley and bread crumbs to bind everything together.

Meanwhile, in a fireproof earthenware casserole with a lid, lightly brown the shad in 3 tablespoons of the remaining oil. Remove the fish, and line the bottom of the casserole with half of the sorrel mixture. Place the shad on top and cover it with the rest of the sorrel mixture. Sprinkle with the remaining oil, put the lid on the casserole and braise the shad in a very slow oven at 250° F. [120° C.] for 8 to 10 hours.

At the end of this long cooking period, the sorrel will have lost its slightly bitter taste, the fish bones will have dissolved and you will have a delicious dish.

MICHEL BOUZY
LES POISSONS-CRUSTACÉS-COQUILLAGES

Martinican Red Snapper Blaff

(Options: angler, snook)

Blaff is a traditional French Caribbean dish of fresh fish poached in a clear stock seasoned with hot pepper.

To serve 6

6	red snapper fillets (about 1½ lb. [¾ kg.])	6
3 tbsp.	fresh lemon juice	45 ml.
3 cups	dry white wine	¾ liter
	salt	
1	medium-sized canned chili pepper, chopped	1
3	garlic cloves, finely chopped	3
2 cups	water	½ liter
3	whole cloves	3
	pepper	
1	small onion, sliced	1
1	rib celery	1
1	bay leaf	1
2	sprigs parsley	2
¼ tsp.	dried thyme	1 ml.

Marinate the fillets for 1 hour in the refrigerator in a shallow glass dish containing the lemon juice, 1 cup [¼ liter] of the wine, salt to taste, the chili, and one of the garlic cloves.

Put 2 cups [½ liter] of water in a large pot. Add the whole cloves, the remaining garlic, pepper, the onion, and the celery, bay leaf, parsley and thyme tied together in a muslin bag. Add the remaining wine. Bring to a gentle boil and reduce by half to about 2 cups. Remove the muslin bag. Add the fish and its marinade, cover and bring to a boil. Boil gently for another 3 to 5 minutes or until done. Serve the fish in the liquid. More lemon juice may be added to taste.

RAYMOND A. SOKOLOV
GREAT RECIPES FROM THE NEW YORK TIMES

Sole Stewed in Cider with Mussels

Sole en Matelote à la Normande

(Options: flounder, fluke)

This is not the elaborate restaurant dish called *sole à la Normande,* but rather the primitive version from which, no doubt, the more luxurious concoction derived. Be sure to use a porcelain or enamel-lined dish for this recipe; tin or unlined cast-iron will turn the cider black.

To serve 2

1	whole sole (1 lb. [½ kg.]), cleaned and skinned on both sides	1
1 quart	small mussels, scrubbed	1 liter
1	large onion, finely sliced	1
1 tbsp.	butter	15 ml.
½ cup	hard cider	125 ml.
	salt and pepper	
	parsley butter, made by mashing 1 tbsp. [15 ml.] butter with 1 tbsp. chopped fresh parsley	

Melt the onion in the butter, stewing it very gently until it is quite soft but still pale yellow. Meanwhile, put the cleaned mussels in a saucepan with the cider, set them over high heat and extract them as soon as they open.

Put the onion mixture, well seasoned, into a long shallow fireproof dish. Put the sole on top. Through cheesecloth, pour in enough stock from the mussels to barely cover it. Cover the dish, and cook in a moderate oven, preheated to 350° F. [180° C.], for 15 minutes. Remove from the oven, put the shelled mussels round the fish, and the parsley butter on top of it. Return the dish to the oven for 5 minutes, just sufficient time for the mussels to heat through. Serve in the same dish.

ELIZABETH DAVID
FRENCH PROVINCIAL COOKING

Soles Stewed in Cream

(Options: flounder, fluke)

The blade of mace called for in this 19th Century recipe is a strip of the whole spice. Ground mace can be substituted.

To serve 3 or 4

3 or 4	medium-sized whole sole, cleaned	3 or 4
	salt	
1 to 2 cups	heavy cream	¼ to ½ liter
	small blade mace, pounded	
	cayenne pepper	
2 tbsp.	fresh lemon juice	30 ml.
2 tsp.	freshly grated lemon peel (optional)	10 ml.
1 tsp.	arrowroot (optional)	5 ml.
1 tbsp.	milk (optional)	15 ml.

Put the soles into lightly salted boiling water, and simmer them for 2 minutes only; lift them out, and let them drain; lay them in a wide stewpan with as much cream as will nearly cover them; add a good seasoning of pounded mace, cayenne and salt; stew the fish gently for 6 to 10 minutes, or until the flesh parts readily from the bones; dish them, stir the lemon juice into the sauce, pour it over the soles, and send them immediately to the table.

Some lemon peel may be boiled in the cream, if approved; and arrowroot may be mixed with milk and stirred into the sauce (if it needs thickening) before the lemon juice is added.

ELIZABETH RAY (EDITOR)
THE BEST OF ELIZA ACTON

Paupiettes of Sole in Lettuce Leaves

(Options: croaker, flounder, scup, tilefish, turbot)

The fumet for this recipe should be made with the carcass of the sole, flavoring vegetables, a piece of lemon peel, a sprig of tarragon, and 2 tablespoons [30 ml.] of dry white wine, dry vermouth or wine vinegar. The technique of filleting a flat fish such as sole is demonstrated on pages 22-23.

	To serve 2 to 4	
1	whole sole (about 3 lb. [1½ kg.]), filleted and the carcass reserved	1
8	Bibb or Boston lettuce leaves	8
	salt and pepper	
3 tbsp.	fresh lemon juice	45 ml.
8	medium-sized, peeled, cooked shrimp	8
	nutmeg	
2 tbsp.	butter	30 ml.
2	eggs	2
½ cup	fish fumet (recipe, page 164)	125 ml.

Choose good lettuce leaves, not the coarse outside ones, but leaves large enough to roll up. Wash them, and blanch them for 2 minutes in boiling salted water; drain them. Season the four fillets of sole with salt, pepper and a little lemon juice. In the center of each, arrange a few shrimp, also seasoned; roll up the fillets. Arrange the lettuce leaves overlapping each other two by two, so that you have four pairs of leaves instead of eight individual ones. Put a rolled fillet in the center of each pair, and roll the leaves around the fish. Squeeze these rolls in the hand, so that each forms a little parcel, which need not be tied. Grate a little nutmeg onto each parcel, or *paupiette*. Melt the butter in a small shallow pan. Put the *paupiettes* in and cook very gently for 30 minutes, with the cover on the pan.

Beat the eggs in a bowl, and add the strained fumet, the remaining lemon juice and a little salt. Remove the *paupiettes* to a warmed serving dish. Strain the egg-and-lemon mixture through a sieve into the butter remaining in the pan, and stir very fast until the sauce has thickened and frothed. Pour over the *paupiettes* and serve at once.

ELIZABETH DAVID
SUMMER COOKING

Stockfish with White Wine and Olives

Le Stockfish à la Niçoise

(Options: salted cod, salted haddock, salted halibut, salted pollock)

Stockfish is a kind of dried cod, which must be soaked for four or five days in several changes of water to prepare it for cooking. Each day, take it out of the water and beat it with a rolling pin to soften it. Don't be alarmed at the smell, which is very disagreeable; just look forward to the result. In the old part of Nice, they sell stockfish entrails; these must be soaked first to soften them, then cut into thin strips and added to the cod; they help to bind the sauce.

	To serve 8	
3 lb.	stockfish, soaked and beaten, skin and bones removed, flesh flaked, rinsed and drained (or substitute salt cod, soaked overnight in water, drained, boned and flaked)	1½ kg.
1	large onion, finely chopped	1
3 or 4	garlic cloves	3 or 4
¼ cup	olive oil	50 ml.
8 to 10	tomatoes, peeled, seeded and chopped	8 to 10
1 cup	dry white wine, warmed	¼ liter
	salt and pepper	
1 or 2	dried red chilies	1 or 2
1	sweet red pepper, seeded, deribbed and cut into strips	1
6	medium-sized potatoes, diced	6
¼ cup	Cognac	60 ml.
5 or 6	salted anchovies, soaked in water for 10 minutes, drained and filleted	5 or 6
½ cup	pitted ripe olives	125 ml.

In a large pan, sauté the onion and garlic in the olive oil. When these are golden, add the flaked fish. Simmer gently over low heat (you must not let the fish toughen). Add the tomatoes, warmed wine, salt, pepper, chilies, and sweet pepper. Simmer very gently, covered, for at least 2 hours; there should then be enough liquid left in which to cook the potatoes. Add them to the pan and, if necessary, pour in a little hot water. Simmer for a further 30 minutes, then add the Cognac, anchovies and a handful of black olives. Stir briefly and serve very hot.

JOSÉPHINE BESSON
LA MÈRE BESSON "MA CUISINE PROVENÇALE"

Russian Sturgeon Stew

Solianka

(Options: burbot, cod, salmon)

To serve 4

1 lb.	sturgeon fillets, cut in 4 serving pieces	½ kg.
2 lb.	fish trimmings (heads, bones, etc.)	1 kg.
1½ quart	water	1½ liters
1 tsp.	salt	5 ml.
	freshly ground white pepper	
2	large tomatoes, peeled, seeded and coarsely chopped	2
¼ cup	corn oil	50 ml.
1 cup	coarsely chopped onion	¼ liter
2	dill pickles, coarsely chopped	2
1 tbsp.	capers	15 ml.
1 tbsp.	pitted green olives, coarsely chopped	15 ml.
1	bay leaf	1
1 tbsp.	finely chopped fresh parsley	15 ml.
4 tbsp.	butter	60 ml.
1 tbsp.	pitted black olives, finely chopped	15 ml.
1	lemon, thinly sliced	1
1	medium-sized cucumber, peeled, halved, seeded and thinly sliced	1
4	sprigs parsley	4

In a large heavy saucepan boil the fish trimmings in water seasoned with the salt and a generous sprinkling of pepper for about 30 minutes. Meanwhile, sauté the tomatoes with the oil in a large heavy skillet. Stir frequently until the tomatoes form a smooth paste. Add the cut-up fillets, onion, pickles, capers and green olives to the skillet.

Strain the fish broth into the skillet and discard the fish trimmings. Add the bay leaf and parsley. Simmer over low heat for about 15 to 20 minutes. Stir in the butter and cook over low heat for another minute.

Top each serving with black olives, lemon, cucumber and a sprig of parsley.

JEROME BRODY AND JOAN AND JOSEPH FOLEY
THE GRAND CENTRAL OYSTER BAR & RESTAURANT SEAFOOD COOKBOOK

Louie's Whiting Stew

(Options: bass, cod, corvina, cusk, haddock, pollock)

To serve 6 to 8

1	whole whiting (4 lb. [2 kg.]), cleaned but not boned, cut into pieces	1
1	medium-sized onion, chopped	1
1 tbsp.	chopped fresh parsley	15 ml.
¼ tsp.	dried rosemary	1 ml.
6 tbsp.	butter	90 ml.
2 cups	milk	½ liter
2 cups	water	½ liter
	salt and pepper	

In a large skillet, brown the onion, with the parsley and rosemary, in the butter. Add the fish, milk and water. Cook uncovered for 25 minutes over medium heat. Season with the salt and pepper. Serve the stew with hot toast.

RAYMOND A. SOKOLOV
GREAT RECIPES FROM THE NEW YORK TIMES

Tuna Chartreuse

Thon à la Chartreuse

(Options: bonito, swordfish)

The technique of larding a tuna steak with anchovies is demonstrated on page 46.

To serve 4

1½ lb.	tuna steak, about 1¼ inches [3 cm.] thick	¾ kg.
3 tbsp.	fresh lemon juice	45 ml.
4	anchovy fillets, soaked in water for 10 minutes, patted dry and halved	4
¼ cup	olive oil	50 ml.
1	medium-sized onion, sliced	1
4	medium-sized carrots, finely sliced	4
4	yellow hearts of Boston lettuce, blanched	4
4 oz.	sorrel, shredded (about ½ cup [125 ml.])	125 g.
	salt and pepper	
¾ cup	dry white wine	175 ml.

To draw out any excess oil, blanch the tuna steak in boiling salted water to which the lemon juice has been added. Remove and drain the fish, then lard it with the anchovy fillets.

Put the oil, onion and carrots into a heavy saucepan. Lay the tuna steak on top, cover the saucepan, place it over low heat and let the fish sweat. Turn the fish over once, arrange the blanched lettuce hearts around it and the sorrel on top of it. Cover the pan again and let the tuna sweat for a few more minutes; then season it with salt and pepper.

When the onion and carrots have begun to brown, and the liquid in the pan has been absorbed, pour in the white wine. Let the fish simmer, covered, for a further 30 minutes. During this time, turn the lettuce hearts over a few times, without disturbing the fish.

To serve, place the sorrel in a heap at one end of a warmed platter, and place the onion and carrots at the other end. Place the tuna steak in the middle and arrange the lettuce hearts around it. Finally, pour the cooking juices over the steak and serve.

J. B. REBOUL
LA CUISINIÈRE PROVENÇALE

Tuna Braised with Spinach or Chard

Thon Braisé aux Épinards ou aux Blettes

(Options: bonito, swordfish)

To serve 4 to 6

1½ lb.	tuna steak, skinned	¾ kg.
⅓ cup	olive oil	75 ml.
3	medium-sized tomatoes, peeled, seeded and quartered	3
2	medium-sized onions, chopped	2
6 to 8	garlic cloves	6 to 8
8 to 10	anchovy fillets, soaked in water for 10 minutes, patted dry and finely chopped	8 to 10
1	bouquet garni of thyme, bay leaf and a celery rib	1
	salt and pepper	
2 lb.	spinach, beet greens or chard, trimmed, parboiled for 2 or 3 minutes and drained	1 kg.
4 tbsp.	butter	60 ml.

Immerse the tuna steak in boiling water for 5 minutes to draw out excess fat. Drain the tuna, put it into a heavy casserole or saucepan just large enough to hold it easily, and add the olive oil, tomatoes, onions, garlic, anchovies and bouquet garni. Season with salt and pepper, but be sparing with the salt because the anchovies will contribute some saltiness. Cook for a minute or two over medium heat, then turn the tuna over and continue cooking, turning frequently, until the steak is colored on both sides. Add water to

cover, bring to a boil, then lower the heat, put the lid half on the casserole and simmer gently for 45 to 50 minutes, or until the tuna is tender. By the end of the cooking, the liquid should be reduced by half. Remove the bouquet garni.

Meanwhile, sauté the parboiled spinach or chard in the butter and season with salt and pepper. Spread the cooked greens on a warmed platter, place the tuna on this bed of greens and pour the contents of the casserole over the fish.

MOHAMED KOUKI
POISSONS MÉDITERRANÉENS

Tuna with Chartreuse

Thon à la Chartreuse

(Options: bonito, swordfish)

To serve 4

1½ lb.	tuna steak, soaked in water and vinegar for 15 minutes	¾ kg.
12	large lettuce leaves	12
2	medium-sized onions, sliced	2
3 or 4	medium-sized tomatoes, peeled, seeded and roughly chopped	3 or 4
4	lemon slices	4
	salt and pepper	
1 tbsp.	olive oil	15 ml.
½ cup	water	125 ml.
½ cup	dry white wine	125 ml.
3 tbsp.	Chartreuse liqueur	45 ml.

Line the base of a round gratin dish with 4 of the lettuce leaves, then put in a layer made up of half of the onion, half of the tomato and 2 lemon slices. Season with salt and pepper. Put the tuna on top and cover with a layer made up of the remaining onion, tomato and lemon, followed by a layer of the remaining lettuce leaves. (This final layer of lettuce has to be thicker than the first, because the top leaves will burn during the cooking and will have to be removed.) Season again, and add the oil, water, wine and Chartreuse.

Cook in a preheated 300° F. [150° C.] oven for 2 hours, basting from time to time. Serve in the same dish, remembering to remove the burnt lettuce leaves from the top.

C. CHANOT-BULLIER
VIEILLES RECETTES DE CUISINE PROVENÇALE

Peruvian Picante

(Options: mackerel, sea robin, rockfish)

To serve 4

1	whole fish (2 lb. [1 kg.]) or several small fish, cleaned and cut into serving pieces	1
	coarse salt	
1	garlic clove, crushed	1
1	yellow or green pepper, seeded, deribbed and chopped	1
½ cup	fresh orange juice, preferably from a bitter Seville orange	125 ml.

Cover the fish thickly on all sides with coarse salt and let stand for 1 hour or more. Place the garlic, pepper and orange juice in a saucepan. Pour in enough water to just cover the fish when they are added, and bring to the boiling point. Wash the salt from the pieces of fish and add the fish to the pan. Bring rapidly back to the boiling point. Cover tightly and simmer for 10 to 15 minutes, or until the fish is done.

CORA, ROSE AND BOB BROWN
THE SOUTH AMERICAN COOK BOOK

Mixed Fish Stew

La Migourée de Matata

(Options: angler, cod, croaker, eel, small ray — the more varieties of fish, the better.)

To serve 6

3 lb.	mixed fish, cut into slices about 1½ inch [4 cm.] thick	1½ kg.
1¼ quarts	dry white wine	1¼ liters
1 quart	water	1 liter
2	garlic cloves, finely chopped	2
2	onions, finely chopped	2
4	shallots, finely chopped	4
1	bouquet garni of parsley, thyme, tarragon and a bay leaf	1
	salt and pepper	
	quatre épices	
10 tbsp.	butter	150 ml.
5 tbsp.	olive oil	75 ml.
1 tbsp.	flour	15 ml.

To prepare the sauce, pour the wine and water into a large pan. Add the garlic, onions, shallots and bouquet garni, and

season with salt and pepper and a good pinch of *quatre épices*. Simmer, covered, for 3 hours.

Lightly fry the fish pieces in a mixture of 6 tablespoons [90 ml.] of butter and the oil until they are firm. Strain the sauce and return it to the pan. Thicken the sauce with the remaining 4 tablespoons [60 ml.] of butter, mixed with flour to make a *beurre manié*. Add the fish to the pan and simmer for 20 minutes over low heat. Serve hot.

AUSTIN DE CROZE
LES PLATS RÉGIONAUX DE FRANCE

Taillevent

A Mediterranean Fisherman's Stew

(Option: cod, sheepshead, wolf fish)

Taillevent, literally, is a four-cornered mainsail. In old French idiom, the word suggested a wind-filled mainsail — and connoted a well-fed person. For that reason Taillevent was the nickname given to a famous 14th Century French chef who made a right hearty fish stew. The name clings; though, one might say, the stew may vary as the wind blows.

To serve 4

2 lb.	fillets, skinned	1 kg.
	salt and pepper	
3 to 4 tbsp.	fresh lemon juice	45 to 60 ml.
¼ cup	olive oil	50 ml.
4	large onions, sliced	4
1	garlic clove, crushed	1
1	large green pepper, seeded, deribbed and cut into rings	1
½ cup	fresh herbs, including parsley, thyme, basil and oregano (optional), crushed	125 ml.
4	tomatoes, sliced	4
2 cups	heated water or fish fumet *(recipe, page 164)*	½ liter
1 cup	dry white wine	¼ liter

Wipe the fillets with a damp cloth and cut them into chunks. Sprinkle with salt, pepper and the lemon juice.

Heat the olive oil in a large iron skillet or kettle. Add the onion, garlic, pepper rings and herbs. Sauté until the onion is translucent. Remove the vegetables with a slotted spoon, discarding the garlic, and reserve. Add the fish and cook lightly until it just begins to color. Return the cooked vegetables and add the tomatoes, water or fumet, and the wine. Test for seasoning. Cover the skillet tightly and cook the fish over low heat until it flakes easily with a fork.

FRANCES MACILQUHAM
FISH COOKERY OF NORTH AMERICA

Fish Stew from Gotland

Gotländsk Fiskgryta

(Options: cod, flounder, haddock, hake, turbot, wolf fish)

	To serve 4 or 5	
2 lb.	fish fillets	1 kg.
5 or 6	large potatoes, peeled and sliced	5 or 6
2	leeks, white parts only, sliced	2
1 tbsp.	finely cut fresh chives	15 ml.
1 tbsp.	finely chopped fresh parsley	15 ml.
	salt and white pepper	

Butter the bottom of a fireproof casserole and add alternate layers of potatoes and leeks, sprinkling each layer with chives and parsley. Add salt and pepper, and enough water to immerse the vegetables. Cook, covered, over low heat for 20 to 30 minutes, or until the potatoes are almost done. Lay the fish fillets on top and put buttered wax paper over them. Cover the casserole and continue cooking for about 10 minutes, or until the fish is done. Season to taste with more salt, and serve directly from the casserole.

OSKAR JAKOBSSON
GOOD FOOD IN SWEDEN

Braised Fish

(Options: bass, carp, snapper)

	To serve 4	
1	whole fish (2 lb. [1 kg.]), cleaned	1
3	carrots, cut into julienne	3
2	ribs celery, cut into julienne	2
3	medium-sized onions, thinly sliced	3
1	garlic clove, thinly sliced	1
3 tbsp.	butter	45 ml.
	salt and pepper	
3	slices bacon or salt pork	3
2 to 3 cups	dry red or white wine, or dry wine and fish fumet (recipe, page 164)	½ to ¾ liter

Sauté the carrots, celery, onions and garlic in the butter for 5 minutes. Arrange the vegetables on the bottom of a baking dish, fish poacher or saucepan. Place the fish on the bed of vegetables, salt and pepper it and place a few strips of bacon or salt pork across the top. Add enough liquid—red or white wine or a mixture of wine and fish fumet—to half-cover the fish. Let it come to a boil very slowly on top of the stove or in a 350° F. [180° C.] oven. Baste carefully during the cooking.

The total cooking time will be about 10 minutes per inch [2½ cm.] of thickness from the time the liquid reaches a boil.

Fish cooked in this manner is usually served with a sauce made of the cooking liquid sieved and mixed with other ingredients. Sometimes part of the skin is removed after cooking and the fish is decorated with garnishes—mushrooms, truffles, pickles, lemon slices or anchovy fillets.

JAMES BEARD
JAMES BEARD'S NEW FISH COOKERY

Baking

Angler with Ratatouille

Gigot de Mer à la Palavasienne

(Options: cod, eel, shark)

This recipe is from Languedoc, on the south coast of France.

	To serve 4	
2 lb.	angler, tail end	1 kg.
4	garlic cloves, cut in slivers	4
	salt and pepper	
	Ratatouille	
3	onions, finely chopped	3
3	garlic cloves, finely chopped	3
¼ cup	olive oil	50 ml.
3	sweet peppers, halved, seeded, deribbed and cut into strips	3
1	small eggplant (about ½ lb. [¼ kg.]), sliced	1
3 or 4	small zucchini (about ½ lb. [¼ kg.]), sliced	3 or 4
3	medium-sized tomatoes (about 1 lb. [½ kg.]), peeled, seeded and chopped	3

Make slits in the flesh of the fish and insert slivers of garlic into them. Season with salt and pepper.

Make the *ratatouille* by cooking the onions and garlic in the olive oil. As they soften, add the peppers. As the peppers soften in turn, add the eggplant and zucchini and, after 10 minutes, the tomatoes. Simmer steadily for 45 minutes, uncovered. When you have a well-flavored, unwatery stew, put it into an ovenproof dish and lay the fish on top. Bake in a preheated 350° to 375° F. [180° to 190° C.] oven for 30 to 45 minutes, turning the fish over from time to time.

JANE GRIGSON
FISH COOKERY

Herb-stuffed Bass in Lettuce Casing

Bar aux Herbes en Chemise

(Options: drum, sea trout, trout)

To serve 4

1	whole sea bass (1½ lb. [¾ kg.]), cleaned and boned, with head and tail left on	1
2	large heads Boston lettuce	2
	salt	
2 to 4 tbsp.	butter	30 to 60 ml.
2 tbsp.	finely chopped shallots	30 ml.
	pepper	
2 tbsp.	dry vermouth	30 ml.
⅓ cup	dry white wine	75 ml.
⅓ cup	heavy cream	75 ml.
Spinach stuffing		
½ lb.	spinach, parboiled, drained, squeezed dry and finely chopped	¼ kg.
3	slices day-old bread, crusts removed, finely crumbled	3
2 tbsp.	butter, softened	30 ml.
½ cup	finely shredded young sorrel leaves	125 ml.
¼ cup	finely chopped fresh parsley	50 ml.
1 tsp.	finely chopped fresh tarragon	5 ml.
	salt and pepper	
1	egg, beaten	1

To make the stuffing, mix the spinach, bread and butter together, mashing each ingredient with a fork before adding the other ingredients and mixing well. Stuff the fish, pressing the filleted flesh and stuffing firmly together to form the fish into its original shape. Place it on its side on the table.

Put about 20 of the largest and most perfectly formed outer lettuce leaves in a saucepan, add salt, pour boiling water over them, simmer for a minute or so and drain, pouring carefully into a sieve or colander so as not to damage the leaves or bunch them up into a mass. Run a bit of cold water over to cool them. Delicately, one by one, lift them out and spread them on a towel to drain.

Have ready an elongated buttered gratin dish, the bottom of which has been scattered with the shallots. Salt and pepper the fish's surface. Wrap the fish from head to tail (muzzle and tail tip remaining exposed); to do this, arrange overlapping leaves of lettuce the length of the belly section with the rib ends of lettuce gently tucked beneath the fish and the fragile leaf extremities pressed to the surface. Repeat the process along the back, tucking rib tips under and pressing the leaves into place. Turn the fish over, placing it

in the prepared dish; salt and pepper the newly exposed surface and repeat the process with the lettuce so that, when finished, the fish is firmly wrapped, mummy-like.

Dribble the dry vermouth over the surface of the fish, and pour the white wine into the bottom of the gratin dish. Add the bones that were removed from the fish, cover the surface of the fish with dabs of butter, press a sheet of aluminum foil or buttered wax paper lightly over the fish and bake for about 30 minutes in a preheated 425° F. [220° C.] oven, basting regularly during the last 15 minutes. Using a spatula, detach the muzzle and tail tip from the sides of the dish if they touch it, and transfer the fish, with the help of two spatulas, to a warmed platter. Discard the bones. Pour the cooking liquid into a small saucepan, reduce to a light syrup, add the cream, and—stirring—boil the liquid rapidly to reduce it by approximately half or until it has the consistency of a light sauce. If you like, whisk in 2 tablespoons [30 ml.] of butter away from the heat. Pour the sauce over the fish and cut into cross sections for serving.

RICHARD OLNEY
SIMPLE FRENCH FOOD

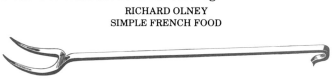

Baked Sea Bass, Corsican-Style

Ragnola au Four

(Options: bluefish, drum, rockfish)

Ragnola is the Corsican name for sea bass. Simone Costantini, in introducing this recipe, explains that it calls for two typically Corsican ingredients: brocciu and gulagna. The former is a fresh, dry goat's-milk cheese, similar to ricotta or brousse. The latter is smoked pork jowl; very thin slices of bacon can be used instead. The original recipe specifies baking the fish in veal stock, but the court bouillon listed here provides an appropriate alternative for cooks who do not have homemade veal stock on hand.

To serve 6

1	whole sea bass (3 lb. [1½ kg.]), cleaned	1
1 cup	fresh bread crumbs	¼ liter
½ cup	milk	125 ml.
½ tsp.	thyme	2 ml.
1	garlic clove, pounded	1
½	medium-sized onion, finely chopped	½
¾ cup	*brocciu, brousse* or ricotta	175 ml.
8	thin slices *gulagna* or bacon	8
2 to 2½ cups	wine court bouillon, made with dry red wine *(recipe, page 163)*	about ½ liter

Lightly oil a shallow baking dish of the right size to accommodate the fish. (Cut off the tail of the fish if necessary).

Gently cook the bread crumbs in the milk, with the

thyme, garlic and onion. After 5 minutes, drain off the excess liquid and combine the seasoned crumbs with the cheese. Stuff the fish with this mixture.

Make several shallow incisions in each side of the fish. Cut two slices of *gulagna* or bacon into thin strips and insert these into the incisions. Place the fish in the prepared dish and cover the fish completely with the remaining *gulagna* or bacon. Pour the court bouillon over all. (The exact quantity of stock will depend on the size of the dish in relation to the fish. The fish should be half-immersed in the court bouillon.)

Put the dish in a preheated 350° F. [180° C.] oven. Bake for 50 to 60 minutes, or until the flesh of the fish parts easily from the bone.

SIMONE COSTANTINI
GASTRONOMIE CORSE ET SES RECETTES

New England Baked Fish

(Options: mackerel, shad)

To serve 4 to 6

1	whole bluefish (3 lb. [1½ kg.]), cleaned	1
	salt and pepper	
	paprika	
	fresh lemon juice	
	melted butter	

Rub the fish with the salt, pepper and paprika to taste, and put it into a buttered baking dish. Pour on equal parts of lemon juice and melted butter. Cover with buttered brown paper and bake in a preheated 350° F. [180° C.] oven for 30 minutes. Serve with the sauce of your choice (New Englanders use a mustard sauce).

JACQUELINE E. KNIGHT
THE COOK'S FISH GUIDE

Bluefish Bustanoby

(Options: bass, drum, trout)

The technique of scoring a fish is demonstrated on page 38.

To serve 6

1	whole bluefish (3 lb. [1½ kg.]), cleaned	1
3 tbsp.	mushroom liquor	45 ml.
1 cup	Chablis or other dry white wine	¼ liter
	salt and pepper	
3 tbsp.	tomato sauce (recipe, page 165)	45 ml.
1 tbsp.	cooked smoked beef tongue, finely minced	15 ml.

Score the bluefish. Dry it and place it in a buttered ovenproof dish. Add the mushroom liquor (obtained by stewing mushrooms gently in butter so that they exude their moisture),

the wine and the seasonings. Cover the dish with buttered wax paper and bake for 30 minutes in a preheated 375° F. [190° C.] oven. Lay the fish on a heated platter and keep it hot. Pour the sauce from the baking dish into a saucepan, add the tomato sauce and the tongue and boil for 2 minutes. Pour the sauce over the fish and serve.

J. GEORGE FREDERICK AND JEAN JOYCE
LONG ISLAND SEAFOOD COOK BOOK

Carp Flemish-Style

Vlaamse Karper

(Options: drum, perch, weakfish)

The parsley root called for in this recipe is a hardy variety of parsley, sometimes called Hamburg parsley, grown for its fleshy, parsnip-shaped root. If it is not obtainable, you can substitute a small parsnip.

To serve 6

1	whole carp (3 lb. [1½ kg.]), cleaned	1
½ cup	vinegar	125 ml.
4 tbsp.	butter	60 ml.
2	medium-sized onions, sliced	2
½ cup	coarsely crumbled gingerbread	125 ml.
	salt and pepper	
1	sprig thyme	1
1	bay leaf	1
1	parsley root, cleaned and sliced	1
2	ribs celery, sliced	2
2 cups	beer	½ liter
2 tbsp.	flour	30 ml.
	sprigs parsley	

Steep the carp for 30 minutes or more in water to which the vinegar has been added.

Heat 4 tablespoons [60 ml.] of the butter, add the onion and cook very gently until softened, about 15 minutes. Add the gingerbread and transfer the mixture to a deep ovenproof dish large enough to hold the carp. Drain the carp and put it in the dish. Season it with salt and pepper. Add the thyme, bay leaf, parsley root and celery, and pour on enough beer to cover the fish. Bake, uncovered, basting regularly, in a preheated 350° F. [180° C.] oven for about an hour, or until the fish is cooked through.

Transfer the fish to a warmed platter and strain the cooking liquid through a fine sieve into a saucepan. Work the remaining butter and the flour together to make a smooth paste, and whisk this *beurre manié* into the cooking liquid. Cook for a few minutes to thicken slightly, and pour the sauce over the fish. Garnish the dish with parsley sprigs before serving.

FONS VERMEERSCH
OP ZOEK NAAR SPIJS EN DRANK

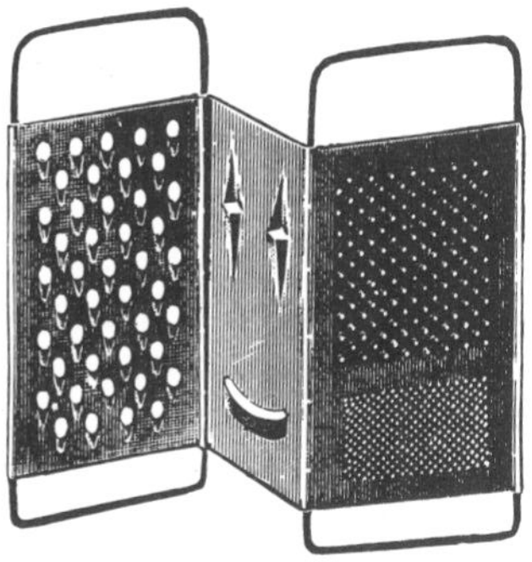

Golden Cod

(Options: haddock, halibut, shark)

To serve 4

4	fresh cod slices, each about 1 inch [2½ cm.] thick	4
1	onion, halved crosswise	1
	salt and pepper	
⅓ cup	oatmeal, pulverized in a blender or in a food processor	75 ml.
4 tbsp.	butter	60 ml.
1	onion, finely chopped	1
1	large parsnip or carrot, finely chopped	1
1 tbsp.	fines herbes	15 ml.
	Cod fumet	
	cod trimmings	
3 cups	water	¾ liter
1	onion, sliced	1
1	carrot, sliced	1
1	bouquet garni	1
¼ tsp.	ground saffron	1 ml.

Combine the fumet ingredients in a pan, bring to a boil, skim, and simmer for 30 minutes.

Meanwhile, rub the fish slices well with the halved onion. Season the fish with salt and pepper, coat as thickly as possible with the oatmeal and quickly fry until golden (but not cooked through) in the butter. (Do not allow the butter to get too hot and darken.) Pack the fried slices into a large, flat ovenproof dish. Chop the halved onion and fry with the remaining chopped onion, and the parsnip or carrot, till golden brown in the butter used for frying the fish. Pack the vegetables around and over the fish, sprinkling in the herbs.

Strain the fumet, which should be clear gold from the saffron, and pour it over the fish. Cover and bake for 40 minutes in a preheated 350° F. [180° C.] oven.

ELISABETH AYRTON
THE COOKERY OF ENGLAND

Gratin of Cod with Vegetables

Trondhjemstorsk

(Options: burbot, haddock, shark, wolf fish)

To serve 4

1½ lb.	cod fillets, cut into 8 equal pieces	¾ kg.
7 tbsp.	butter	105 ml.
1	medium-sized onion, grated	1
3	medium-sized carrots, grated (about ¾ cup [175 ml.])	3
6 oz.	celeriac, grated (about ¾ cup [175 ml.])	200 g.
6	slices firm-textured white bread with the crusts removed	6
	salt and pepper	
1 tbsp.	chopped fresh parsley	15 ml.
¼ cup	dry bread crumbs	50 ml.

Melt half of the butter in a small skillet and add the grated onion, carrots and celeriac. Stir everything together over low heat, stirring occasionally, for 10 to 15 minutes or until "stewed" but not browned.

Butter a large, shallow baking dish and line the bottom with the bread slices. Arrange the fish pieces on top, season with salt and pepper, then spread over the vegetables. Sprinkle with the parsley and bread crumbs, and dot with small bits of the remaining butter. Bake in a preheated 350° F. [180° C.] oven for about 40 minutes, or until the fish is cooked and the topping is golden brown.

HROAR DEGE
FRA NEPTUNS GAFFEL

Creamed Salt Cod, Brittany-Style

Morue Bretonne

(Options: salted haddock, salted halibut, salted pollock)

To serve 4 to 6

2 lb.	salt cod, soaked in water overnight and drained	1 kg.
2 cups	dried white beans (about 1 lb. [½ kg.]), soaked in water overnight	½ liter
¼ cup	béchamel sauce (recipe, page 165)	50 ml.
3 tbsp.	heavy cream	45 ml.
2 cups	milk	½ liter
3 tbsp.	butter	45 ml.
½ cup	freshly grated Parmesan cheese	125 ml.

Add enough fresh water to the beans to cover them by 1 inch [2½ cm.]. Boil for 10 minutes, reduce the heat and simmer uncovered until the beans are tender—up to 3 hours. Drain the beans, and bind them with the béchamel and the cream. The beans should be filmed with a creamy veil.

Meanwhile put the cod into a large pan with 2 quarts [2 liters] of fresh water and the milk. Bring to a boil. Reduce the heat and cook very slowly, making sure that the liquid no more than trembles, for about 10 minutes.

Drain the cod and flake it into slivers the size of rose petals. Generously butter a large ovenproof porcelain dish. Spread a quarter of the beans over the bottom of the dish. Cover with one third of the flaked cod. Continue layering in this way, finishing with a layer of beans. Sprinkle with the grated cheese. Melt the remaining butter and pour it over the top. Put the dish into a preheated 350° F. [180° C.] oven for 30 minutes, or until golden brown. Serve very hot.

ÉDOUARD NIGNON
LES PLAISIRS DE LA TABLE

"Grandmother's" Gratin of Salt Cod

Gratin de Morue "Grand-Mère"

(Options: salted haddock, salted halibut, salted pollock)

To serve 4 to 6

2 lb.	salt cod, soaked overnight in water and drained	1 kg.
4 or 5	medium-sized leeks (about 1 lb. [½ kg.]), white parts only, chopped	4 or 5
4	medium-sized onions, chopped	4
4 tbsp.	butter	60 ml.
1 cup	spinach, parboiled for 2 minutes, squeezed dry and finely chopped	¼ liter
1 cup	heavy cream	¼ liter
4 to 6	eggs, hard-boiled and halved lengthwise	4 to 6
8	anchovy fillets, soaked in cold water for 10 minutes, patted dry and halved lengthwise	8
½ cup	freshly grated Parmesan or Gruyère cheese	125 ml.
2 tbsp.	dry bread crumbs	30 ml.

Poach the cod—preferably in milk—for 10 to 20 minutes, according to the thickness of the fish. Drain the cod, then flake and bone it.

Put the leeks, onions and half of the butter into a heavy casserole, cover with a tightly fitting lid and cook over very low heat for 1½ hours.

Meanwhile, in a large saucepan, cook the spinach in the remaining butter for 3 to 5 minutes over low heat. Remove the pan from the heat and stir in one third of the cream.

When the leeks and onions are ready, mix them with the spinach, and stir in the remaining cream.

Cover the bottom of a buttered gratin dish with half of the vegetable mixture, add the flaked fish and cover it with the rest of the vegetables. Set the halved hard-boiled eggs, yolks facing upward, in a circle around the edge of the dish. Crisscross two anchovy fillets between each pair of eggs. Sprinkle all over with the grated cheese, then with the bread crumbs, and bake in a preheated 400° F. [200° C.] oven for 10 to 15 minutes.

MICHEL BARBEROUSSE
CUISINE PROVENÇALE

Salt Cod with Tomatoes and Peppers

Morue à la Cantabrica

(Options: salted haddock, salted halibut, salted pollock)

To serve 4 or 5

1½ lb.	salt cod fillets, soaked in water overnight and drained	¾ kg.
2 tbsp.	olive oil	30 ml.
2	large onions, thinly sliced	2
6	garlic cloves, crushed	6
2	leeks, white parts only, chopped	2
6	sweet red peppers, seeded, deribbed and cut into strips	6
6	tomatoes, peeled, halved and seeded	6
1	bouquet garni	1
¾ cup	dry white wine	175 ml.
	salt and pepper	

Put the cod fillets in a large heavy saucepan and cover them with fresh cold water. Bring the water to a boil, then remove the saucepan from the heat.

Heat the olive oil in a sauté pan. Lightly fry the onions, garlic and leeks in it; then add the peppers, tomatoes and bouquet garni. Let the vegetables simmer for a few minutes, then add the white wine with an equal quantity of the water in which the fish has been poached. Season with pepper and a very little salt, and let cook uncovered, over medium heat, for 15 minutes.

Drain the cod fillets, flake them and remove any bones.

Mix the fish and the sauce together in a baking dish, put it in a preheated 350° F. [180° C.] oven and cook for 20 to 30 minutes. Remove the bouquet garni and serve.

IRENE LABARRE
LA CUISINE DES TROIS B

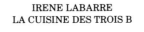

Maltese Dolphin Pie

Torta Tal-Lampuki

(Options: haddock, perch, pompano, porgy, whiting)

	To serve 4 to 6	
1	whole dolphin (1 ½ lb. [¾ kg.]), head and tail removed, cleaned and cut into thick slices	1
	sifted flour	
8 tbsp.	olive oil	120 ml.
1	large onion, chopped	1
2	medium-sized tomatoes, peeled, seeded and chopped	2
1 cup	freshly shelled peas (about 4 oz. [125 g.]), parboiled for 3 to 4 minutes and drained	¼ liter
2 cups	cauliflower florets (about ½ lb. [¼ kg.])	½ liter
1 tsp.	mixed dried thyme, oregano, marjoram and savory	5 ml.
1 cup	pitted ripe olives, sliced	¼ liter
2 tsp.	freshly grated lemon zest	10 ml.
	short-crust pastry (recipe, page 167, but double the quantities called for)	
	salt and pepper	
2	eggs, lightly beaten	2
1	egg yolk, beaten with 1 tbsp. [15 ml.] water	1

Dip the fish slices in the sifted flour. Heat 4 tablespoons [60 ml.] of the oil in a skillet and fry the fish gently, just until lightly browned, on both sides. Remove the fish, let it cool, then cut out and remove all the bones.

Using the remaining oil, sauté the onions, then add the tomatoes. Reduce the heat, then add the peas, cauliflower, herbs, olives, lemon zest and fish. Cover and simmer for 5 minutes. Meanwhile, grease a deep 1-quart [1-liter] pie dish or casserole, and line it with two thirds of the pastry. Season the fish mixture with salt and pepper and add the beaten eggs. Simmer again for 5 minutes and pour the mixture into the pie dish. Cover with pastry, brush with the beaten yolk and cut slits in the pastry lid. Bake in a preheated 375° F. [190° C.] oven for 40 minutes, or until golden.

ANTON B. DOUGALL
KCINA MALTIJA: MALTESE CUISINE

Baked Eel with Olives

Terrine d'Anguilles

(No options)

	To serve 4	
1	whole eel (3 lb. [1 ½ kg.]), skinned and cleaned, with head and tail left on	1
5	medium-sized leeks, including 1 inch [2 ½ cm.] of the green leaves, finely chopped	5
2	garlic cloves, finely chopped	2
¼ cup	finely chopped fresh parsley	50 ml.
	salt and pepper	
1	bay leaf	1
½ cup	pitted ripe olives (or ripe and green olives mixed)	125 ml.
1 cup	dry white wine	200 ml.
¼ cup	dry bread crumbs	50 ml.
½ cup	olive oil	100 ml.

Arrange the leeks in a thick layer in the bottom of a gratin dish or terrine. Cover with the chopped garlic and parsley. Season with salt and pepper and add the bay leaf. Sprinkle in the olives and moisten with the wine. Place the eel on this bed with its tail in its mouth. Scatter the bread crumbs over the whole surface and sprinkle with the oil.

Cook in a preheated 350° F. [180° C.] oven for about 1½ hours, basting occasionally.

IRENE BORELLI
LA CUISINE PROVENÇALE

Eels Volendam-Style

Paling op Zijn Volendams

(No options)

The technique for skinning eels is demonstrated on page 45.

	To serve 4	
2 lb.	thumb-thick eels, cleaned, skinned and cut into 3 ½-inch [9-cm.] pieces	1 kg.
	freshly ground black pepper	
	salt	
4 tbsp.	butter	60 ml.
3 tbsp.	wine vinegar	45 ml.

Pack the eels, not too tightly, in an upright position in a small, deep, straight-sided saucepan that fits in the oven; the easiest way to pack in the eels is to place the pan on its side. Sprinkle generously with pepper and lightly with salt. Cover the pan and cook the eels over moderate heat for 20 minutes without adding any liquid. Then set the pan lid askew, and cook for a further 10 minutes.

Remove the pan from the heat and dot the eels with the butter. Cover the pan and place it in a preheated 350° F. [180° C.] oven for 10 minutes. Remove the lid and cook uncovered for another 10 minutes, until the contents start to crackle and splutter. Sprinkle with the vinegar and cook for a further 3 minutes.

Serve with parslied, boiled new potatoes and provide each diner with a fork and a small dish of melted butter mixed with vinegar and pepper. Take a piece of eel on the fork, dip it in the vinegar-butter and nibble it off. Do the same with the potatoes.

HUGH JANS
BISTRO KOKEN

Eel-Pie Island Pie

(No options)

The technique of skinning eels is demonstrated on page 45.

To serve 6 to 8

1	whole eel (3 lb. [1½ kg.]), skinned, cut into 1½-inch [4-cm.] pieces and bones removed	1
8 tbsp.	butter	120 ml.
2	shallots, chopped	2
2 tsp.	chopped fresh parsley	10 ml.
	grated nutmeg	
	salt and pepper	
1 cup	dry sherry or dry white wine	¼ liter
1 cup	flour	¼ liter
2 to 3 tbsp.	fresh lemon juice	30 to 45 ml.
3	eggs, hard-boiled and sliced	3
	rough puff pastry (recipe, page 167)	
1	egg, beaten with a little milk or water	1

Melt half of the butter in a saucepan and cook the shallots for a few minutes without letting them color, then add the parsley, nutmeg, salt, pepper and the sherry or white wine. Put the eels into this mixture, with just enough water to cover; bring slowly to a boil. When the boiling point is reached, remove the eels and place them in a 1½-quart [1½-liter] casserole. Strain the cooking liquid and reserve it.

Melt the remaining butter in a clean saucepan; stir in the flour and gradually add the reserved cooking liquid. Bring to a boil, stirring. Add the lemon juice, correct the seasoning and pour the sauce over the fish. Arrange slices of hard-boiled egg on top, cover with the pastry and brush the top with the beaten egg mixture. Bake in a preheated 450° F. [230° C.] oven for 15 minutes. Then reduce the heat to 350° F. [180° C.] and continue to bake for 45 minutes.

LIZZIE BOYD (EDITOR)
BRITISH COOKERY

Baked Grouper

(Options: bass, drum, snapper)

To serve 4

2 lb.	grouper steaks or fillets	1 kg.
1	lemon, sliced	1
1	onion, sliced	1
	salt and pepper	
1 cup	sour cream	¼ liter
1 tsp.	prepared mustard	5 ml.
¼ tsp.	paprika	1 ml.

Arrange the lemon and onion slices in a greased baking dish and sprinkle with salt and pepper. Add the steaks or fillets and bake, covered with a lid or foil, in a preheated 400° F. [200° C.] oven for about 20 minutes. Meanwhile, make a sauce of the cream, ½ teaspoon [2 ml.] of salt, the mustard and paprika. Spread the sauce on the fish and broil 3 inches [8 cm.] below the heat until brown.

HUGH ZACHARY
THE BEACHCOMBER'S HANDBOOK OF SEAFOOD COOKERY

Halibut in Lemon Cream

(Options: flounder, fluke, pollock)

To serve 4

2 lb.	halibut fillets, cut into serving pieces and wiped with a damp cloth	1 kg.
	salt	
1 cup	heavy cream	¼ liter
1 tbsp.	grated onion	15 ml.
1 tsp.	freshly grated lemon peel	5 ml.
4 tsp.	fresh lemon juice	20 ml.
	freshly ground black pepper (optional)	
	thin lemon slices	

Sprinkle the fish pieces lightly with salt. Arrange them in a single layer in a shallow, buttered baking dish. Combine the cream, onion, lemon peel, lemon juice and ½ teaspoon [2 ml.] of salt, and pour over the fish. Bake, uncovered, in a preheated 400° F. [200° C.] oven for 20 minutes. Spoon the cream sauce over the fish as you serve it. Grind on black pepper, if liked. Garnish with the lemon slices.

SHIRLEY SARVIS
CRAB & ABALONE: WEST COAST WAYS WITH FISH & SHELLFISH

Herring and Apple Casserole

Sild med Epler

(Options: sablefish, smelt)

To serve 4

2	whole herring (1 lb. [½ kg.] each), filleted and the roes reserved	2
2 tsp.	salt	10 ml.
3 tbsp.	butter	45 ml.
2	medium-sized onions, finely chopped	2
4	cooking apples, peeled, cored and grated	4
2 tbsp.	fresh bread crumbs	30 ml.
2 tbsp.	freshly grated Gruyère cheese	30 ml.

Sprinkle the fillets with the salt. Heat 2 tablespoons [30 ml.] of the butter in a skillet and gently fry the roes and onions.

Cover the bottom of a buttered baking dish with the apples. Sprinkle with the roes and onions, and place the herrings close together on top, backs uppermost.

Sprinkle with the bread crumbs and the cheese. Dot with the remaining butter. Bake in a preheated 475° F. [240° C.] oven for 15 minutes. Serve hot with mashed potatoes.

BORGSTRÖM AND DANFORS
SCANDINAVIAN COOKBOOK

Salted Herring with Anchovy Stuffing

Paupiettes de Hareng

(Option: salted mackerel)

To serve 6

6	whole salted herring, heads removed, skinned, filleted, and soaked in milk overnight	6
16 to 20	anchovy fillets, soaked in water for 10 minutes and patted dry	16 to 20
9 tbsp.	butter	135 ml.
2	egg yolks	2
2 tbsp.	fines herbes	30 ml.
	cayenne pepper	
¼ cup	dry bread crumbs	50 ml.
2 to 3 tbsp.	fresh lemon juice	30 to 45 ml.

Trim the herring fillets into neat rectangles. Pound the trimmings with the anchovies in a mortar, or chop the trimmings and anchovies together very finely. Add 7 tablespoons

[105 ml.] of the butter to the mixture, then mix in the egg yolks, the fines herbes and cayenne pepper very thoroughly.

Lay the herring fillets flat. Cover them with a layer of stuffing. Roll them up and arrange them close together in a buttered gratin dish large enough to hold them in a single layer. Sprinkle over the bread crumbs. Melt the remaining butter and sprinkle a little over each rolled fillet. Bake in a preheated 425° F. [220° C.] oven for 15 to 20 minutes, or until the crumb topping is golden brown.

Remove the dish from the oven, pour the lemon juice over the fish and serve.

ALOIDE BONTOU
TRAITÉ DE CUISINE BOURGEOISE BORDELAISE

Swedish Herring Gratin

Sillgratäng Fran Gamla Opris

(Options: smelt, mackerel)

This is a specialty of the Opera Cellar restaurant in Stockholm, where Baltic herring are used for the dish. If you substitute salt herring, first soak the fillets overnight in cold water.

To serve 4

4	herring fillets	4
8	medium-sized potatoes, thinly sliced	8
2	onions, thinly sliced	2
1½ cups	light cream	375 ml.
1	bay leaf, crumbled	1
1 tsp.	thyme	5 ml.
	white pepper	
3 tbsp.	coarsely cut fresh dill	45 ml.
¼ cup	fresh bread crumbs	50 ml.
3 tbsp.	grated Cheddar or Gruyère cheese	45 ml.
4 tbsp.	butter	60 ml.

Put the potatoes and onions into a saucepan. Add enough cream to barely cover them, and season with the bay leaf, thyme and white pepper. Cook, covered, until the potatoes are tender, about 20 minutes.

Place half of the potato mixture in a buttered gratin dish, and sprinkle with half of the dill. Arrange the herring fillets on top and sprinkle with the remaining dill. Cover with the rest of the potato mixture and pour in the remaining cream. Mix the bread crumbs and cheese, and sprinkle over the surface. Dot with the butter. Brown in a preheated 400° F. [200° C.] oven for 20 minutes, or until the fish is cooked and the surface is crisp.

TORE WRETMAN
SVENSK HUSMANSKOST

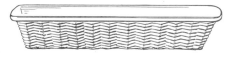

Mackerel Baked with Tomatoes and Potatoes

Maquereaux La Varenne

(Options: herring, smelt, trout)

To serve 8

8	small whole mackerel (about ¾ lb. [⅓ kg.] each), cleaned	8
1 tsp.	fresh thyme	5 ml.
1	bay leaf, finely crumbled	1
	salt and pepper	
4 tbsp.	butter	60 ml.
2	potatoes, peeled, diced, rinsed and dried in a towel	2
2	tomatoes, peeled, seeded and diced	2
2 tbsp.	chopped fresh parsley	30 ml.
2 tsp.	fresh lemon juice	10 ml.
	Duxelles	
3 tbsp.	olive oil	45 ml.
1	small onion, chopped	1
1	shallot, chopped	1
2 cups	finely diced fresh mushrooms (about ⅓ lb. [150 g.])	½ liter
	salt and pepper	
½ cup	dry white wine	100 ml.

To make the *duxelles*, heat the oil and sauté the onion and shallot over low heat until softened. Add the mushrooms, increase the heat and season with salt and pepper. Cook for 5 minutes, stirring. Moisten with the wine. Boil rapidly, stirring, until nearly all the liquid has evaporated. Spread the *duxelles* in a large, oval fireproof dish.

Mix together the thyme, bay leaf, and salt and pepper. Rub the fish, inside and out, with this seasoning mixture. Lay the fish on top of the *duxelles*.

Heat half of the butter, and sauté the potatoes for 10 minutes or until they are almost tender. Add the tomatoes and cook for 2 minutes more. Cover the fish with the potatoes and tomatoes, and dot with the remaining butter, cut into small bits. Heat the dish on the stove for 2 or 3 minutes, then transfer it to a preheated 400° F. [200° C.] oven. Bake for 12 to 14 minutes. Sprinkle with the parsley and the lemon juice, and serve in the cooking dish.

PROSPER MONTAGNÉ
MON MENU

Mullet Papillote

(Options: butterfish, mackerel, trout)

To serve 4

2	whole mullet (about 1 lb. [½ kg.] each), halved and boned	2
	salad oil	
½ tsp.	salt	2 ml.
1 cup	béchamel sauce *(recipe, page 165)*	¼ liter
½ lb.	shelled raw shrimp, chopped	¼ kg.
¼ tsp.	grated nutmeg	1 ml.

Brush salad oil on one side of four 10-inch [25-cm.] aluminum foil squares. Salt both sides of each mullet half and lay one half on each foil square. Mix the other ingredients and divide among the four servings of mullet. Fold the foil over the mullet halves and seal each foil package. Bake in a preheated 325° F. [160° C.] oven for 20 minutes or until done.

THE JUNIOR LEAGUE OF TAMPA
THE GASPARILLA COOKBOOK

Mullet and Yams

(Options: butterfish, carp)

To serve 4

2 lb.	mullet fillets	1 kg.
3 or 4	slices salt pork	3 or 4
1	onion, chopped	1
3 or 4	sweet potatoes, peeled and cut into ¼-inch [6-mm.] slices	3 or 4
	salt and pepper	

Render the fat from the salt pork and remove the pork from the pan. Fry the onions in the pork fat until tender.

In a heavy, covered iron pot, place alternate layers of sweet potatoes and mullet, adding salt and pepper. Put enough water in the bottom of the pot to make steam, but not enough to cover the first layer of fish. Pour the onions and the fat on top of the final layer. Cover and bake for about 40 minutes in a 350° F. [180° C.] oven, until the sweet potatoes are done and the fish flakes easily.

HUGH ZACHARY
THE BEACHCOMBER'S HANDBOOK OF SEAFOOD COOKERY

Pompano Stuffed with Shrimp

(Options: flounder, rockfish, snapper)

To serve 4

4	whole pompano (1½ lb. [¾ kg.] each), cleaned, with heads and tails left on	4
8 tbsp.	butter	120 ml.
1 lb.	raw shrimp, shelled and deveined	½ kg.
4 to 6	medium-sized scallions, trimmed, washed and cut crosswise into rounds ⅛ inch [3 mm.] thick (about ½ cup [125 ml.]), including 2 inches [5 cm.] of the green tops	4 to 6
1 cup	fresh crumbs, made from day-old homemade-type white bread, pulverized in a blender or finely shredded with a fork	¼ liter
¼ cup	finely chopped fresh parsley	50 ml.
¼ cup	pale dry sherry	50 ml.
4 tsp.	salt	20 ml.
	freshly ground black pepper	

Preheat the oven to 400° F. [200° C.].

Drop the shrimp into enough lightly salted boiling water to immerse them completely and boil briskly, uncovered, for 3 minutes, or until they are firm and pink. Drain the shrimp and pat them completely dry with paper towels. Then chop the shrimp coarsely and place them in a bowl.

In a heavy 8- to 10-inch [20- to 25-cm.] skillet, melt 2 tablespoons [30 ml.] of the butter over medium heat. When the foam begins to subside, add the scallions and, stirring frequently, cook for 2 to 3 minutes, until they are soft and translucent but not brown. With a slotted spoon, transfer the scallions to the bowl of shrimp.

Melt 2 more tablespoons of butter in the same skillet, add the bread crumbs and, stirring constantly, fry over medium heat until the crumbs are crisp and golden brown. With a rubber spatula, scrape the entire contents of the skillet over the shrimp and scallions. Add the parsley and sherry, and toss all the stuffing ingredients together gently but thoroughly. Taste for seasoning.

Season the cavities and skin of the fish with the salt and a few grindings of pepper. Spoon the shrimp stuffing into the cavities, dividing it evenly among them. Press the edges of the flaps together with your fingers.

Arrange the pompanos side by side on a buttered jelly-roll pan and brush the tops of the fish with the remaining 4 tablespoons [60 ml.] of butter, softened. Bake in the middle of the oven for 30 minutes, or until the pompanos feel firm when prodded gently with a finger. Arrange the fish attractively on a warmed platter and serve at once.

FOODS OF THE WORLD/AMERICAN COOKING: SOUTHERN STYLE

Stuffed Pike

Täytetty Hauki

(Options: perch, trout)

In Finland the stuffed fish is often arranged in a circle, tail in mouth, and cooked in a round casserole.

This recipe goes back to the turn of the century. The prunes in the stuffing may seem surprising, but they are very good and very nutritious.

To serve 4 to 6

1	whole pike (2½ to 3 lb. [1¼ to 1½ kg.]), cleaned, head left on	1
Prune stuffing		
½ cup	brown rice, cooked	125 ml.
2	eggs, hard-boiled and chopped	2
1 tbsp.	butter, softened	15 ml.
6 to 8	pitted prunes, soaked in warm water for 1 hour and drained	6 to 8
Bread-crumb topping		
2 tbsp.	dry bread crumbs	30 ml.
1	egg white, lightly beaten	1
½ tsp.	sea salt	2 ml.
⅛ tsp.	white pepper	½ ml.
1 tbsp.	butter, cut into small bits	15 ml.

Dry the fish well. Mix together the rice, chopped eggs and softened butter. Loosely fill the cavity of the fish with this mixture. Arrange the prunes on top of the filling. Sew up the opening of the cavity with strong thread.

Preheat the oven to 350° F. [180° C.]. Butter the bottom and sides of an ovenproof glass casserole that will hold the fish snugly, and put the fish in it. Brush the top of the fish with the egg white; sprinkle with the bread crumbs, salt and pepper. Dot with the bits of butter and bake the fish for 1 to 1½ hours. Test for doneness by pulling a fin. If the fin feels loose, the fish is done.

Remove the sewing thread and serve the fish from the casserole, accompanied by a light salad.

ULLA KÄKÖNEN
NATURAL COOKING THE FINNISH WAY

Ray with Cheese

Raie au Fromage

(Option: skate)

To serve 4

4	ray wings (½ lb. [¼ kg.] each), skinned	4
2 tsp.	butter	10 ml.
1 tsp.	flour	5 ml.
1 cup	milk	¼ liter
2	whole cloves	2
2	scallions, chopped	2
1	garlic clove, crushed	1
1	bay leaf	1
2	sprigs thyme	2
	salt and pepper	
12	small boiling onions	12
2½ cups	grated Gruyère cheese	625 ml.
2 cups	croutons *(recipe, page 167)*	½ liter

Melt the butter in a large saucepan, blend in the flour and stir in the milk. Add the cloves, scallions, garlic, bay leaf, thyme, salt and pepper. Place the fish in the pan, bring to a boil, cover and cook for 8 to 10 minutes over low heat. Remove and drain the fish. Sieve the cooking liquid and return it to the cleaned pan. Add the small onions, cover and cook for 10 minutes. Remove the onions. Over high heat reduce the cooking liquid until it thickens into a sauce.

Cover the bottom of a large, buttered gratin dish with half of the grated cheese. Put the fish and the onions in the dish, and arrange the croutons around the edge. Pour in the sauce and cover with the remaining cheese. Put the dish in a preheated 425° F. [220° C.] oven for 10 minutes or until the top has browned.

CHARLES MONSELET
LETTRES GOURMANDES

Baked Salmon

Paistettu Lohi

(Options: sea trout, swordfish, tuna)

To serve 4

4	salmon steaks (1 inch [2½ cm.] thick)	4
1 tbsp.	unsalted butter, melted	15 ml.
½ tsp.	sea salt	2 ml.
2 tsp.	finely cut fresh dill	10 ml.
4	lemon wedges	4

Preheat the oven to 450° F. [230° C.]. Brush a baking dish lightly with melted butter, and place the salmon steaks in it.

Mix the salt with the remaining melted butter and brush some of the mixture very lightly over the tops of the steaks. Bake the steaks in the oven for about 10 minutes.

Remove the steaks from the oven. Turn on the broiler to its highest setting. Brush the steaks again with butter. Put them under the broiler for about 2 minutes, or until they take on an appetizing brown color. Turn the steaks carefully; do not pierce them. After turning, brush the steaks with the rest of the butter and broil for 2 minutes more. Sprinkle the steaks with the dill and serve with the lemon wedges, accompanied by steamed or creamed spinach.

ULLA KÄKÖNEN
NATURAL COOKING THE FINNISH WAY

Baked Salmon with Wine and Tarragon Sauce

(Options: bass, bluefish)

To serve 6

3 lb.	salmon in 1 piece	1½ kg.
14 tbsp.	butter (7 oz. [225 g.]), softened	210 ml.
	salt and pepper	
4	lemons, halved	4
	parsley sprigs	

Wine and tarragon sauce

1½ tbsp.	dry white wine	22 ml.
½ tsp.	fresh tarragon	2 ml.
⅛ tsp.	soy sauce	½ ml.
	salt and pepper	

Preheat the oven to 425° F. [220° C.]. Rinse the salmon and dry it on paper towels. Select a deep, covered baking dish that will hold the salmon snugly. Place the salmon in the dish and smear the fish all over, inside and out, with 8 to 10 tablespoons [120 to 150 ml.] of the butter. Sprinkle it with the salt and pepper. Squeeze on the juice of 1 lemon. Cover the dish and bake for 10 minutes per inch [2½ cm.] of thickness. Baste the salmon once or twice during baking.

While the salmon is baking, prepare the sauce. In a small pot melt the remaining 4 tablespoons [60 ml.] of the butter with the wine, tarragon, soy sauce, salt and pepper. Bring just to the boiling point and remove the pot from the heat.

Remove the salmon to a warmed serving platter. Spoon 4 tablespoons of the butter from the baking dish into the sauce and reheat the sauce. Spoon some sauce over the fish. Decorate the platter with the remaining lemon halves and the parsley sprigs. Serve the remaining sauce separately.

CAROL CUTLER
THE SIX-MINUTE SOUFFLÉ AND OTHER CULINARY DELIGHTS

Shad Stuffed with Stuffed Dates

Alose Farcie aux Dattes Fourrées

(Options: bluefish, mackerel)

This dish is just as good if prunes are used instead of dates. Rice may be used instead of farina.

To serve 8 to 10

1	whole shad (6 lb. [3 kg.]), cleaned and washed in salted water	1
½ cup	slivered blanched almonds	125 ml.
1 tbsp.	sugar	15 ml.
7 tbsp.	butter	105 ml.
	salt and black pepper	
½ tsp.	ground ginger	2 ml.
3½ oz.	farina (1 cup [¼ liter]), boiled or steamed, and cooled	125 g.
1 lb.	large pitted dates (2½ cups [625 ml.])	½ kg.
1	small onion, thinly sliced	1
1 cup	water	¼ liter
½ tsp.	ground cinnamon	2 ml.

First prepare the stuffing for the dates. Pound the almonds in a large mortar, then pound in the sugar, 2 tablespoons [30 ml.] of the butter, a little pepper, and half of the ginger. Add the cool, cooked farina, and stuff the dates with this mixture.

Fill the fish with the stuffed dates and sew up the belly carefully with cotton thread. Rub a large gratin dish with half of the remaining butter and line the dish with the sliced onion. Put in the fish and dot with the rest of the butter. Add the water and sprinkle with plenty of pepper, a little salt and the remaining ginger. Bring to a simmer over low heat and cook, covered, either on the stove or in a preheated 325° F. [160° C.] oven, for about 1½ hours.

When the fish is cooked, pull out the thread and remove the dates. Arrange the dates in the gratin dish around the fish and spoon the braising liquid over them.

Place the dish in the oven at 425° F. [220° C.] or under the broiler. Cook, basting, for 10 to 15 minutes, or until nearly all the liquid has evaporated, leaving only a syrupy juice, and the skin of the shad is crisp and golden. The dates should be caramelized but still soft. Sprinkle the cinnamon over the fish and serve.

Z. GUINANDEAU
FEZ VU PAR SA CUISINE

Baked Boned Fresh Shad

(Options: mackerel, pike)

To serve 4 to 6

1	whole boned shad (2½ to 3 lb. [1¼ to 1½ kg.])	1
2 tbsp.	olive oil	30 ml.
8 tbsp.	unsalted butter, melted	120 ml.
¼ cup	finely chopped shallots or grated onion	50 ml.
2 tbsp.	flour	30 ml.
½ tsp.	salt	2 ml.
	freshly ground black pepper	
¼ cup	milk, heated	50 ml.
2	egg yolks	2
¼ cup	heavy cream	50 ml.
¼ cup	dry white wine	50 ml.

Preheat the oven to 350° F. [180° C.]. Oil a baking pan with some of the olive oil. Combine the remaining oil and half of the melted butter in the pan and heat on top of the stove. Add the chopped shallots or grated onion and sauté gently for 5 minutes. Arrange the shad on the shallots or onion. Put the pan in the oven and bake for 10 minutes.

Combine the flour and the remaining melted butter, the salt and pepper, and stir over low heat. Add the milk and cook for 1 minute, stirring constantly. Beat the egg yolks in a bowl, add the cream and beat again. Dribble the egg and cream mixture into the hot sauce, beating all the while. Spoon the sauce over the fish and sprinkle the wine over the top. Bake for 15 minutes, then transfer the dish from the oven to a preheated broiler for 10 minutes.

Serve with hot boiled potatoes on the same plate. Spoon chives and hot butter over the potatoes and shad. This goes well with a chilled bottle of Chablis.

GENE LEONE
LEONE'S ITALIAN COOKBOOK

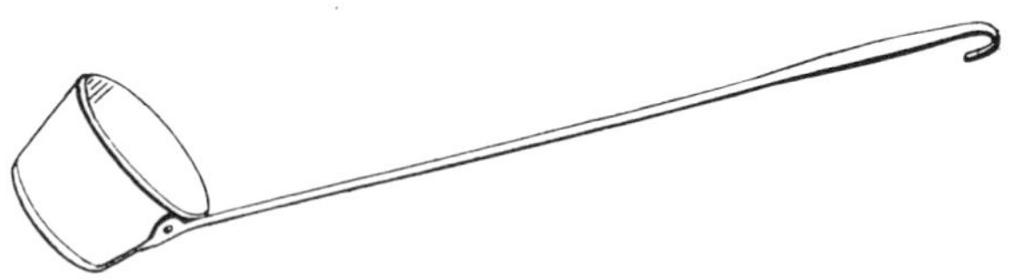

Shark Baked with a Tomato and Citrus Juice Sauce

Ngamantha Khayanchinthi si Piyan

(Options: grouper, marlin, swordfish)

The key to shark cookery is to first leach out the ammonia that sharks retain in their bodies. Soak the meat in salted water for 3 hours, or in milk if a deep-frying recipe is to be used, or in fresh lemon juice if the meat is to be broiled. This recipe is from Vietnam.

	To serve 3	
1 lb.	shark meat, cut into 6 pieces, marinated for 3 hours in salted water and drained	½ kg.
1 tsp.	salt	5 ml.
¼ cup	oil	50 ml.
2 to 4	garlic cloves, crushed	2 to 4
8	sprigs coriander	8
6 tbsp.	puréed tomato	90 ml.
2 tbsp.	fresh citrus juice (lime, lemon or bitter orange)	30 ml.
1 tsp.	freshly pulverized dried red chilies	5 ml.
½ cup	water	125 ml.

Rub the salt well into the pieces of fish. Oil a suitable shallow baking dish (large enough to take the pieces of fish side by side, but no larger) and put in the fish.

Heat the remaining oil in a skillet, and gently fry the garlic until it turns golden. Then add the coriander, followed a few minutes later by the puréed tomato and the citrus juice. Keep stirring the mixture. It will soon give off an irresistible aroma, the sort of smell which creates total confidence in the cook. At this point, pour it over the fish, sprinkle on the chili, and add the water.

Bake in a preheated 425° F. [220° C.] oven for 25 to 30 minutes. The exact baking time will depend on the thickness of the pieces of shark, but you can tell when the dish is ready by looking to see that oil has collected on top of the pieces and by probing the meat with a fork.

ALAN DAVIDSON
SEAFOOD OF SOUTH-EAST ASIA

———◆———

Baked Maine Smelts

(Options: anchovy, mackerel, silversides)

	To serve 4	
1½ lb.	whole smelts, cleaned	¾ kg.
8	thin slices lean salt pork, without the rind, or bacon (about ½ lb. [¼ kg.])	8

Preheat the oven to 400° F. [200° C.].

In a flat baking pan, interweave the smelts with slices of pork or bacon much as if you were weaving a basket. Bake for 10 to 15 minutes, or until the smelts and pork or bacon are molded into a crisp cake.

MARJORIE PAGE BLANCHARD
TREASURED RECIPES FROM EARLY NEW ENGLAND KITCHENS

Baked Snapper with Green Sauce

Pargo Asado con Salsa Esmeralda

(Options: bass, bluefish, drum, perch, sheepshead)

	To serve 6	
1	whole red snapper (5 to 6 lb. [2½ to 3 kg.]), cleaned, with the head and tail left on	1
2 tsp.	salt	10 ml.
¼ tsp.	freshly ground pepper	1 ml.
4	garlic cloves, crushed	4
¼ tsp.	oregano	1 ml.
¼ tsp.	ground cumin	1 ml.
½ cup	fresh lime juice	125 ml.
1 tbsp.	butter	15 ml.
6 to 8	medium-sized potatoes (about 2 lb. [1 kg.]), cut into slices ½ inch [1 cm.] thick	6 to 8
1 cup	olive oil	¼ liter
½ cup	chopped fresh parsley	125 ml.
2	pimientos, cut into strips	2
Green sauce		
3	garlic cloves, crushed	3
2 tbsp.	chopped capers, preferably Spanish, rinsed and drained well	30 ml.
4	hard-boiled egg yolks, mashed	4
1 tsp.	salt	5 ml.
¼ tsp.	white pepper	1 ml.
2 tbsp.	chopped fresh parsley	30 ml.
½ cup	whole almonds, toasted in a moderate oven and ground	125 ml.
¾ cup	olive oil	175 ml.
¼ cup	white vinegar	50 ml.

Mix together the salt, pepper, garlic, oregano, cumin and lime juice, and rub the mixture into the fish, inside and out. Set the fish aside to marinate for 30 minutes.

Butter a shallow baking dish large enough to hold the fish easily. Arrange the potatoes on the bottom of the dish; place the fish on top, pouring the marinade over the fish. Pour the oil over the fish and potatoes. Cook in a preheated 400° F. [200° C.] oven for 40 to 45 minutes.

Meanwhile, make the sauce. In a mortar, mash together the garlic, capers, egg yolks, salt, white pepper, parsley and almonds. Beat in the oil, little by little. At the last minute, add the vinegar. Decorate the fish with parsley and pimientos, and serve with the green sauce.

ELISABETH LAMBERT ORTIZ
THE COMPLETE BOOK OF CARIBBEAN COOKING

Red Snapper, Veracruz-Style

Pescado a la Veracruzana

(Options: bass, drum, sheepshead, snook)

A classic Mexican dish.

	To serve 6	
2 lb.	red snapper fillets	1 kg.
1	large onion, chopped	1
¼ cup	olive oil	50 ml.
3½ cups	canned tomatoes, drained and chopped	875 ml.
	salt and pepper	
2	pimientos, drained and coarsely chopped	2
2 tbsp.	capers, rinsed and drained	30 ml.
½ cup	pitted green olives, rinsed	125 ml.

Wilt the onion in the olive oil; add the tomatoes, salt and pepper, and cook for about 5 minutes to blend the flavors. Place the red snapper fillets in a buttered baking dish; add the pimientos, capers and olives; pour the tomato sauce over the fillets and bake in a preheated 350° F. [180° C.] oven for 25 to 30 minutes or until the fish flakes easily with a fork.

ELENA ZELAYETA
ELENA'S SECRETS OF MEXICAN COOKING

Pensacola Red Snapper

(Options: bass, bluefish, pompano, snook)

	To serve 4	
4	red snapper fillets (½ lb. [¼ kg.] each), with the skin left on	4
1 tsp.	salt	5 ml.
	freshly ground black pepper	
¼ cup	strained fresh lemon juice	50 ml.
2 tbsp.	olive oil	30 ml.
1½ tsp.	finely chopped garlic	7 ml.
1 tsp.	crumbled dried oregano	5 ml.
2	medium-sized firm ripe tomatoes, sliced ¼ inch [6 mm.] thick	2
1 tbsp.	finely chopped fresh parsley	15 ml.

Preheat oven to 400° F. [200° C.]. Pat the red snapper fillets completely dry with paper towels and season them on both sides with the salt and a few grindings of pepper. Combine the lemon juice, olive oil, garlic and ½ teaspoon [2 ml.] of the oregano in a shallow baking-serving dish just large enough to hold the fillets in one layer.

Stir the lemon mixture until the ingredients are well blended, then add the fillets and turn them to moisten them evenly. Arrange the fillets skin side up, place the tomato slices over them and sprinkle the remaining oregano on top.

Bake in the middle of the oven for 10 to 12 minutes, or until the fillets flake easily when prodded gently with a fork. Sprinkle with the parsley and serve the fillets at once, directly from the baking dish.

FOODS OF THE WORLD/AMERICAN COOKING: SOUTHERN STYLE

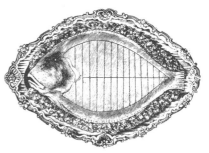

Sole Fillets, Zandvoort-Style

Zandvoortse Tongfilets

(Options: dolphin, flounder, pike, turbot)

The Dutch fishing fleet produces something like four out of every five soles caught in the North Sea. Although many of these are exported, sole is something of a Dutch specialty. Zandvoort is a Dutch seaside village.

	To serve 4	
8	sole fillets	8
4	large tomatoes, halved crosswise, seeded, and loose pulp removed	4
	salt and freshly ground pepper	
14 tbsp.	butter	210 ml.
1	garlic clove, chopped	1
3 tbsp.	chopped fresh parsley	45 ml.
1	lemon, sliced	1

Sprinkle the tomato halves with salt and pepper, then set them side by side in a shallow, buttered casserole. Lightly salt the fish fillets and roll them up. Fit one rolled fillet, upright, into each tomato half.

Take about half of the butter, divide it into eight pieces and put one piece on top of each rolled fillet. Put the dish in a preheated 400° F. [200° C.] oven and leave it for 15 minutes.

Meanwhile melt the remaining butter in a skillet. Fry the garlic in the butter until this sauce is lightly colored. Add the parsley. Take the dish out of the oven and pour the sauce over the fish. Garnish the dish with lemon slices and serve with fluffy mashed potatoes.

TON VAN ES
HET VOLKOMEN VISBOEK

Gratin of Sole

Sole au Gratin

(Options: flounder, fluke, pompano)

To serve 4

4	sole fillets, ½ lb. [¼ kg.] each	4
12 tbsp.	butter (6 oz. [175 g.])	180 ml.
4 tbsp.	chopped fresh parsley	60 ml.
4	scallions, white parts only, or shallots, chopped	4
2 cups	chopped fresh mushrooms	½ liter
	salt and white pepper	
4 tbsp.	toasted bread crumbs	60 ml.
½ cup	dry white wine, or 2 tbsp. [30 ml.] brandy mixed with ½ cup fish fumet (recipe, page 164)	125 ml.

Butter a large gratin dish and sprinkle the base with half of the parsley, scallions or shallots, and mushrooms. Season with salt and white pepper, and lay the fish on top. Cover with the rest of the chopped ingredients and top with the bread crumbs. Add the wine or brandy and fumet, melt the remaining butter and sprinkle it over.

Bake in a preheated 425° F. [220° C.] oven for 15 minutes, or until the fish is cooked and the top is crisp and golden. At the end of the cooking, the dish may be broiled quickly if necessary to color the top.

L. E. AUDOT
LA CUISINIÈRE DE LA CAMPAGNE ET DE LA VILLE

Sole Albert

(Options: flounder, fluke)

This recipe is from the famous Paris restaurant Maxim's.

To serve 1

1	whole sole (9 oz. [275 g.]), cleaned and skinned	1
	salt and pepper	
5 tbsp.	butter	75 ml.
1 or 2	shallots or scallions, finely chopped	1 or 2
1 cup	dry vermouth	¼ liter
2 tbsp.	fresh bread crumbs	30 ml.

Season the sole with salt and pepper. Butter a baking dish and sprinkle it with the shallots or scallions. Set aside.

Make a shallow incision along the backbone of the sole. Melt 4 tablespoons [60 ml.] of the butter in a skillet and lightly brown the sole on both sides. Remove at once to the prepared baking dish. Pour the vermouth down the sides of the dish and sprinkle the exposed surface of the sole with bread crumbs. Finish the cooking in a preheated 450° F. [230° C.] oven, baking the sole until the bread-crumb coating is golden. Remove the sole, trim the sides, lift out the center bone and reshape the fillets on a heated, buttered serving dish. Keep warm.

Strain the cooking liquid into a saucepan, and rapidly reduce it over high heat until it is lightly thickened. Beat in the remaining tablespoon [15 ml.] of butter, but do not bring the sauce to a boil. Rim the sole with a little sauce. Serve the remainder in a sauceboat. Accompany the sole with two small steamed potatoes.

LOUISETTE BERTHOLLE (EDITOR)
SECRETS OF THE GREAT FRENCH RESTAURANTS

Swordfish Casserole

Teglia di Pesce al Forno

(Options: grouper, salmon)

To serve 6

1½ lb.	swordfish steaks, cut ½ inch [1 cm.] thick	¾ kg.
	salt and pepper	
⅔ cup	olive oil	150 ml.
6	medium-sized potatoes, thinly sliced	6
1	large onion, sliced	1
1	garlic clove, finely chopped	1
4	sprigs parsley, finely chopped	4
½	fresh hot chili, stemmed, seeded and finely chopped	½

Sprinkle the swordfish steaks with salt and pepper on both sides. Brush a large, moderately deep baking dish with some of the oil, and cover the bottom with half of the potato and onion slices. Sprinkle with salt and pepper, and add all the fish steaks in a single layer. Sprinkle them with more oil, and all the garlic and parsley; and scatter the chopped chili over the top. Cover with the remaining potato and onion slices, sprinkle with a little more salt and pepper, and pour in the rest of the oil. Bake in a preheated 350° F. [180° C.] oven for at least 1 hour, or until the potatoes are soft.

ADA BONI
ITALIAN REGIONAL COOKING

Swordfish Pie

Impanata di Pesce Spada

(Options: cod, halibut, shark)

The waters around Sicily are rich fishing grounds for the swordfish. Sicilians have more recipes for this fish than any other people in Europe, and this is one of the best.

To serve 4 to 6

14 oz.	swordfish steak, skinned, cut into 1-inch [2½-cm.] cubes	400 g.
½ cup	olive oil	125 ml.
1	medium-sized onion	1
1 tbsp.	tomato paste, diluted with a little water	15 ml.
1	rib celery, thinly sliced	1
½ cup	pitted green olives, chopped	125 ml.
1 tbsp.	capers, rinsed and drained	15 ml.
	salt and pepper	
2	eggs	2
4	medium-sized zucchini, trimmed and cut into julienne	4
½ cup	flour	125 ml.
1 tbsp.	butter	15 ml.
3 or 4 tbsp.	dry bread crumbs	45 or 60 ml.

Orange-peel pastry

2 tbsp.	finely grated orange peel	30 ml.
3 cups	flour	¾ liter
	salt	
½ cup	sugar	125 ml.
3	egg yolks, lightly beaten	3
4 tbsp.	lard, cut into small pieces	60 ml.
8 tbsp.	butter, cut into small pieces and slightly softened	120 ml.

First make the pastry. Put the flour on a pastry board together with the grated orange peel, a pinch of salt and the sugar. Mix these ingredients and make a well in the center. Pour the egg yolks into the well and add the lard and butter. Knead everything together, but only enough to amalgamate the ingredients. Then form the dough into a ball, wrap it in wax paper and refrigerate it for an hour.

Heat ¼ cup [50 ml.] of the olive oil in a fireproof casserole, preferably an earthenware one, and add the onion. Cook it over very low heat, stirring frequently, until the onion is lightly colored.

When the onion is ready, add to it the diluted tomato paste, the celery, olives, capers and fish. Sprinkle with salt and pepper, mix all together, cover the casserole and simmer over very low heat for about 15 minutes, stirring often. At the end of the cooking, the sauce should be greatly reduced.

Break one of the eggs into a shallow bowl, season it and beat it lightly with a fork. Coat the zucchini julienne with flour, then dip them in the beaten egg, turning them carefully so they are well coated.

Heat the remaining olive oil in a skillet. When the oil is hot, add the zucchini and let the julienne brown over medium heat, turning them from time to time. When they are done, after 8 to 10 minutes, drain them on paper towels.

Butter an 8-inch [20-cm.] spring-form pan. Sprinkle the bottom of the pan with the bread crumbs, then shake out any loose crumbs. Divide the pastry dough into three parts. Roll out one part into a disk just large enough to cover the bottom of the pan. Put the pastry disk into the pan and prick it all over with a fork. Spread half of the fried zucchini evenly over this base, then pour in half of the fish mixture. Roll out a second piece of dough the same size as the first and place it in the pan, followed by the remaining zucchini, then the rest of the fish mixture. Take care that all these layers of zucchini and fish are uniform. Finally, roll out the third piece of dough into a disk slightly larger than the first two. Place it on top of the pie, pressing it firmly against the inside wall of the mold to ensure a proper seal. Cut two or three slits in the pastry lid. Beat the remaining egg and use a pastry brush to brush it over the top of the pie.

Bake the pie in a preheated 350° F. [180° C.] oven for about 45 minutes. Remove it when done, let it rest for a few minutes, then slide a knife blade around the edge. Undo the clasp of the pan and transfer the pie to a serving dish.

A. GOSETTI DELLA SALDA
LA CUCINA ITALIANA

Baked Swordfish

Kilic Firinda

(Options: bass, drum, halibut, tuna)

To serve 2 to 4

2	swordfish steaks (1 inch [2 cm.] thick)	2
	salt and pepper	
¼ cup	olive oil	50 ml.
2	bunches scallions, including green tops, chopped	2
¼ cup	chopped fresh parsley	50 ml.
¼ cup	finely cut fresh dill	50 ml.
¼ cup	tomato juice	50 ml.
¼ cup	fresh lemon juice	50 ml.
6	pitted green olives (optional)	6

Preheat the oven to 350° F. [180° C.]. Place the steaks on an oiled baking dish. Sprinkle with salt and pepper and pour the olive oil over them. Mix the scallions, parsley and dill, and spread over the fish. Pour the tomato juice and lemon juice on top. Decorate the steaks with the olives, if using. Bake for 25 minutes, or until the fish is cooked. Serve hot.

NESET EREN
THE ART OF TURKISH COOKING

Baked Trout Stuffed with Sorrel

Truites à l'Oseille au Four

(Options: bass, butterfish, grayling, whiting)

The technique of boning a fish through the back is demonstrated on pages 56-57. If sorrel is not available, spinach may be substituted.

To serve 4

4	whole medium-sized trout (about ¾ lb. [⅓ kg.] each), boned through the back, cleaned, washed and sponged dry with paper towels	4
1 lb.	fresh sorrel, stems and ribs removed, coarsely chopped	½ kg.
8 tbsp.	butter	120 ml.
	salt and pepper	
1	small onion, finely chopped	1
¼ cup	dry white wine	50 ml.
¼ cup	heavy cream	50 ml.

Melt half of the butter in a saucepan and gently stew the sorrel leaves, seasoned with salt and pepper, stirring frequently until they have "melted" to a near purée.

Spread the onion over the bottom of an earthenware or enameled cast-iron baking or gratin dish just large enough to hold the fish easily. Season the fish, inside and out, with salt and pepper. Arrange them in the dish, belly sides down. Place a small piece of butter inside each of the fish and stuff the cavities with the sorrel purée. Place a thin slice of butter on top of each fish and sprinkle the white wine over and around them. Press a piece of buttered wax paper, cut slightly smaller than the top of the baking dish, gently on the surface. Bake in a hot oven, preheated to 400° F. [200° C.], for about 15 minutes. Upon removing the dish from the oven, pour a tablespoon [15 ml.] of heavy cream over each fish and serve them immediately in their baking dish.

RICHARD OLNEY
THE FRENCH MENU COOKBOOK

Baked Trout with Dill and Lemon

Truite en Papillote à l'Aneth et au Citron

(Options: rockfish, scup, sea robin)

To serve 4

4	whole trout (about ½ lb. [¼ kg.] each), cleaned	4
	salt and pepper	
4	sprigs dill or fennel	4
1	shallot, chopped	1
1 tbsp.	pale dry sherry	15 ml.
¼ cup	fish fumet (recipe, page 164)	50 ml.
2 tsp.	olive oil	10 ml.
1	lemon, peeled and the pith removed, thinly sliced	1

Wipe the trout thoroughly with paper towels. Season the insides of the fish with salt and pepper, and put a sprig of dill or fennel in each one.

Preheat the oven to 450° F. [230° C.]. Prepare four sheets of aluminum foil, cut into circles 12 inches [30 cm.] in diameter. Fold the circles of aluminum foil in half; at the ends of the folds turn up and pinch the corners to make a sort of boat to hold the trout. Put the fish in their foil, sprinkle them with the minced shallot, pour ¾ teaspoon [4 ml.] of sherry, one tablespoon [15 ml.] of fish fumet and ½ teaspoon [2 ml.] of olive oil over each one, and cover them with the slices of lemon. Close the foil by folding over the edges and pinching them together securely; the shape should be rather like that of an apple turnover.

Place the *papillotes* (little parcels) in an oval ovenproof gratin dish and bake for 8 minutes. To serve, put the foil *papillotes* on heated plates. With scissors, cut all around the top of the foil so it can be opened easily at the table.

MICHEL GUÉRARD
MICHEL GUÉRARD'S CUISINE MINCEUR

Baked Turbot

(Options: flounder, pompano, sole)

To serve 3

1	turbot (1 lb. [½ kg.]), cleaned	1
1 cup	unflavored yogurt, lightly beaten	¼ liter
1 tbsp.	fresh lemon juice	15 ml.
2 tbsp.	dry white wine	30 ml.
1	blade mace, pounded (or substitute ¼ tsp. [1 ml.] ground mace)	1
1	egg yolk, lightly beaten	1
	salt and pepper	
½ cup	dry bread crumbs, lightly sautéed in butter	125 ml.
2 tbsp.	finely chopped fresh parsley	30 ml.

Place the fish in a buttered baking dish. Mix together the yogurt, lemon juice, wine, mace and egg yolk, and pour the mixture over the fish. Add the salt and pepper. Cover with the sautéed bread crumbs, and bake in a preheated 350° F. [180° C.] oven for 45 to 50 minutes.

Serve hot, garnished with parsley.

IRFAN ORGA
COOKING WITH YOGURT

Turbot Fillets with Leeks and Cream Sauce

Suprême de Turbotaux Poireaux

(Options: flounder, halibut, sole)

To serve 4

4	turbot fillets (about ½ lb. [¼ kg.] each), unskinned	4
6 tbsp.	butter	90 ml.
2	shallots, thinly sliced	2
	salt and pepper	
1 cup	fish fumet (recipe, page 164)	¼ liter
4	leeks, white parts only, finely sliced	4
½ cup	heavy cream	125 ml.
4	thin slices truffle (optional)	4

Place the turbot fillets, skin side down, side by side in a buttered sauté pan. Add the shallots, salt and pepper, and fish fumet to just cover the fillets. Cover with buttered wax paper, and cook in a preheated 350° F. [180° C.] oven for about 10 minutes.

Meanwhile, put the leeks into a saucepan with salt and pepper, 1 tablespoon [15 ml.] of the butter and a couple of tablespoons [30 ml.] of water and cook, covered, for about 5 minutes. Keep the leeks warm.

When the fish fillets are cooked, remove them from the pan and keep them hot. Over high heat, reduce the cooking liquid to a syrupy consistency. Add the cream and reduce the sauce mixture until it coats a spoon. Remove the pan from the heat, whisk in the remaining 4 tablespoons [60 ml.] of butter, previously softened or cut into cubes.

Remove the skin from the turbot fillets, and arrange them on a warmed serving dish, surrounded by the leeks. Coat the fillets with the sauce, put a slice of truffle (if using) on each fillet, and serve.

LA REYNIÈRE
200 RECETTES DES MEILLEURES CUISINIÈRES DE FRANCE

Baked Whitings

(Options: butterfish, haddock, mackerel, porgy)

The chili vinegar called for here can be made by steeping crushed chilies in vinegar for several weeks, then straining the vinegar. Alternatively, substitute wine vinegar for the chili vinegar and increase the quantity of cayenne pepper.

To serve 4

4	whole whiting, heads removed, cleaned, and the roe, if any, reserved	4
¼ cup	port, sherry or dry wine	50 ml.
1 or 2 tsp.	chili vinegar	5 or 10 ml.
	salt	
	cayenne pepper	
	ground mace	
6 tbsp.	butter	90 ml.
1 to 2 tsp.	flour	5 to 10 ml.

Wash the fish and wipe them dry, then fold them in a soft cloth, and let them remain in it awhile. Replace the roe, and put the fish into a buttered baking dish of suitable size with the wine, chili vinegar, a little salt, cayenne pepper and ground mace and 4 tablespoons [60 ml.] of the butter, well blended with the flour. The fish must be turned with the heads and tails toward each other, that they may lie compactly in the dish, and the backs should be placed downward, that the sauce may surround the thickest part of the flesh.

Lay two buttered pieces of wax paper over the dish, and press them down upon the fish; set the dish into a gentle oven, preheated to 325° F. [160° C.], for 20 minutes, or until cooked. Take off the papers and send the fish to the table in their sauce. When preferred so, they can be re-dished for the table, and the sauce poured over them.

ELIZA ACTON
MODERN COOKERY

Baked Whiting in Sesame Sauce

(Options: bass, bluefish, corvina, sea trout)

Boning roundfish is demonstrated on pages 24-25.

To serve 3 or 4

4	whole whiting (1 lb. [½ kg.] each), cleaned and boned, with heads and tails left on	4
1	medium onion, sliced	1
2 tbsp.	chopped fresh parsley	30 ml.
2	lemons, cut into wedges	2
	parsley sprigs	
Sesame sauce		
¼ cup	sesame seeds	50 ml.
½ cup	dry white wine	125 ml.
¼ cup	olive oil	50 ml.
¼ tsp.	crushed hot red pepper	1 ml.
½ tsp.	salt	2 ml.
1	garlic clove, finely chopped	1

Preheat the oven to 350° F. [180° C.]. Rinse the fish well with cold water and drain it. Place the fish in a shallow, oiled baking pan. Blend the sesame sauce ingredients together and pour the sauce over the fish. Cover with the sliced onion and chopped parsley.

Bake in the oven, basting occasionally, until the fish flakes at the touch of a fork and the flesh is opaque—30 to 40 minutes. Arrange the fish on a warmed platter. Discard the onion and chopped parsley. Pour the sauce over the fish. Garnish with lemon wedges and parsley sprigs.

ANNA MUFFOLETTO
THE ART OF SICILIAN COOKING

Fish Baked in Sour Cream

Ryba Zapechennaya v Smetane

(Options: carp, cod, drum, haddock)

To serve 3 or 4

1 lb.	fish fillets	½ kg.
	salt and pepper	
2 tbsp.	flour	30 ml.
10 tbsp.	butter	150 ml.
2 cups	fresh chopped mushrooms (about ½ lb. [¼ kg.])	½ liter
5	medium-sized potatoes, cut into ¼-inch [6-mm.] slices	5
2	eggs, hard-boiled and sliced	2
¼ cup	grated Cheddar cheese	50 ml.
2 to 3 tbsp.	finely chopped fresh parsley	30 to 45 ml.
Sour cream sauce		
1 cup	sour cream	¼ liter
	beurre manié, made from 1 tbsp. [15 ml.] flour, kneaded with 1 tbsp. butter	
	salt	

Season the fish fillets with salt and pepper and coat them with the flour. Sauté them in 4 tablespoons [60 ml.] of the butter for 8 to 10 minutes, or until they are lightly browned on both sides.

In separate skillets, sauté the mushrooms in 1 tablespoon [15 ml.] of the butter over high heat until their liquid has evaporated, and sauté the potato slices in 4 tablespoons of the butter until they are soft and pale golden on both sides.

Arrange the fish in a buttered casserole. Place a few slices of hard-boiled egg and a spoonful of mushrooms on each fillet. Cover the fish with the potato slices.

To make the sauce, bring the sour cream to a boil over low heat. Mix in the *beurre manié*. Simmer for a minute or two, add salt to taste, then strain the sauce over the contents of the casserole.

Sprinkle the cheese over the top, dot with the remaining butter and put the casserole in a preheated 450° F. [230° C.] oven for 5 to 10 minutes, or until brown on top. Just before serving, sprinkle with the chopped parsley.

O. P. MOLCHANOVA
KNIGA O VKUSNOĬ I ZDOROVOĬ PISCHE

Spiced Baked Fish

Kerala

(Options: burbot, butterfish, perch, rockfish, snapper, whiting)

The original version of this recipe calls for pomfret, the European name for several members of the butterfish family.

	To serve 8	
2	whole fish (about 2 lb. [1 kg.] each), cleaned	2
1	large garlic clove, crushed	1
3	large onions, sliced	3
½-inch	cube fresh ginger root	1-cm.
2 tsp.	cayenne pepper	10 ml.
½ tsp.	ground turmeric	2 ml.
2 tsp.	vinegar	10 ml.
2 tsp.	salt	10 ml.
¼ cup	oil	50 ml.
½ cup	water	125 ml.

Keeping the fish whole, make three or four cuts on either side of both of them. Pound the garlic, one of the sliced onions, the ginger, cayenne pepper and turmeric in a mortar with the vinegar and salt.

Rub the fish with a little of this spice paste. Heat 3 tablespoons [45 ml.] of oil in a large skillet and lightly fry each fish on both sides. Remove the fish from the pan.

If all the oil has been absorbed by the fish, add 1 more tablespoon [15 ml.] of oil. Fry the two remaining sliced onions until brown. Add the remaining spice paste and fry well.

Stuff the fish with this mixture, inside the stomach cavities and the incisions, and then place the fish in a large, shallow baking dish.

Pour the water over the fish. Bake in a preheated 325° F. [160° C.] oven for 30 minutes.

RACHEL C. MUTHACHEN
INDIAN REGIONAL RECIPES (FOR NEWLY-WEDS)

Fish Baked in Vine Leaves

Psari Fournou me Ambelofila

(Options: mullet, perch, whiting)

	To serve 4	
4	whole fish (about ¾ lb. [⅓ kg.] each), cleaned but heads left on	4
2 to 3 tbsp.	olive oil	30 to 45 ml.
2 to 3 tbsp.	fresh lemon juice	30 to 45 ml.
1 tbsp.	chopped fresh parsley	15 ml.
1 tbsp.	chopped fresh thyme	15 ml.
1 tbsp.	chopped fresh fennel leaves	15 ml.
	salt and freshly ground pepper	
3 or 4	anchovy fillets, soaked in water for 10 minutes, patted dry and pounded to a paste	3 or 4
2 tbsp.	butter	30 ml.
8 to 12	large fresh grapevine leaves, parboiled for 5 minutes, drained and patted dry	8 to 12
1	lemon, sliced	1
1 tbsp.	fennel leaves	15 ml.

In an earthenware or glass bowl, beat together the oil, lemon juice, chopped parsley, thyme and fennel and a pinch each of salt and pepper. Put the fish in the mixture, turning to coat well, and marinate for an hour or two in the refrigerator.

Remove the fish from the marinade and drain. Beat the anchovies and butter together and spread the mixture onto the fish with a knife. Wrap each fish in two or three vine leaves and place it seam side down in a baking dish. Bake in a preheated 350° F. [180° C.] oven for 30 minutes. Serve hot, garnished with lemon slices and fennel leaves.

VILMA LIACOURAS CHANTILES
THE FOOD OF GREECE

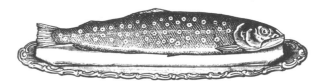

Roman Fish Omelet

Patina Zomoteganon

(Options: bass, cod, mullet, sole)

The liquamen called for in this adaptation of an ancient Roman recipe is a salty fish sauce. You can substitute pounded anchovies or one of the Oriental fermented-fish sauces. The wine called for can be white or red wine —or even a mixture of dry white wine and port.

	To serve 4	
1½ lb.	fish fillets	¾ kg.
¼ cup	olive oil	50 ml.
1 tbsp.	*liquamen*	15 ml.
1 cup	dry wine	¼ liter
1	bouquet garni of leek and fresh coriander leaves	1
2	sprigs lovage	2
1 tsp.	dried oregano	5 ml.
	pepper	
4	eggs, lightly beaten	4

Place the fish in a shallow pan. Add the oil, *liquamen*, wine and bouquet of leek and coriander. Cover and poach over low heat for 10 to 12 minutes.

Meanwhile pound the lovage and oregano with some pepper. When the fish is cooked, arrange the fillets in a shallow oven dish. Add the leek and coriander to the pounded herbs. Pound all together. Transfer the mixture to a bowl and strain over the fish stock. Stir in the eggs until blended, then pour the mixture through a sieve onto the fish fillets. Cook in a preheated 300° F. [150° C.] oven for 20 minutes, or until the egg custard is set. Sprinkle with pepper and serve.

BARBARA FLOWER AND ELISABETH ROSENBAUM
THE ROMAN COOKERY BOOK, A CRITICAL TRANSLATION OF THE ART OF COOKING BY APICIUS

Fish Pudding from the Azores
Pudim de Peixe dos Açores

(Options: dolphin, grouper, hake, rockfish, wolf fish)

The fish originally recommended for this pudding is what the Portuguese call cherne; it is closely related to the grouper.

	To serve 4	
1¼ lb.	firm, white fish fillets, skinned and cut into almond-sized pieces	⅔ kg.
4 tbsp.	butter	60 ml.
1	large onion, chopped	1
2	medium-sized tomatoes, peeled, seeded and chopped	2
	salt	
1 cup	fresh bread crumbs	¼ liter
3	eggs, beaten	3
½ cup	pitted olives	125 ml.

Melt the butter in a large saucepan, and cook the onion until softened but not colored, then add the tomatoes, salt and

fish. Cook over moderate heat until the fish is done, about 7 to 8 minutes. Then add the bread crumbs, eggs and olives. Mix well and pour the mixture into a buttered 1 quart [1 liter] baking dish. Put the dish in a pan set on an oven rack, pour hot water into the pan to a depth of about 1 inch [2½ cm.] and bake the pudding in a preheated 350° F. [180° C.] oven for about 1 hour. Chill the pudding overnight in the refrigerator.

On the following day, turn the pudding out onto a platter, garnish it with olives, lettuce and radishes, and serve it cold.

MARIA ODETTE CORTES VALENTE
COZINHA REGIONAL PORTUGUESA

Fish Pudding
Le Poupeton

This Provençal dish provides a good way of using up fish left over from a stew.

	To serve 3 or 4	
10 to 14 oz.	leftover cooked fish	300 to 425 g.
4	slices French or Italian bread with the crusts removed, soaked in milk and squeezed	4
3	eggs, yolks separated from whites	3
¾ cup	freshly grated Parmesan cheese	175 ml.
	salt and pepper	
1 tbsp.	butter	15 ml.
8	slices tomato, sautéed in olive oil or butter	8

Carefully remove all skin and bone from the fish. In a large mortar, pound the fish flesh and the bread. Beat in the egg yolks, one at a time, then the Parmesan cheese. Beat the egg whites until they stand in soft peaks and fold them into the mixture; lightly season with salt and pepper.

Butter a 1-quart [1-liter] soufflé dish or charlotte mold and pour in the mixture. Place the dish in a large pan and pour enough water into the pan to come about halfway up the sides of the dish. Bake the pudding in a preheated 325° F. [160° C.] oven for about 40 minutes, or until it is firm to the touch. Turn the pudding out onto a warmed platter and surround it with sautéed tomatoes.

IRÈNE BORELLI
LA CUISINE PROVENÇALE

Fish Baked with Chard, as in Majorca

Peix en es Forn

(Options: cod, dogfish, haddock, swordfish, whiting)

To serve 4

1½ to 2 lb.	fish slices or fillets	¾ to 1 kg.
1 cup	olive oil	¼ liter
3	large potatoes, sliced	3
1	large onion, finely chopped	1
¼ cup	chopped fresh parsley	50 ml.
2 to 2½ lb.	chard, chopped	1 kg.
2	large tomatoes, peeled, seeded and chopped	2
	salt and pepper	
⅓ cup	dry white wine	75 ml.

Oil a large, shallow baking dish and cover the bottom with the slices of potato. Add half of the onion, parsley, chard and tomatoes. Season with salt and pepper. Lay the slices or fillets of fish on top, and cover them with the remaining onion, parsley, chard and tomatoes. Season again, pour the remaining olive oil over all and bake in a preheated 400° F. [200° C.] oven for about 15 minutes. Then turn the oven to 325° F. [160° C.] and bake for a further 45 minutes. About 15 minutes before the cooking is completed, add the white wine.

ALAN DAVIDSON
MEDITERRANEAN SEAFOOD

Fish Fillets in Sesame Sauce

Tajen Samak bi Tahini

(Options: bass, haddock, rockfish, sea trout)

To serve 6

3 lb.	trout or red snapper fillets, rubbed with lemon juice, sprinkled with salt and refrigerated for a few hours	1½ kg.
⅔ cup	olive oil	150 ml.
2	medium-sized onions, sliced	2
1½ cups	*tahini*	375 ml.
½ cup	fresh lemon juice	125 ml.
2	garlic cloves, crushed	2
1½ tsp.	salt	7 ml.

Remove the fish fillets from the refrigerator 30 minutes before cooking time. Wash and dry the fillets. Rub them with

olive oil and bake them in a shallow baking dish in a preheated 400° F. [200° C.] oven for 10 minutes. Baste the fish with a little more olive oil and place them under a preheated broiler for a minute or two.

Lower the heat of the oven to 350° F. [180° C.]. In a skillet, sauté the onions in the remaining olive oil and spread them over the fish in the baking dish. Blend the *tahini*, lemon juice, garlic and salt thoroughly, adding water until the sauce is creamy. Bring to a boil and pour the sauce over the fish. Return the dish to the oven and bake for about 20 minutes or until the sauce thickens. Serve with rice.

AIDA KARAOGLAN
A GOURMET'S DELIGHT

Fish Pie

(Options: cod, grouper, haddock, halibut, pollock, whiting)

It is important to use a deep baking dish for this recipe so that there will be ample room for covering the fish with the sauce; otherwise the sauce will tend to bubble out over the edges of the dish.

To serve 5 or 6

2 lb.	mixed white-fleshed fish, cleaned, whole or cut into pieces, depending on size	1 kg.
1 quart	fish fumet *(recipe, page 164)*	1 liter
3	eggs, hard-boiled and finely chopped	3
5 tbsp.	butter	75 ml.
¾ cup	flour	175 ml.
	salt and black pepper	
2 tbsp.	fresh parsley and capers, chopped together	30 ml.
5	medium-sized potatoes, boiled, peeled and mashed with butter	5

Poach the fish in the fumet for 5 or 6 minutes. With a perforated spoon or fish server, transfer the fish to a baking dish. Remove the heads, bones and skin from the fish and break the flesh so that it is spread out evenly in the dish. Then add the chopped eggs.

To make a thick velouté sauce, melt the butter in a saucepan and stir in the flour to make a roux. Pour in the hot fumet, bring to a boil, stirring, and simmer and skim for about 20 minutes. Season with salt and pepper, and stir in the parsley and capers.

Pour the velouté over the fish. Cover with the mashed potatoes, and cook at the top of a preheated 375° F. [190° C.] oven for 25 minutes. For the last few minutes, raise the heat to 400° F. [200° C.] to brown the potatoes. Alternatively, brown the potatoes under the broiler.

GEORGE LASSALLE
THE ADVENTUROUS FISH COOK

Fish Fillets with Noodles

Mes Daurades aux Nouilles

(Options: bass, bluefish, dolphin, drum, pompano, porgy, sheepshead)

The original version of this recipe by Marinette Vacheron, of Le Râtelier restaurant, Lyons, France, calls for sea bream—a European name for several members of the porgy family.

	To serve 6	
3	whole fish, about 1½ to 2 lb. [¾ to 1 kg.] each, skinned and filleted	3
	salt and pepper	
1 cup	dry white vermouth	¼ liter
1¼ cups	heavy cream	300 ml.
7 oz.	fresh sorrel, cut with scissors into very fine strips	200 g.

Arrange the unadorned pieces of fish on an ovenproof dish so that they don't overlap, and place the dish in a preheated 400° F. [200° C.] oven for 8 to 10 minutes.

Keep the fish warm without cooking it any longer. Salt and pepper it lightly.

While the fish is cooking, reduce the vermouth to a syrup over medium heat, then add the cream. Reduce the sauce some more until it coats a wooden spoon. Add pepper, then begin adding the sorrel, little by little, so you can judge when you have added enough. Bring to a boil, salt if necessary, then remove from the heat.

Arrange the fish fillets on a heated serving platter, spoon the sauce over them and serve.

Homemade noodles, cooked *al dente* and served buttered, make a very nice accompaniment.

MADELEINE PETER
FAVORITE RECIPES OF THE GREAT WOMEN CHEFS OF FRANCE

Galician Fish Pie

Pastel de Pescado

(Options: burbot, haddock, rockfish)

	To serve 4 to 6	
1 lb.	fresh cod or hake fillets	½ kg.
24	blanched almonds	24
3 tbsp.	olive oil	45 ml.
2	garlic cloves, chopped	2
4	onions, finely chopped	4
1	bay leaf	1
6	tomatoes, peeled, seeded and chopped	6
	salt	
2 tbsp.	butter	30 ml.
6	potatoes, boiled, peeled, puréed and well seasoned with salt and pepper	6

In a skillet, fry the almonds in the oil until lightly golden. Remove the almonds, drain them on paper towels and crush them in a mortar. Put the garlic, onions and bay leaf into the skillet and cook slowly, uncovered, for about 15 minutes, or until the onions are tender. Add the tomatoes, season with salt and cook for 10 minutes. Remove about one third of this mixture and reserve for use as a sauce. Add the crushed almonds to the remainder and cook for 5 to 10 minutes longer. Take out the bay leaf.

Butter an ovenproof dish, line the bottom and sides with about two thirds of the puréed potatoes, then fill the dish with alternating layers of the fried-tomato mixture and of fish fillets, starting with the fried mixture. Cover with a layer of the puréed potatoes and bake the pie in a preheated 400° F. [200° C.] oven for 40 minutes.

Serve in the same dish, accompanied by the sauce. Or carefully turn out the pie onto a warmed platter and coat with the reserved sauce.

ANNA MAC MIADHACHÁIN
SPANISH REGIONAL COOKERY

Baked Fish with Horseradish

Ryba Zapiekana w Sosie Chrzanowym

(Options: cod, haddock, perch, sole)

To serve 4

1	whole fish (1½ lb. [¾ kg.]), left whole or filleted	1
	salt	
1 tsp.	vinegar	5 ml.
2 tbsp.	butter, melted	30 ml.

Horseradish and apple sauce

½ cup	grated horseradish	125 ml.
1	medium-sized apple, peeled, cored and shredded	1
¾ cup	sour cream	175 ml.
	salt	
	sugar	

Sprinkle the fish with salt and vinegar. Place it in a buttered baking dish and sprinkle with the melted butter. Bake in a preheated 400° F. [200° C.] oven for 10 minutes. Meanwhile, mix the horseradish with the apple. Stir in the sour cream and season with salt and a pinch of sugar. Pour the horseradish sauce over the fish. Bake for another 15 minutes, and serve with boiled potatoes.

ALINA ZERÁNSKA
THE ART OF POLISH COOKING

Lemon Fish

Psari Lemonato

(Options: bluefish, haddock, sheepshead, trout)

The technique of scoring each side of a fish is demonstrated on page 61.

To serve 5 or 6

1	whole fish (2 lb. [1 kg.]), cleaned	1
4 to 6 tbsp.	fresh lemon juice	60 to 90 ml.
	salt and pepper	
3	medium-sized potatoes, thinly sliced	3
½ cup	olive oil	125 ml.
2 tsp.	dried oregano	10 ml.

Slash the fish on each side in two or three places. Sprinkle the fish inside and out with some of the lemon juice and season with salt and pepper.

Place the fish in an oiled, shallow baking dish. Arrange the sliced potatoes around the fish and pour the remaining lemon juice over the potatoes and fish. Pour the olive oil over the contents of the dish, and season the potatoes with salt and pepper. Sprinkle with the oregano and cover the dish with a lid or foil.

Bake in a moderate oven, preheated to 350° F. [180° C.], for 40 minutes. Remove the cover and continue to bake for an additional 20 minutes, or until the fish and potatoes are cooked. Serve immediately with a boiled, leafy green vegetable such as spinach.

As a variation, 2 tablespoons [30 ml.] of drained capers, mixed with a little olive oil, may be added during the last 10 minutes of cooking.

TESS MALLOS
GREEK COOKBOOK

Fish Stuffed with Buckwheat

Ryba, Farshirovannaya Kashei

(Options: carp, cod, haddock, perch, snapper)

Buckwheat groats, which are often called kasha, are available plain and roasted. This recipe specifies roasted groats. The technique of gutting a fish through the gills is demonstrated on page 19.

To serve 3 or 4

1	whole fish (1½ lb. [¾ kg.]), head removed, cleaned without slitting the belly open	1
⅔ cup	roasted buckwheat groats	150 ml.
1 cup	boiling water	¼ liter
	salt	
4 tbsp.	butter	60 ml.
1	medium-sized onion, chopped	1
2	hard-boiled eggs, chopped	2
	pepper	
1 tbsp.	flour	15 ml.
1 cup	sour cream	¼ liter

The first step is to prepare the buckwheat. Put the groats in a casserole and pour in the boiling water: this should just cover the groats. Add salt and 1 tablespoon [15 ml.] of the butter, stir well, cover tightly and bake in a preheated 350° F.

[180° C.] oven for 20 minutes or until all the water is absorbed and the buckwheat is light and fluffy.

To make the stuffing, fry the onion in 1 tablespoon [15 ml.] of the remaining butter, and combine it with the buckwheat and the hard-boiled eggs. Sprinkle a little salt into the inside of the fish and then put in the stuffing.

Dust the stuffed fish with pepper and the flour, and fry it in the remaining butter until lightly browned on both sides. Place the fish in a shallow baking dish and put it in a preheated 350° F. [180° C.] oven for 5 minutes. Remove the fish and pour the sour cream over it. Return it to the oven and continue cooking, basting it with the liquid, until the fish is cooked right through. This is likely to take a further 20 to 25 minutes, depending on the size and shape of the fish. Serve the fish in the dish in which it has been cooked.

Pickled cucumber, a vegetable, and fruit salad or marinated apple slices may be served with the fish.

O. P. MOLCHANOVA
KNIGA O VKUSNOĬ I ZDOROVOĬ PISHCHE

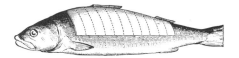

Whole Fish in Chablis

Daurade Djénane

(Options: crappie, porgy, scup, sheepshead)

The original version of this recipe calls for daurade (gilt-head bream), a commonly used French name for several members of the porgy family.

	To serve 4 to 6	
1	whole fish (2 lb. [1 kg.]), cleaned	1
3 cups	Chablis or other dry white wine	¾ liter
	salt and pepper	
1	whole clove	1
2	fresh sage leaves	2
1	bay leaf	1
1½ cups	fresh mushrooms (about ¼ lb. [125 g.])	375 ml.
½ cup	pitted ripe olives	125 ml.
2	large tomatoes, each cut into 6 slices	2
2	slices lemon	2

Place the fish in an oval, ovenproof earthenware dish. Pour in the wine and add salt and pepper, the clove, sage and bay leaves, mushrooms and olives. Arrange the tomato and lemon slices on the fish. Cook uncovered in a preheated 350° F. [180° C.] oven, basting every 10 minutes, for about 45 minutes. Serve straight from the dish.

GASTON DERYS
L'ART D'ÊTRE GOURMAND

Fish with Normandy Sauce

Carrelet à la Sauce Normande

(Options: drum, flounder, sheepshead, turbot)

The original version of this recipe calls for plaice, a popular European flounder.

	To serve 2	
1	whole fish (about 1 lb. [½ kg.]), cleaned	1
7 tbsp.	butter	105 ml.
	salt and pepper	
1¼ cups	dry white wine	300 ml.
2 tsp.	flour	10 ml.
30	live mussels, scrubbed	30
10 or 12	fresh mushrooms	10 or 12
2 tbsp.	fresh lemon juice	30 ml.
4	egg yolks	4
¼ cup	heavy cream	50 ml.

Put the fish in a generously buttered ovenproof dish. Season the fish, pour in ½ cup [125 ml.] of the wine and put the dish in a preheated 350° F. [180° C.] oven for about 20 minutes, or until the flesh of the fish is cooked.

Put 2 tablespoons [30 ml.] of butter in a saucepan and, over medium heat, stir in the flour until the mixture becomes golden. Moisten this with butter and wine from the fish, leaving in the dish only enough liquid to ensure that the fish does not dry up. Reduce the sauce mixture by half.

Put the mussels in another saucepan with the remaining wine, cover and shake over high heat until all the shells have opened. Poach the mushrooms for 2 or 3 minutes in a little water with the lemon juice, 1 tablespoon [15 ml.] of butter and a pinch of salt.

Add the strained juice from the mussels and from the mushrooms to the reduced sauce; reduce the mixture by half, then bind it with the egg yolks, mixed with the cream.

Arrange the mussels and mushrooms around the fish, and pour the sauce on top. Dot the dish here and there with the remaining butter, cut into small pieces; let the fish sit in the oven for 2 minutes, then serve it.

ALAN AND JANE DAVIDSON
DUMAS ON FOOD

Baked Fish, Spanish-Style

Besugo Asado con Piriñaca

(Options: porgy, scup, sheepshead)

The original version of this recipe calls for sea bream, a common European name for several members of the porgy family.

	To serve 4	
1	whole fish (2¼ lb. [1 kg.]), cleaned	1
3	tomatoes, sliced	3
½	small cucumber, sliced	½
1	medium-sized onion, finely chopped	1
3	garlic cloves, finely chopped	3
1	bay leaf, finely crumbled	1
2 tsp.	chopped fresh parsley	10 ml.
1	green pepper, seeded, deribbed and finely chopped	1
	salt	
1 or 2 tbsp.	fresh lemon juice	15 or 30 ml.
2 tbsp.	oil	30 ml.

Put the fish in an oiled baking dish. Place the slices of tomato and cucumber on the fish. Mix the rest of the ingredients together and sprinkle them on the top. Bake the fish in a preheated 375° F. [190° C.] oven, for about 30 minutes or until the fish flakes easily when tested with a fork.

ELIZABETH CASS
SPANISH COOKING

Baked Fish in Hot Sauce

Samaki Harra

(Options: croaker, bonito, grouper, bass)

	To serve 6 to 8	
1	whole fish (4 to 5 lb. [2 to 2½ kg.]), cleaned	1
	salt	
6	sprigs coriander	6
15	garlic cloves, crushed	15
	pepper	
1 cup	olive oil	¼ liter
½ cup	walnuts, ground	125 ml.
½ cup	fresh lemon juice	125 ml.
	cayenne pepper	

Rub the fish well inside and outside with salt. Pound the coriander with the garlic, season with pepper and rub the inside of the fish with this mixture. Tie the fish with cotton string, if necessary, to close the opening. Put the fish on a piece of aluminum foil, pour on the oil and wrap the foil around the fish. Place it on a baking sheet and bake in a preheated 350° F. [180° C.] oven for about 40 minutes, or until the fish is tender.

Meanwhile, blend the walnuts, lemon juice and a pinch of cayenne pepper to a smooth sauce. Put the fish on a warmed platter, and serve the sauce separately in a gravy boat.

AIDA KARAOGLAN
A GOURMET'S DELIGHT

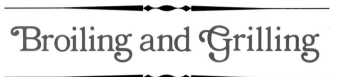

Broiling and Grilling

Grilled Striped Bass with Fennel

(Options: bluefish, drum, lake trout)

This is the American version of a famous Mediterranean dish, *loup de mer* with dried fennel. *Loup de mer* is unavailable here, and even a whole striped bass is not easy to come by, although you can usually find fillets. Dried fennel is found in specialty herb shops.

	To serve 6	
1	whole striped bass (about 6 lb. [3 kg.]), cleaned with the head and tail removed, or 2 striped bass fillets (3 lb. [1½ kg.] each)	1
1 tbsp.	fennel seeds	15 ml.
1 tsp.	salt	5 ml.
	freshly ground black pepper	
¼ cup	olive oil	50 ml.
1 tbsp.	brandy	15 ml.
	lemon wedges	

Rinse the fish and dry it on paper towels. Cut three or four slashes in the skin of a whole fish or fillets, but not all the way through. Place the fillets together, sandwich-style.

Crush the fennel seeds either by placing them between two sheets of wax paper and using a rolling pin, or with a mortar and pestle. Combine the crushed fennel with the salt, pepper, oil and brandy.

Beat the mixture well and brush it over the skin of the fish on both sides, being sure extra amounts are put in the slashes. Place the whole fish, or the fillets laid together flesh to flesh, in a hinged grill and cook over a charcoal fire about 5 inches [13 cm.] from the coals for about 8 minutes on each side, until the skin is crisp and well browned and the flesh flakes easily with a fork.

Remove the fish from the grill. Remove the bones from the fish. Slice into six servings and serve with lemon wedges.

MARIAN BURROS
PURE & SIMPLE

Broiled Butterfish Steaks

(Options: bluefish, salmon, swordfish)

To serve 6

2 lb.	butterfish steaks or fillets	1 kg.
3 to 4 tbsp.	fresh lemon juice	45 to 60 ml.
½ tsp.	cut fresh dill	2 ml.
½ tsp.	oregano	2 ml.
1	garlic clove, finely chopped	1
	salt	
	paprika	

Arrange the fish on a well-oiled broiler pan. Brush the fish with the lemon juice, and sprinkle with the dill, oregano, garlic and a little salt. Set the pan about 3 inches [8 cm.] from the heat source, and broil the fish for about 15 to 20 minutes, or until the fish flakes when tested with a fork. Sprinkle paprika over the fish.

UNIVERSITY OF CALIFORNIA COOPERATIVE EXTENSION
CALIFORNIA SEAFOOD RECIPES

Fish Kebabs

Portuguese Assaduras de Peixe

(Options: cod, flounder, pollock, sole)

The technique of skewering fillet strips is shown on page 59.

To serve 8

4 to 5 lb.	haddock fillets	2 to 2½ kg.
4	garlic cloves	4
1 tsp.	paprika	5 ml.
1 tbsp.	salt	15 ml.
1 cup	wine vinegar	¼ liter
2 cups	water	½ liter
2	bay leaves, crushed	2

Combine all the ingredients except the fish. (This makes a marinade called *vinha de alhos.*) Pour the mixture over the haddock fillets and marinate them overnight. Drain the fillets; save the marinade. Cut the fillets into long strips about 1 inch [2½ cm.] wide. Wind each strip onto a skewer, making loops in opposite directions by running the skewer through the fish at each turn. Place the skewers on a grill about 4 inches [10 cm.] above hot coals. Broil for 15 minutes, or until the fish is golden brown, turning the skewers often and brushing the fish with marinade.

MASSACHUSETTS SEAFOOD COUNCIL
SEAFOODS 'N SEAPORTS...A COOK'S TOUR OF MASSACHUSETTS

Broiled Herring with Mustard

(Options: butterfish, mackerel, smelt)

To serve 4

4	whole fresh herring	4
2 tbsp.	flour, seasoned with salt and freshly ground black pepper	30 ml.
2 to 3 tbsp.	olive oil	30 to 45 ml.
2 to 3 tbsp.	Dijon-style prepared mustard	30 to 45 ml.
½ cup	fresh bread crumbs	125 ml.
4 tbsp.	butter, melted	60 ml.

Clean and scale the herring, taking care not to break the delicate skin; cut off the heads; wash and dry the herring carefully. Make three shallow incisions on both sides of each fish with a sharp knife.

Dip the herring into the seasoned flour, brush them with olive oil and broil them on a well-oiled baking sheet for 3 to 4 minutes on each side.

Arrange the herring in a shallow ovenproof gratin dish, brush them with the mustard, sprinkle with the bread crumbs and melted butter, and put in a preheated 475° F. [240° C.] oven for 5 minutes. Serve in the gratin dish with boiled new potatoes.

ROBERT CARRIER
THE ROBERT CARRIER COOKERY COURSE

Broiled Kippers

(Options: salted and dried or smoked herring, mullet, smelt)

To serve 4

4	kippers, soaked in milk for 3 hours	4
	dry bread crumbs	

Onion and parsley marinade

1	medium-sized onion, finely chopped	1
	pepper	
1 tbsp.	chopped fresh parsley	15 ml.
¼ cup	olive oil	50 ml.

Drain and dry the kippers, then soak them for at least 3 hours in the marinade, turning them several times. Remove the kippers and roll them in the bread crumbs. Broil them 4 inches [10 cm.] from the heat for 5 minutes on each side, and serve with brown bread and butter.

AMBROSE HEATH
HERRINGS, BLOATERS AND KIPPERS

Grilled Mackerel with Cumin

Maquereaux Grillés au Cumin

(Options: bluefish, butterfish, smelt)

The harissa called for in this recipe is a seasoning paste made from red chili peppers and garlic, seasoned with coriander, caraway and salt. Widely used in Tunisian cooking, it is obtainable where North African foods are sold. If unavailable, substitute Hungarian paprika. The technique for scoring each side of a fish is demonstrated on page 61.

To serve 4

4	whole medium-sized mackerel (about ½ lb. [¼ kg.] each), cleaned and heads removed	4
½ tsp.	*harissa*, mixed with 3 tbsp. [45 ml.] water	2 ml.
3 tbsp.	oil	45 ml.
2	garlic cloves, crushed	2
2 tsp.	ground cumin	10 ml.
	salt	
1	lemon, quartered	1

Make two diagonal cuts in both sides of each fish. Put the *harissa* into a large shallow bowl with the oil, garlic, cumin

and salt. Mix together well, and put the mackerel into the bowl to marinate for 15 minutes, turning over the fish from time to time. Then grill the fish for about 5 minutes on each side, over charcoal or under an oven broiler. Arrange them on a platter and serve very hot, with the lemon quarters.

EDMOND ZEITOUN
250 RECETTES CLASSIQUES DE CUISINE TUNISIENNE

Mackerel with Fennel and Gooseberries

Maquereaux au Fenouil et Groseilles dans la Saison

(Options: bass, bluefish, snapper)

For best results, the fish should be cooked in a fish grill: line one side of the grill with fennel stalks, place the fish in the grill, arrange the rest of the fennel stalks on top and close the grill. The technique of boning a fish through the back is demonstrated on pages 56-57. When fresh gooseberries are not obtainable, you can substitute rhubarb, cut into ½-inch [1-cm.] pieces, or currants.

To serve 4

4	whole mackerel (½ lb. [¼ kg.]), cleaned and boned through the back	4
	salt and pepper	
2 tbsp.	butter, melted	30 ml.
8	fennel stalks	8
4 tbsp.	butter	60 ml.
1 tbsp.	finely cut fennel leaves	15 ml.
	grated nutmeg	
1 tsp.	flour	5 ml.
1 tbsp.	vinegar	15 ml.
½ cup	water	125 ml.
4 oz.	white or green gooseberries	125 g.

Lay the mackerel in a dish, season them with salt and pepper, pour on the melted butter and turn the fish to coat them on both sides. Put four of the fennel stalks on a hot barbecue grill and lay a fish on each one. When the fish are cooked on one side, after 5 to 7 minutes, put four more fennel stalks on the grill and turn the fish over, onto the fresh fennel, and grill for a further 5 to 7 minutes.

Meanwhile, melt the butter in a saucepan. Add the chopped fennel leaves and season with salt, pepper and nutmeg. Stir in the flour, then add the vinegar and water. When the sauce has thickened, add the gooseberries and simmer for 10 minutes. Taste for seasoning.

When the fish are done, arrange them on a warmed serving platter side by side, open up the slits in the backs, and pour the sauce into the slits and over the fish.

VINCENT DE LA CHAPELLE
LE CUISINIER MODERNE

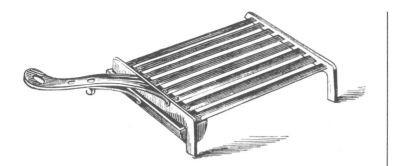

Grilled Mullet with Green Herb Sauce

Rougets Grillés Sauce Verte

(Options: bass, perch, sea robin, scup, trout)

The original version of this recipe specified red mullet, a firm-fleshed, lean Mediterranean fish. The fish can be grilled over charcoal or broiled in an oven, 4 inches [10 cm.] from the heat.

	To serve 6	
6	whole mullet (about 1 lb. [½ kg.] each), cleaned	6
3 tbsp.	oil	45 ml.
	salt and pepper	
1	onion, finely chopped	1
1	bay leaf	1
1	sprig thyme	1
	Green herb sauce	
1 tbsp.	finely cut fresh chives	15 ml.
1 tbsp.	finely chopped fresh parsley	15 ml.
1 tbsp.	finely chopped fresh chervil	15 ml.
1 tsp.	finely chopped fresh tarragon	5 ml.
¼ cup	oil	50 ml.
1 tbsp.	wine vinegar	15 ml.
1 tbsp.	finely chopped gherkins	15 ml.
1 tbsp.	finely chopped capers	15 ml.
	salt and pepper	

Marinate the fish in a dish containing the oil, salt and pepper, the chopped onion, bay leaf and thyme. After 30 minutes to 1 hour, remove the fish from the marinade and grill them for 5 to 10 minutes on each side (depending on the size of the fish), basting with the marinade.

To make the sauce, put the oil and vinegar in a serving dish; add the chives, parsley, chervil, tarragon, gherkins and capers. Mix together well, and season with salt and pepper. Lay the grilled mullet on this green sauce and serve.

ALOIDE BONTOU
TRAITÉ DE CUISINE BOURGEOISE BORDELAISE

Flaming Perch

(Options: bluefish, drum, snapper)

	To serve 4	
1	whole perch (3 to 4 lb. [1 ½ to 2 kg.]), cleaned	1
2 tsp.	salt	10 ml.
3 tbsp.	melted butter	45 ml.
2	small bunches fennel greens	2
⅓ cup	brandy, heated	75 ml.

Rub the perch with salt inside and out. Dip the perch in the melted butter and grill over coals for about 10 minutes, basting often with melted butter. The fish is done when it flakes easily. Place the fish in a shallow baking dish and cover it with the fennel greens, which have been washed and dried. Pour the brandy over the fennel and set it aflame.

RENÉ VERDON
THE WHITE HOUSE CHEF COOKBOOK

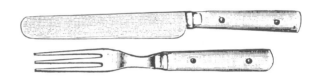

Salmon Barbecue, Seattle

(Options: arctic char, mackerel, sea trout)

	To serve 10	
1	whole salmon (10 lb. [4 ½ kg.]), filleted, skin left on	1
8 tbsp.	butter, melted	120 ml.
¼ cup	fresh lemon juice	50 ml.
¼ tsp.	dried oregano	1 ml.
	salt and pepper	

Make a basting sauce with the melted butter, lemon juice and oregano, and brush it over the salmon flesh. Salt the fish fillets heavily and pepper them generously. Let the salmon stand at room temperature for 1 hour or more. Place each fillet, skin side down, on a separate piece of aluminum foil; crimp up the edges of the foil to form trays. Place the trays on a barbecue grill over wood or charcoal embers. Cover the trays with the grill hood or additional pieces of foil. Lift the hood or the foil covers, baste, and check for doneness about every 5 to 10 minutes. The fish is cooked when it flakes with a fork—after about 25 to 30 minutes. To serve, cut the flesh into serving-sized pieces and lift from the skin.

SHIRLEY SARVIS
CRAB & ABALONE: WEST COAST WAYS WITH FISH & SHELLFISH

Barbecued Stuffed Coho Salmon

(Options: muskellunge, pike, lake trout)

The technique of lacing the opening of a fish with skewers and string is demonstrated on pages 52-53.

To serve 6 to 8

1	whole coho salmon (5 lb. [2½ kg.]), cleaned	1
1 tbsp.	vegetable oil	15 ml.
White wine marinade		
1½ cups	dry white wine	375 ml.
½ cup	strained fresh lemon juice	125 ml.
½ cup	vegetable oil	125 ml.
1	onion, thinly sliced	1
3	garlic cloves, crushed	3
3	sprigs parsley	3
1 tsp.	ground ginger	5 ml.
½ tsp.	crumbled dried thyme	2 ml.
¼ tsp.	Tabasco sauce	1 ml.
1 tsp.	salt	5 ml.
¼ tsp.	freshly ground black pepper	1 ml.
Rice stuffing		
1 cup	freshly cooked rice	¼ liter
¼ cup	finely chopped scallions, including 2 inches [5 mm.] of the green tops	50 ml.
¼ cup	finely chopped fresh parsley	50 ml.
	the peel of ½ lemon, cut into julienne	
1	lemon, sliced ¼ inch [6 mm.] thick	1

First prepare the marinade in the following manner: combine the wine, lemon juice, ½ cup [125 ml.] of the oil, the onion, garlic, parsley sprigs, ginger, thyme, Tabasco, salt and pepper in a small enameled saucepan and, stirring occasionally, bring to a boil over high heat. Pour the marinade into an enameled casserole or roasting pan large enough to hold the salmon, and set it aside to cool to room temperature.

With a sharp knife, score both sides of the fish by making four or five evenly spaced diagonal slits about 4 inches [10 cm.] long and ¼ inch [6 mm.] deep. Place the salmon in the cooled marinade and turn it over to moisten it evenly. Cover tightly with foil or plastic wrap and marinate at room temperature for about 3 hours, or in the refrigerator for about 6 hours, turning the fish occasionally.

Light a layer of coals in a charcoal grill and let them burn until a white ash appears on the surface, or preheat the broiler of your stove to its highest setting.

Transfer the salmon to paper towels and pat it completely dry with more paper towels. Strain the marinade through a fine sieve set over a bowl. To prepare the stuffing, combine the rice, scallions, chopped parsley and lemon strips in a small bowl. Pour in ¼ cup [50 ml.] of the strained marinade and mix well. Set the remaining marinade aside.

Loosely fill the salmon with the stuffing, then close the opening with small skewers and kitchen cord. With a pastry brush, spread the tablespoon [15 ml.] of oil over the hot grill or the broiler rack. Place the salmon on top and brush it with a little of the reserved marinade. Broil 3 to 4 inches [8 to 10 cm.] from the heat, basting the salmon frequently with marinade. The salmon should be broiled for about 15 minutes on each side, or until it is evenly and delicately browned and feels firm when prodded gently with a finger.

Serve the salmon at once from a heated platter, with the lemon slices arranged attractively in a row along the top of the fish. Garnish it further, if you like, with red and green pepper strips and onion rings.

FOODS OF THE WORLD
AMERICAN COOKING: THE EASTERN HEARTLAND

Salmon and Cucumber Kebabs

(Options: swordfish, tuna)

To serve 5 or 6

2½ lb.	salmon steaks, preferably center-cut, 1¼ inches [3 cm.] thick, bones removed	1¼ kg.
3	cucumbers, peeled, halved lengthwise and seeded	3
½ cup	dry white wine	125 ml.
3 tbsp.	Japanese soy sauce	45 ml.
1 tsp.	sugar	5 ml.
2 tbsp.	butter, melted	30 ml.

Cut the salmon into 1½-inch [4-cm.] chunks and the cucumbers into 1-inch [2½-cm.] chunks, and place them in a bowl.

Combine the wine, soy sauce, sugar and melted butter. Pour the mixture over the salmon and cucumber chunks. Mix, and marinate in the refrigerator for at least an hour.

Just before serving, thread alternate pieces of salmon and cucumber on skewers. Broil, preferably over charcoal, turning the skewers until the salmon is lightly browned all over—about 10 to 15 minutes. Brush occasionally with the marinade while broiling.

PAULA PECK
PAULA PECK'S ART OF GOOD COOKING

Potlatch Salmon

(Options: mackerel, sturgeon, swordfish, tuna)

The salmon steaks called for in this recipe may also be broiled 4 inches [10 cm.] from the heat or pan fried.

	To serve 6	
6	salmon steaks (about 2 lb. [1 kg.])	6
1 tbsp.	juniper berries (about 50), lightly crushed	15 ml.
¼ cup	oil	50 ml.
2 tsp.	salt	10 ml.
⅛ tsp.	pepper	½ ml.
	lemon or lime wedges	

Push six to eight juniper berries into each steak. Coat the fish with oil to prevent sticking. Sprinkle the fish with salt and pepper. Grill over hot coals for 5 to 6 minutes on each side. Garnish with lemon or lime wedges.

U.S. DEPARTMENT OF COMMERCE
A SEAFOOD HERITAGE

Sardines Grilled in Vine Leaves

Sardines Grillées aux Feuilles de Vigne

(Options: anchovy, herring, mullet)

	To serve 2	
12	fresh small sardines, cleaned and patted dry	12
¼ cup	olive oil	50 ml.
2 tbsp.	fresh lemon juice	30 ml.
	salt and pepper	
	rosemary	
12	tender fresh young grapevine leaves, parboiled for 5 minutes and patted dry	12

Mix the oil, lemon juice, salt and pepper in a shallow dish. Quickly roll the sardines in this mixture, and put a little rosemary inside each one. Wrap each fish in a vine leaf, using the stem of the leaf to secure it. (Alternatively, tie the wrapped sardine rolls with fine cotton string.)

Grill the sardine rolls over glowing embers for about 3 minutes on each side, or until the vine leaves start to blacken. Serve immediately. When the rolls are opened, the skin of the fish will peel off with the leaves, revealing the delicious fillets inside.

MICHEL BARBEROUSSE
CUISINE PROVENÇALE

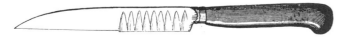

Broiled Shad

(Options: mackerel, salmon, trout)

	To serve 4 to 6	
2½ lb.	shad fillets, with the skin left on	1¼ kg.
6 tbsp.	butter	90 ml.
	salt	
	freshly ground black pepper	
	lemon wedges	

Melt the butter in a shallow, fireproof dish large enough to hold the fillets in one layer. Dry the fillets and lay them in the dish, turning them to coat both sides with butter.

Cook the fish, skin side down, 4 inches [10 cm.] from the heat in a broiler preheated to its highest setting. Baste occasionally with the butter. Do not turn the fillets. Cook 6 to 8 minutes, until the flesh is opaque and flakes when prodded with a fork. Sprinkle with salt and a few grindings of pepper, surround the fillets with lemon wedges and serve in the dish.

FOODS OF THE WORLD/AMERICAN COOKING

Broiled Sole

Sole Grillée

(Options: flounder, fluke)

	To serve 2	
2	whole sole (about 10 oz. [300 g.] each), cleaned and skinned	2
	salt and pepper	
¼ cup	fresh lemon juice	50 ml.
2 tbsp.	butter	30 ml.
1 cup	fresh bread crumbs	¼ liter
Anchovy sauce		
2	anchovy fillets, soaked in water for 10 minutes and patted dry	2
2 tbsp.	butter	30 ml.
¼ cup	dry white wine	50 ml.
2 tbsp.	fresh lemon juice	30 ml.

Season the sole with salt and pepper and the lemon juice. Melt the butter. Brush the fish with the melted butter, then coat with the bread crumbs. Broil 4 inches [10 cm.] from the heat for about 10 minutes, turning once.

Meanwhile, cook the anchovy fillets in the butter over low heat, stirring and crushing to a purée. Add the wine and lemon juice, and bring to a boil. Pour the anchovy sauce over the fish and serve.

CHARLES DURAND
LE CUISINIER DURAND

Saint Germain Sole

Sole Saint-Germain

(Options: drum, flounder, pompano)

To serve 4

2 lb.	sole fillets	1 kg.
6 to 8 tbsp.	melted butter	90 to 120 ml.
½ cup	fresh bread crumbs	125 ml.

Season the sole; dip the fillets in the melted butter and cover with the fresh bread crumbs, taking care to pat them in with the flat of a knife so that they combine with the butter to form a crust. Sprinkle with some more melted butter, and broil the fish fillets about 4 inches [10 cm.] from the heat for about 6 minutes so that the coating of bread crumbs may acquire a nice golden brown color. Surround the fillets with potatoes cut in the shape of olives and cooked in butter. Send a béarnaise sauce *(recipe, page 166)* to the table separately.

AUGUSTE ESCOFFIER
THE ESCOFFIER COOK BOOK

Barbecued Swordfish Rolls

Involtini di Pescespada

(Options: shark, whitefish)

To serve 4

1 lb.	swordfish, cut into 12 thin slices	400 g.
2 oz.	swordfish flesh, poached and chopped	50 g.
2 cups	fresh bread crumbs	½ liter
1 oz.	*pecorino*, grated	30 g.
1 tbsp.	capers, chopped	15 ml.
10	pitted green olives, chopped	10
3 or 4	sprigs parsley, chopped	3 or 4
1 tbsp.	tomato sauce *(recipe, page 165)*	15 ml.
	salt	
	cayenne pepper	
2 to 3 tbsp.	olive oil	30 to 45 ml.
16	bay leaves	16
1	large onion, quartered and separated into 16 pieces	1

Pound the fish slices to widen them as much as possible without breaking them. In a bowl mix together the cooked swordfish, bread crumbs, cheese, capers, olives and parsley. Add the tomato sauce, season with salt and cayenne pepper, and moisten with oil. Stir thoroughly.

Spread the stuffing on the fish slices, roll up the slices and thread the rolls onto skewers (allowing three rolls per skewer), alternating the rolls with bay leaves and onion wedges. Barbecue over a charcoal fire, basting the rolls once or twice with a few drops of olive oil, for about 10 minutes or until the flesh is firm to the touch.

PINO CORRENTI
IL LIBRO D'ORO DELLA CUCINA E DEI VINI DI SICILIA

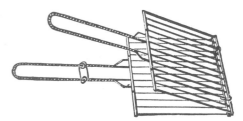

Barbecued Trout, Armenian-Style

Forel'na Vertele

(Options: bass, grayling)

In Armenia the pink-fleshed Ishkhan trout from Lake Sevan are barbecued by this method and served with pomegranate seeds. You can use any small trout, but if you want the traditional garnish, fresh pomegranates are available in the United States in September and October. The technique of gutting fish through the gills is demonstrated on page 19.

To serve 4

4	whole trout (about ½ lb. [¼ kg.] each), gutted through the gills	4
	salt	
	cayenne pepper or Hungarian paprika	
4 tbsp.	butter, melted	60 ml.
2	lemons, sliced	2
8	sprigs tarragon	8
2 oz.	pomegranate seeds (optional)	75 g.

With a sharp knife, make a few shallow, diagonal incisions in the skin on both sides of each fish to ensure that the trout will not lose their shape when cooked. Sprinkle each fish inside and out with salt and cayenne pepper or paprika. Roll them in melted butter and cook for 10 to 12 minutes over glowing charcoal or under a broiler, turning the fish periodically and basting with butter. Serve the cooked trout on a dish decorated with slices of lemon and sprigs of tarragon.

A. S. PIRUZYAN
ARMYANSKAYA KULINARIYA

Fish Flamed with Herbs

Riba-Flambé

(Options: bluefish, mackerel, mullet, rockfish)

This Bulgarian dish is very easy to prepare, and is a particularly suitable way of treating the mullet that are found in the coastal waters of the Black Sea, as well as those of Western Europe and the United States.

	To serve 2	
1	whole mullet (about 1½ lb. [¾ kg.]), scaled and cleaned	1
	salt and pepper	
1 tbsp.	finely cut dill	15 ml.
1 tbsp.	finely chopped fresh parsley	15 ml.
¼ cup	brandy, warmed	50 ml.

Season the fish with salt and pepper. Grill the fish over charcoal, or under an oven broiler, about 4 inches [10 cm.] from the heat for about 10 minutes on one side and about 5 minutes on the other.

Place the grilled fish neatly in a fireproof serving dish of a shape that fits it, and sprinkle the dill and parsley over it. Pour the warmed brandy over the fish and ignite it. The herbs will burn and give the fish a special aroma, while the flaming dish will create an air of festivity.

KNISA ZA VSEKI DEN I VSEKI DOM

Grilled Fish, Javanese-Style

Panggang Ikan Bawal Djawa

(Options: flounder, fluke)

	To serve 2	
1	whole flatfish (1 lb. [½ kg.]), cleaned and skinned	1
2 tbsp.	soy sauce	30 ml.
1 tbsp.	brown sugar	15 ml.
1	garlic clove, crushed	1
1 tbsp.	water	15 ml.
1 tbsp.	butter, melted	15 ml.
5	fresh red chilies, stemmed, seeded and thinly sliced	5
1 tbsp.	fresh lemon juice	15 ml.

Mix half the soy sauce and half the sugar with the garlic and water. Place the whole fish in a bowl and marinate it in this mixture for about 1 hour. Grill the fish on both sides over very low heat, basting with the remaining marinade as it cooks. (You can do this under the oven broiler, but a charcoal fire produces a more delicious result.) When the fish is tender, after about 15 to 20 minutes, remove it from the grill and lay it on a warmed plate. Pour the melted butter over it, then sprinkle with a final spice mixture made from the chilies, the remaining soy sauce and sugar, and the lemon juice.

ROSEMARY BRISSENDEN
SOUTH-EAST ASIAN FOOD

Fish Grilled with Aromatic Oils

La Daurade Grillée à la Niçoise

(Options: porgy, scup, sheepshead)

The original version of this recipe calls for daurade (gilt-head bream), a common French name for several members of the porgy family. The various oils called for should be made at least two weeks ahead of time by steeping aromatics in olive oil. Put several dried red chilies in one small bottle of the oil, a large sprig of thyme into another and sprigs of dried fennel into a third. Tightly covered, the oils can be stored in a cool, dark, dry place for six weeks without losing fragrance. The technique of cutting incisions in fish is shown on page 61.

	To serve 4	
1	whole fish (2 to 2½ lb. [1 kg.]), cleaned	1
1 tsp.	aromatic chili oil	5 ml.
1 tsp.	aromatic thyme oil	5 ml.
1 tsp.	aromatic fennel oil	5 ml.
2 tbsp.	olive oil	30 ml.
	salt	
2 to 3 tbsp.	lemon juice or 1 tsp. [5 ml.] aromatic oil (optional)	30 to 45 ml.

Make several shallow, diagonal incisions in each side of the fish. Heat a grill rack over a charcoal grill in which the embers are glowing but already covered with white ash. (Preheating the rack will prevent the fish from sticking.)

Mix the aromatic oils with the olive oil. Add a little salt and, using a brush, daub both sides of the fish with the mixture. Grill the fish about 15 minutes per side, or until done.

Lift the fish onto a warmed platter and, if desired, sprinkle with lemon juice or aromatic oil. Serve immediately.

JACQUES MÉDECIN
LA CUISINE DU COMTÉ DE NICE

Fish Teriyaki

(Options: halibut, mackerel, rockfish)

Teriyaki refers to the cooking process of first marinating foods in a mixture of soy sauce, *mirin* (sweet rice wine) and *sake* (stronger rice wine), and then broiling them, preferably over charcoal.

To serve 6		
6	fish fillets (about 2 lb. [1 kg.] in all)	6
⅓ cup	soy sauce	75 ml.
⅓ cup	*mirin*	75 ml.
⅓ cup	*sake*	75 ml.
1	garlic clove, finely chopped (optional)	1

Mix the soy sauce, *mirin* and *sake* together in a small saucepan and bring to a boil. Add the garlic, if using. Remove the pan from the stove, pour the soy-sauce mixture over the fish fillets and marinate them for 15 to 20 minutes.

Preheat the broiler or charcoal grill, and cook the pieces 4 inches [10 cm.] from the heat for 5 to 10 minutes on each side, brushing them three or four times with the marinade. When finished, the fish should be coated with a rich brown glaze. Serve immediately.

PETER AND JOAN MARTIN
JAPANESE COOKING

Frying

Batter-fried Bluegills

(Options: catfish, crappie, scup, spot)

To serve 4

1 lb.	bluegill fillets, skinned	½ kg.
	vegetable oil for deep frying	
½ cup	cake flour, not the self-rising variety	125 ml.
2 tbsp.	cornstarch	30 ml.
½ tsp.	salt	2 ml.
½ tsp.	freshly ground black pepper	2 ml.
1	egg, yolk separated from white	1
½ cup	water	125 ml.
1	lemon, quartered	1

Pour the vegetable oil into a deep fryer or large heavy saucepan to a depth of about 3 inches [8 cm.], and heat the oil until it reaches 375° F. [190° C.] on a deep-frying thermometer.

Meanwhile, prepare the batter in the following fashion: combine the flour, cornstarch, salt and pepper, and sift them together onto a plate or a sheet of wax paper. With a wire whisk, beat the egg yolk and water to a smooth cream and then incorporate the flour mixture, a few tablespoons at a time. Just before using the batter, beat the egg white with a wire whisk or a rotary or electric beater until it is stiff enough to stand in unwavering peaks on the beater when it is lifted from the bowl. Scoop the egg white over the batter and fold it in gently with a rubber spatula.

Pat the fish fillets dry with paper towels. Pick up one fillet with tongs, immerse it in the batter, and drop it into the oil. Turning them with a slotted spoon, deep fry four or five fillets at a time for 3 minutes or until golden brown. As they brown, transfer the fillets to paper towels to drain.

Arrange the fillets attractively on a warmed platter and serve them at once, accompanied by the lemon quarters.

FOODS OF THE WORLD
AMERICAN COOKING: THE EASTERN HEARTLAND

Bonito with Peas

Palamita con Piselli

(Options: bluefish, mackerel, salmon)

To serve 4

1	whole bonito (about 2 lb. [1 kg.]) with head and tail removed, cleaned and cut into 4 slices	1
½ cup	olive oil	125 ml.
3	garlic cloves, chopped	3
4 tbsp.	chopped fresh parsley	60 ml.
3	medium-sized tomatoes, peeled, seeded and coarsely chopped, or drained, canned tomatoes	3
	salt and pepper	
2 lb.	fresh peas (if shelled about 2 cups [½ liter]), parboiled for 5 minutes in salted water with 1 garlic clove and 1 sprig parsley	1 kg.

Heat the olive oil in a large skillet and lightly sauté the garlic and 3 tablespoons [45 ml.] of the parsley. Before the garlic is golden, add the tomatoes. Season with salt and pepper and, after 5 minutes, add the fish slices. Cook, uncovered, for 10 minutes, then add the drained, parboiled peas. Simmer, covered, over low heat for another 10 minutes. Sprinkle with the remaining parsley and serve.

PAOLO PETRONI
IL LIBRO DELLA VERA CUCINA MARINARA

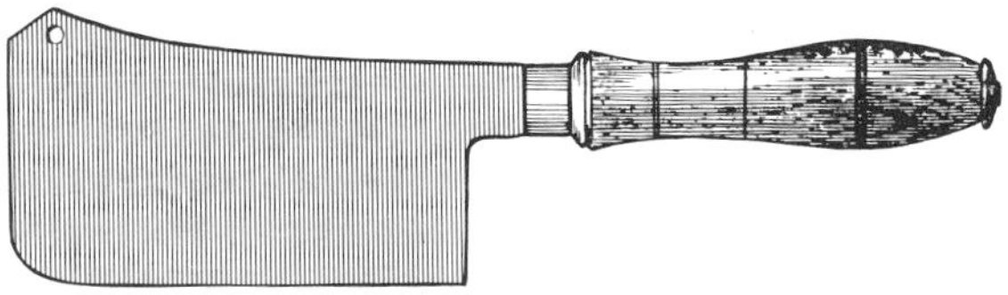

Chinese Fish Strips

(Options: dolphin, drum, grouper, snook)

To serve 3 or 4

1½ lb.	sea bass fillets, cut into diagonal strips about ¼ inch thick	¾ kg.
1	egg white	1
4 tsp.	water	20 ml.
2 tsp.	cornstarch	10 ml.
	salt	
3 tbsp.	sesame oil	45 ml.
1	small garlic clove, thinly sliced	1
¼ lb.	fresh snow peas	125 g.
¼ lb.	water chestnuts, sliced	125 g.
2 tsp. plus 1 tbsp.	dry sherry	25 ml.
1 tsp.	sugar	5 ml.

Combine the egg white with 2 teaspoons [10 ml.] of the water, 1 teaspoon [5 ml.] of the cornstarch and a pinch of salt. Marinate the fish in this mixture for 2 or 3 minutes.

Cover the bottom of a wok or skillet with 2 tablespoons [30 ml.] of the oil and heat until just warm. Add the fish strips; cook for about 3 minutes and drain on paper towels.

Add the remaining oil to the pan and heat with the garlic. Stir in the snow peas and water chestnuts and cook for 1 or 2 minutes. Combine 2 teaspoons of the sherry with the remaining water and cornstarch, the sugar and a dash of salt; add to the vegetables. Stir in the fish strips carefully. Cook for about 3 minutes, or until the sauce is thickened and the fish is heated through. Sprinkle with 1 tablespoon [15 ml.] of sherry before serving.

JACQUELINE E. KNIGHT
THE COOK'S FISH GUIDE

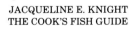

Butterfish Norfolk

(Options: bluegill, crappie, scup)

To serve 6

6	whole butterfish (½ lb. [¼ kg.] each), cleaned, heads and tails left on	6
¼ cup	flour	50 ml.
1½ tsp.	salt	7 ml.
⅛ tsp.	pepper	1 ml.
½ cup	white cornmeal	125 ml.
3 tbsp.	butter or shortening	45 ml.
6	sprigs mint	6

Wipe the butterfish with a damp cloth. Sift the flour, salt and pepper into an oblong dish or onto a mixing board; stir in the cornmeal. Roll the butterfish in the cornmeal mixture.

Heat the butter or shortening in a skillet. Brown the fish quickly for about 4 minutes on each side, being careful not to overcook them. Serve the fish piping hot on preheated plates. Garnish with sprigs of mint.

MILO MILORADOVICH
THE ART OF FISH COOKERY

Tennessee Fried Catfish

(Options: bluegill, crappie, sunfish)

To serve 6

6	whole catfish, skinned, heads removed, and cleaned	6
2 tsp.	salt	10 ml.
¼ tsp.	pepper	1 ml.
2	eggs	2
2 tbsp.	milk	30 ml.
2 cups	cornmeal	½ liter
	lard for frying	

Sprinkle both sides of the fish with salt and pepper. Beat the eggs lightly and blend in the milk. Dip the fish in the egg mixture and roll them in the cornmeal. Place the fish in a heavy skillet containing about ⅛ inch [3 mm.] of hot but not smoking fat. Fry over medium heat. When the fish are brown on one side, turn them carefully and brown the other side. Cooking time is about 10 to 15 minutes, depending on the thickness of the fish. Drain the fish on absorbent paper. Serve immediately on a warmed serving platter.

U.S. DEPARTMENT OF COMMERCE
COUNTRY CATFISH

Pan-fried Catfish

(Options: grouper, haddock, scup)

To serve 4

1	whole catfish (2 lb. [1 kg.]), cleaned, left whole or cut into pieces	1
1 cup	milk	¼ liter
1 cup	fresh bread crumbs or cornmeal	¼ liter
	lard or oil for frying	
	salt and pepper	

Dip the fish in the milk, then coat with the crumbs or the cornmeal. Cook rapidly in a skillet, in hot lard or oil about 1 inch [2½ cm.] deep. Drain the fish, season to taste and serve.

JAMES BEARD
JAMES BEARD'S NEW FISH COOKERY

Salt Cod with Spinach

Morue à la Lessiveuse

(Options: salted cusk, salted haddock, salted halibut, salted pollock)

The bitter Seville orange juice called for in this recipe may be replaced by the juice from one sweet orange mixed with the juice from one lemon.

To serve 4

1½ lb.	salt cod, soaked in water overnight, drained and cut into 2-inch [5-cm.] squares	¾ kg.
½ cup	flour	125 ml.
¼ cup	olive oil	50 ml.
1 lb.	spinach, chopped, lightly salted, squeezed to remove excess liquid, then rinsed and squeezed dry	½ kg.
½ cup	boiling water	125 ml.
2 tbsp.	finely chopped fresh parsley	30 ml.
1	garlic clove, finely chopped	1
1 tsp.	finely chopped orange peel, preferably from a bitter Seville orange	5 ml.
2	anchovy fillets, soaked in cold water for 10 minutes, patted dry and finely chopped	2

Flour the pieces of cod and half-cook them in the oil over low heat (allow about 2 minutes on each side). Remove the cod from the pan, then add the spinach and cook over high heat for 1 to 2 minutes, tossing it frequently. Add 1 teaspoon [5 ml.] of flour, the water, parsley, garlic, orange peel and anchovy fillets. Reduce the heat to medium once the mixture has reached a boil. When the spinach is cooked (after about 5 minutes), mix in the cod and cook for a further 2 to 3 minutes, shaking the pan vigorously. Then serve.

CHARLES DURAND
LE CUISINIER DURAND

Gloucester Codfish Balls

(Options: salted cusk, salted haddock, salted halibut, salted pollock)

This dish may be served with either tomato sauce (recipe, page 165) or tartare sauce (recipe, page 162).

To serve 2 or 3

⅓ lb.	salt cod (about 1 cup [¼ liter]), soaked in cold water overnight	150 g.
2 or 3	medium-sized potatoes, diced (about 2½ cups [625 ml.])	2 or 3
½ tbsp.	butter or margarine	7 ml.
	salt and pepper	
1	egg, or 2 egg yolks, lightly beaten	1
	oil for deep frying	

Drain the fish and shred it by placing the pieces on a cutting board and using a fork. Steam, rather than boil, the potatoes until tender; drain the potatoes thoroughly and return them to the pot in which they were cooked. Shake over medium heat until the potatoes are dry, then mash them thoroughly. Add the butter and pepper and beat until the potatoes are very light. Add the flaked codfish and egg, and continue beating until the mixture is light and fluffy. Taste and add salt if necessary. Heat the oil to 375° F. [190° C.] in a deep skillet. Slip in tablespoonfuls of the mixture and cook until light brown—about 1 minute. Cook a few at a time. Drain on paper towels.

CLEMENTINE PADDLEFORD
HOW AMERICA EATS

Codfish Balls

(Options: salted haddock, salted pollock)

To serve 4 to 6

1 lb.	salt cod fillets, soaked overnight and drained	½ kg.
2	medium-sized potatoes	2
1 cup	bread crumbs	¼ liter
¼ cup	chopped fresh parsley	50 ml.
2 tbsp.	freshly grated Parmesan cheese	30 ml.
2	garlic cloves, finely chopped	2
	salt	
	pepper	
2	eggs, lightly beaten	2
	oil for deep frying	

Boil and mash the potatoes; set them aside. Boil the codfish until it flakes easily. Drain, and flake the fish with a fork. Mix the flaked fish, the potatoes and the rest of the ingredients together well by hand. Form the mixture into cakes or balls, and fry them in hot oil.

THE FISHERMEN'S WIVES OF GLOUCESTER
THE CAPE ANN LEAGUE OF WOMEN VOTERS
THE TASTE OF GLOUCESTER

Dutch Mess

(Options: salted haddock, salted halibut, salted pollock)

This dish, which was popular among the Germans who settled Lunenburg in Nova Scotia, was soon adopted by English-speaking settlers. The "Dutch" in the title is probably a corruption of "Deutsch."

To serve 4

1 lb.	salt cod, soaked in one or two changes of cold water for 6 to 10 hours	½ kg.
4	large potatoes, cut into large pieces	4
4 oz.	lean salt pork, diced	125 g.
1	large onion, chopped	1
1 cup	heavy cream (optional)	¼ liter
	pepper	

Drain the salt cod, reserving the water in which it has been soaked. Flake the fish and discard the skin and bones. Cook the potatoes in the reserved water. When the potatoes are about half done, after about 15 minutes, add the fish and simmer for 10 minutes, or until the potatoes are tender.

Meanwhile, fry the salt pork in a skillet until the fat begins to run, then add the onion and cook until both the pork and the onion are golden brown. Drain off the excess fat. Add the cream, if desired, and heat through, stirring.

Drain the potatoes and salt cod and place on a warmed platter, top with the salt pork and onion mixture and season generously with pepper.

Any leftovers can be mashed and made into fish cakes.

MARIE NIGHTINGALE
OUT OF OLD NOVA SCOTIA KITCHENS

Dogfish Croquettes

Plaombo da Augustarello a Estaccio

(Options: cod, pike, shark, swordfish)

This recipe from Lazio, in Italy, is highly effective in transforming the humble dogfish into an unmistakably Mediterranean delicacy.

To serve 6

2 lb.	dogfish, cut into 12 slices, each about ½ inch [1 cm.] thick	1 kg.
2	eggs, beaten	2
	salt	
3	garlic cloves, chopped	3
3½ tbsp.	chopped fresh parsley	52 ml.
¾ cup	freshly grated Parmesan cheese	175 ml.
1½ tbsp.	dry bread crumbs	22 ml.
½ cup	olive oil	125 ml.
	pepper	
3	lemons, halved	3

Wash, skin and pat dry the slices of fish. Immerse them in the beaten egg, lightly salted, for 45 minutes, turning them several times.

Remove the fish slices, and drain off any excess egg. Pound together the garlic, 1½ tablespoons [22 ml.] of the parsley, the cheese and bread crumbs to a paste. Spread the paste on the fish slices, pressing to make it adhere.

Heat the oil very hot in a wide skillet. Fry the slices of fish for about 5 minutes on each side, until golden and crisp. Drain them and season with salt and pepper to taste. Arrange them, slightly overlapping, on a warmed serving platter. Garnish with lemon halves and the remaining chopped parsley, and serve at once.

LUIGI CARNACINA AND LUIGI VERONELLI
LA BUONA VERA CUCINA ITALIANA

Flounder Puffs

(Options: bluegill, crappie, perch, pompano)

To serve 2

½ to ¾ lb.	flounder fillets, cut into serving pieces	¼ to ⅓ kg.
1	egg, yolk separated from white	1
1 tbsp.	flour	15 ml.
1 tbsp.	water	15 ml.
¼ to ½ tsp.	salt	1 to 2 ml.
½ cup	olive or salad oil	125 ml.

Beat the egg white until it is very stiff. In a separate bowl beat the egg yolk until smooth, fold in the flour, water and salt, then fold the egg white into the yolk mixture.

Heat the oil in a skillet. When the oil is sizzling hot, dip the pieces of fish in the egg mixture, then fry until golden brown on one side and turn to brown on the other side. Drain the fillets and serve them hot.

BETTY WASON
BRIDE IN THE KITCHEN

Ham and Haddie

(Options: smoked cod, smoked pollock)

This dish is a favorite in Scotland. To convince her readers elsewhere that it is as good as it sounds, the author quotes a visitor to Scotland who described it as "altogether delectable" and declared that the combination of fried smoked ham and haddock was as perfect as the wedding of bacon and egg. She adds, however, for the benefit of those who prefer not to fry foods, that the dish can be successfully made by cooking the ham and haddock together, with a little water, in a cooking vessel with a tightly fitting lid.

To serve 4

1¼ lb.	lightly smoked finnan haddock, skinned by passing it briefly over a flame until the skin buckles, and cut into neat pieces	⅔ kg.
4	thin slices ham	4
2 tbsp.	butter (optional)	30 ml.
	pepper	

Fry the ham, which will provide its own fat for the purpose, then remove it and keep it hot while you fry the pieces of fish in the ham fat that is left in the pan. Add the butter if the ham fat is insufficient. Turn the fish once during the frying.

When the fish is done, after 5 to 10 minutes, depending on the thickness of the pieces, season it with pepper. Serve the fish pieces wrapped up in the slices of ham.

F. MARIAN MC NEILL
THE SCOTS KITCHEN

Fried Perch Fillets, Milanese-Style

Filetti di Pesce Persico alla Milanese

(Options: burbot, flounder, sucker)

To serve 6

6	whole perch (about ½ lb. [¼ kg.] each), cleaned and filleted	6
¼ cup	flour	50 ml.
1	egg, beaten	1
1 cup	dry bread crumbs	¼ liter
10 tbsp.	butter	150 ml.
2	lemons, cut into wedges	2

Scallion marinade

4	scallions, including 2 inches [5 cm.] of the green tops, finely chopped	4
⅓ cup	olive oil	75 ml.
3 tbsp.	fresh lemon juice	45 ml.
	salt and freshly ground white pepper	

Mix all the marinade ingredients together in a large shallow dish, and marinate the fish fillets for 1 hour. Drain them and dry with a clean cloth. Dredge the fillets in the flour, dip them in the beaten egg and then in the bread crumbs.

Melt 7 tablespoons [105 ml.] of the butter in a skillet and fry the coated fillets until they are golden. Drain the fillets and transfer them to a warmed platter. Add the remaining butter to the skillet and cook until it foams; pour it over the fish. Garnish with the lemon wedges and serve.

The fillets can be served on a bed of boiled rice, or accompanied by boiled potatoes.

GIANNI BRERA AND LUIGI VERONELLI
LA PACCIADA

Salmon Scallops with Sorrel Sauce

Escalopes de Saumon à l'Oseille Troisgros

(Options: bluefish, dolphin, pompano)

The crème fraîche called for in this recipe may be available at French food markets. If not, make it from the heavy —but not ultra-pasteurized —cream usually sold in health food stores. Add about 1 teaspoon [5 ml.] of buttermilk to 1 cup [¼ liter] of cream. Cover the mixture, and let it rest in a warm place for 12 to 24 hours, or until it thickens. Refrigerate until ready to use.

	To serve 4	
2 lb.	middle cut of salmon, boned, skin removed and trimmed	1 kg.
1 quart	fish fumet *(recipe, page 164)*	1 liter
⅓ cup	dry white wine, preferably Sancerre	75 ml.
3 tbsp.	dry vermouth	45 ml.
2	shallots, finely chopped	2
1⅔ cups	crème *fraîche*	400 ml.
4 oz.	sorrel leaves (1 cup [¼ liter]), ribs removed, washed and large leaves torn into 2 or 3 pieces	125 g.
3 tbsp.	butter	45 ml.
1 tbsp.	fresh lemon juice	15 ml.
	coarse salt	
	freshly ground pepper, preferably white	
1 to 2 tbsp.	peanut oil	15 to 30 ml.
	fine sea salt	

With the aid of tweezers, pick out any small bones embedded in the salmon. You will find them by running your fingers against the grain of the fish. Divide each fillet in two horizontally, making four pieces of about 6 ounces [200 g.] each. Slip the pieces between two sheets of lightly oiled wax paper and, with a wooden mallet or the flat of a meat cleaver, flatten them slightly to scallops of equal thicknesses.

Put the fish fumet, wine, vermouth and shallots together in a large, heavy saucepan or casserole and, over high heat, boil down the liquid until it is bright and syrupy and reduced nearly to a glaze. Add the *crème fraîche* and boil until the sauce becomes slightly thickened.

Drop the sorrel into the sauce and cook together for just 25 seconds, then remove the pan from the heat. Swirling the casserole, or stirring with a wooden spoon (do not use a whisk, as it will catch on sorrel leaves), incorporate the butter, cut into tiny pieces. Complete the seasoning with a few drops of lemon juice and salt and pepper.

Warm a large skillet, adding just barely enough oil to coat the bottom. If you use a nonstick pan, no oil is needed. Season the salmon scallops with salt and pepper on their less presentable sides, then place them in the skillet, seasoned side up. Cook for 25 seconds, then turn carefully to the second side and cook for 15 seconds longer. The salmon must be undercooked to preserve its tenderness.

Distribute the hot sorrel sauce in the centers of four large, warmed plates and, after having first sponged off any excess oil with a paper towel, place the salmon scallops, seasoned side down, on the sauce. Sprinkle lightly with coarse salt. This dish suffers if it must wait and should be prepared at the last moment.

JEAN & PIERRE TROISGROS
THE NOUVELLE CUISINE OF JEAN & PIERRE TROISGROS

Sautéed Shad Roe

(No options)

	To serve 4	
2	pairs shad roe	2
	salt	
	freshly ground black pepper	
½ cup	flour	125 ml.
8 tbsp.	butter, cut into small pieces	120 ml.
1 tsp.	Worcestershire sauce	5 ml.
2 tsp.	fresh lemon juice	10 ml.
2 tbsp.	finely cut fresh chives	30 ml.
1 tbsp.	finely chopped fresh parsley	15 ml.
	cooked crisp bacon slices (optional)	

With scissors or a small, sharp knife, slit the membranes connecting the pairs of roes. Sprinkle the roes with salt and a few grindings of black pepper, then flour both sides and shake off the excess.

Over medium heat, melt 6 tablespoons [90 ml.] of the butter in a heavy 8-inch [20-cm.] skillet. When the foam subsides, add the roes and cook them for about 6 minutes on each side, regulating the heat so that the roes brown evenly and quickly without burning. Carefully transfer them to a warmed platter and quickly make the sauce.

Stir the Worcestershire sauce, lemon juice, chives and parsley into the butter remaining in the skillet. Add the remaining 2 tablespoons [30 ml.] of butter and heat until the butter melts. Pour over the roes and serve at once, accompanied by slices of crisp bacon if you like.

FOODS OF THE WORLD/AMERICAN COOKING

Deep-fried Smelts

Friture d'éperlans

(Options: grunion, herring, small mackerel, silversides)

	To serve 4	
1½ lb.	whole smelts, cleaned	¾ kg.
2 cups	flour	½ liter
	salt and pepper	
	oil for deep frying	
2	lemons cut in half	2

Rinse the smelts and roll them in a towel to dry. Spread them on a large plate or piece of wax paper and sprinkle liberally with salt and pepper. Pour on about ¾ cup [75 ml.] of flour and, using both hands, toss the fish with the flour to coat them thoroughly. Let stand for at least 15 minutes. Meanwhile, in a deep fryer or pan at least 5 inches [13 cm.] deep, heat 3 inches [8 cm.] of oil to 375° F. [190° C.].

Just before frying, pour more flour on the smelts. This second coating with flour is most important. The previously applied flour will have become damp and sticky. The second coating will adhere to the first and present a completely dry surface for frying.

Take a handful of smelts, shake off the excess flour, and plunge the smelts into the hot oil, scattering them through the pan with a long fork or skimmer. Do not overcrowd; overcrowding will greatly reduce the heat of the oil so the smelts clump together and the coating does not crisp. The smelts will turn a dark golden color in just a few minutes. Remove the smelts with a skimmer and place them in a baking dish lined with paper towels; keep warm in a slow oven while continuing to fry the remaining fish.

Sprinkle the smelts with salt and heap them onto a warmed platter. Serve with lemon halves.

CAROL CUTLER
THE SIX-MINUTE SOUFFLÉ AND OTHER CULINARY DELIGHTS

Pan-fried Brook Trout

(Options: bass, sunfish)

	To serve 4	
4	whole brook trout (¾ to 1 lb. [⅓ to ½ kg.] each), cleaned but with heads and tails left on	4
8	slices bacon	8
	salt	
	freshly ground black pepper	
2 cups	white or yellow cornmeal	½ liter

In a large, heavy skillet, cook the bacon over medium heat until it renders all its fat and is brown and crisp. Transfer the bacon to paper towels to drain, leaving the fat in the pan.

Dry the trout thoroughly with paper towels. Sprinkle them inside and out with salt and a few grindings of black pepper, then dip them in the cornmeal, shaking them gently to remove the excess. Heat the bacon fat in the skillet, add the fish and cook them for about 5 minutes on each side, turning them over carefully with tongs. Regulate the heat so that the trout will brown evenly without burning. Remove them to paper towels to drain. Place the trout on a heated platter, arrange the bacon around the fish and serve at once.

FOODS OF THE WORLD/AMERICAN COOKING

Trout Amandine

(Options: pike, pompano, snook, sole)

	To serve 3 or 4	
2 lb.	trout fillets	1 kg.
1	egg, lightly beaten	1
1 cup	milk	¼ liter
8 tbsp.	flour	120 ml.
8 tbsp.	butter	120 ml.
⅓ cup	slivered almonds	75 ml.
¼ cup	fresh lemon juice	50 ml.
2 tbsp.	Worcestershire sauce	30 ml.
1 tbsp.	chopped fresh parsley	15 ml.

Salt and pepper the trout. Dip in batter made by mixing the egg and milk. Drain and dredge in the flour. In a 9-inch [23-cm.] skillet, melt the butter and sauté the trout for 5 to 8 minutes, or until golden brown. Remove the trout to a warmed platter. Add the almonds to the skillet and brown lightly. Add the lemon juice, Worcestershire sauce and parsley, heat through and pour over the fish.

HERMANN B. DEUTSCH AND DEIRDRE STANFORTH
BRENNAN'S NEW ORLEANS COOKBOOK

Trout à la Meunière

(Options: bass, sole, sunfish)

	To serve 6	
6	small whole trout (about ¾ lb. [⅓ kg.] each)	6
6 tbsp.	butter	90 ml.
6 tbsp.	cream	90 ml.
1 tbsp.	fresh lemon juice	15 ml.
1 tsp.	grated lemon peel	5 ml.
3 tbsp.	chopped parsley	45 ml.

Clean the trout and pat dry with paper towels. Melt the butter in a heavy sauté pan and brown the trout carefully over fairly high heat. Reduce the heat and cook for 5 to 8 minutes longer, or until the fish flakes when tested with a fork. Remove to a heated platter and keep warm.

Add the cream, lemon juice and lemon peel to the juices remaining in the pan. Blend well and cook only until thoroughly heated. Do not allow to boil.

Pour over the trout, sprinkle with the parsley and serve.

CEIL DYER
THE NEWPORT COOKBOOK

Deviled Whitebait

(Options: anchovy, grunion, herring, silversides, smelt)

To serve 6 to 8

2 lb.	whitebait	1 kg.
½ cup	flour, seasoned with salt and pepper	125 ml.
	oil or fat for deep frying	
1 tsp.	cayenne pepper	5 ml.

Wash and carefully dry the whitebait; coat them with the seasoned flour. Deep fry in 375° F. [190° C.] oil or fat until crisp. Drain on paper towels, and sprinkle with cayenne pepper before serving.

LIZZIE BOYD (EDITOR)
BRITISH COOKERY

Whiting with Orange Sauce

(Options: angler, cod, flounder, sole, turbot)

This recipe was inspired by a similar one for scallops, published in 1747 in Hannah Glasse's Art of Cookery.

To serve 6

¾ lb.	whiting fillets	⅓ kg.
3	Seville oranges, or 2 sweet oranges and 1 lemon	3
¼ cup	heavy cream	50 ml.
3	large egg yolks	3
½ cup	dry white wine	125 ml.
	salt and black pepper	
	cayenne pepper	
8 tbsp.	butter	120 ml.
	flour seasoned with salt and pepper	
	chopped fresh parsley	

Sprinkle the fish with the juice of half a Seville orange (or half of the lemon) and leave in a cool place while the sauce is being made. Beat together in a large heatproof bowl the

cream, egg yolks, wine and the juice of 1½ Seville oranges; cut the last Seville orange down into wedges for the garnish. With sweet oranges, beat in the juice of 1 orange and of the second lemon half, and cut the second orange into wedges.

Set the bowl over a pan of simmering water, or transfer the sauce to a heavy pan set directly over the heat if you are used to cooking egg-thickened sauces. Stir until the sauce reaches the consistency of heavy cream or is a little thicker. Season with salt, and both black and cayenne pepper. Beat in 4 tablespoons [60 ml.] of the butter. Reduce the heat so that the sauce keeps warm without cooking more.

Dip the whiting fillets in the flour, and fry to golden brown in the remaining butter. Arrange the whiting on a platter with the orange wedges tucked in between them, and a little parsley scattered on top. Serve the sauce separately in a warmed sauceboat.

The whiting are good with boiled parsnip rings tossed in butter, and natural brown rice.

JANE GRIGSON
FISH COOKERY

Deep-fried Whiting

Merlan Frit

(Options: burbot, cod, hake)

For instructions on boning a whole fish, see pages 24 and 25. Ideally, the fish should be boned through the back, but if they are already cleaned when you buy them, you can bone them through the existing slit in the belly.

To serve 4

4	whole whiting (about ½ lb. [¼ kg.] each), cleaned, boned and opened out	4
	salt and pepper	
½ cup	milk	125 ml.
½ cup	flour	125 ml.
	oil for deep frying	
1	bunch parsley, stems removed	1
	lemon wedges	

Season the fish with salt and pepper, dip them in the milk, then roll them in the flour until well coated.

Heat the oil until moderately hot, 365° F. [185° C.], and fry the fish for 4 minutes. Turn up the heat and complete the cooking with 3 minutes at 375-385° F. [190-195° C.]. This graduated cooking will produce crisp, golden fish.

Drain the fish and salt them lightly. As soon as the fish are removed from the hot oil, plunge in the parsley and remove it with a slotted spoon as soon as the explosion of spluttering has ceased. Serve the fish garnished with deep-fried parsley and with the lemon wedges.

JULES GOUFFÉ
LE LIVRE DE CUISINE

Fried Fish with Peanut Sauce

(Options: bluegill, crappie, trout, whiting)

The best curry powders to use for a spicy effect are those made in, or in the style of, Madras, India.

To serve 4

4	small whole fish, cleaned	4
	salt	
½ cup	oil	125 ml.
2	onions, chopped	2
1 tsp.	curry powder	5 ml.
2	tomatoes, peeled, seeded and chopped	2
½ cup	unsalted dry-roasted peanuts, pulverized in a mortar	125 ml.
1½ cups	water	375 ml.

Sprinkle the fish with salt. Heat the oil and fry the fish slowly until light brown on both sides. Remove the fish and discard all but 2 tablespoons [30 ml.] of the oil from the skillet. Add the onions and curry powder to the skillet and fry until brown. Then add the tomatoes and fry lightly for 3 to 4 minutes. Mix the peanuts with the water and add them to the onions and tomatoes. Cook slowly for about 5 minutes. Place the fried fish in the sauce and heat through slowly. Season with salt and serve.

JANNY VAN DER MEER AND BEATRICE R. MANSUR
TANZANIAN FOOD WITH TRADITIONAL AND NEW RECIPES

Kegeree

This Victorian breakfast dish—often spelled kedgeree—originated in British India. Any cold, cooked fish can be used, but smoked haddock is a traditional favorite in Britain.

To serve 1 or 2

¼ lb.	cold cooked fish, bones and skin removed	125 g.
2 tbsp.	butter	30 ml.
½ cup	boiled rice	125 ml.
1 tsp.	prepared mustard	5 ml.
2	eggs, soft-boiled	2
	salt	
	cayenne pepper	

Melt the butter in a heavy saucepan. Add all the other ingredients and heat carefully over low heat. Adjust the seasoning and serve very hot.

MRS. ISABELLA BEETON
THE BOOK OF HOUSEHOLD MANAGEMENT

Pan-fried Fish

(Options: bluegill, catfish, crappie)

To serve 6 to 8

2 lb.	fish fillets, steaks or small whole, cleaned fish	1 kg.
½ cup	milk, mixed with 1 tsp. [5 ml.] salt	125 ml.
½ cup	flour	125 ml.
¾ cup	fine, dry bread crumbs	175 ml.
	oil for deep frying	

Dip the fish in the salted milk and then in the flour. For a crispy coating, dip the fish in the milk again and then in the bread crumbs. Fry the fish in hot oil until they are golden brown on each side; drain and serve immediately. The complete cooking time will be about 10 minutes per inch [2½ cm.] of thickness.

GOVERNMENT OF CANADA, FISHERIES & OCEANS,
FISHERIES FOOD CENTER
THE WAY TO COOK FISH

Mixed Fried Fish Cake

La Sartagnado à la Toulonnaise

(Options: anchovies, grunion, herring, silversides, whitebait)

This dish is made from very small fish, no more than 2 inches [5 cm.] long. The fish are left intact and washed well, but they are not cleaned.

The French name of this recipe derives from la sartan, Provençal for the pan in which the dish is traditionally fried.

To serve 2

½ lb.	mixed small, whole fish, washed and dried	¼ kg.
¼ cup	flour	50 ml.
	salt and pepper	
4 to 5 tbsp.	olive oil	60 to 75 ml.
2 tbsp.	vinegar	30 ml.

Toss the fish in the flour until they are evenly coated and cling together in a mass. Season with salt and pepper. Heat the oil in a skillet until very hot, then add the fish. Reduce the heat to medium and fry the fish, without stirring, for about 6 to 7 minutes, or until the undersides turn golden brown. The fish will resemble a flat cake or omelet. Turn the fish and fry the other side. Slide the fish onto a warmed platter. Add the vinegar to the skillet, stir and pour the pan juices over the fish.

JOSÉPHINE BESSON
LA MÈRE BESSON "MA CUISINE PROVENÇALE"

Jellied Egyptian Fish with Lemon

(Options: bass, cod, halibut)

The best curry powders to use for a spicy effect are those made in, or in the style of, Madras, India.

	To serve 6 to 8	
2½ lb.	fish steaks	1¼ kg.
5 tbsp.	olive oil	75 ml.
2	garlic cloves, chopped	2
1 quart	water	1 liter
¾ cup	fresh lemon juice	175 ml.
2 tsp.	salt	10 ml.
	pepper	
1 tsp.	curry powder (optional)	5 ml.
5 tbsp.	chopped fresh parsley	75 ml.

Heat the oil in a large pan and fry the garlic in it. Add the water, lemon juice, seasonings and parsley. Add the steaks. Simmer slowly for 30 minutes. Transfer the fish and the liquid to a deep serving dish. Serve the fish cold in its jelly.

MOLLY LYONS BAR-DAVID
THE ISRAELI COOK BOOK

❖

Sweet-Sour Fish

(Options: burbot, rockfish, pike)

The technique of scoring a whole fish is shown on page 61.

	To serve 8	
1	whole fish (3 to 4 lb. [1½ to 2 kg.]), cleaned	1
1 tbsp.	flour	15 ml.
	oil or lard for frying	
1	scallion, including the green top, cut into 1-inch [2½-cm.] sections	1
4 or 5	slices fresh ginger root	4 or 5
½ cup	sugar	125 ml.
½ cup	vinegar	125 ml.
3 tbsp.	dry sherry	45 ml.
¼ cup	cornstarch, dissolved in 2 cups [½ liter] water	50 ml.
1 tsp.	salt	5 ml.
¼ cup	soy sauce	50 ml.

Clean the fish and make some slashes on each side. Rub the outside of the fish with flour. In a large skillet, heat about 1 inch [2½ cm.] of oil, until very hot. Fry the fish for 2 minutes on each side over high heat. Reduce the heat to medium and fry the fish for 4 minutes longer on each side. Then turn up the heat again and fry for 1 more minute on each side. The outside of the fish will be very crisp while the inside will be soft. Take the fish out of the pan, drain, put it on a warmed platter and keep it hot.

Pour off all but about 1 tablespoon [15 ml.] of oil from the skillet. Put in the scallion and ginger first. Lightly cook them, stirring all the time. Then stir in the remaining ingredients one at a time. When the sauce becomes translucent, pour it over the fried fish and serve. If you like, you can add some shreds of green pepper or sweet pickle to the sauce with the seasonings.

BUWEI YANG CHAO
HOW TO COOK AND EAT IN CHINESE

❖

Stir-fried Fish and Bean Sprouts

(Options: corvina, dolphin, flounder, sole)

To blanch the bean sprouts for this recipe, place them in a bowl, pour boiling water over them, drain them immediately and pour in cold water to cool the bean sprouts and preserve their crispness. Drain the bean sprouts and dry them with paper towels before using.

	To serve 4 to 6	
2 lb.	fish fillets, skinned	1 kg.
½ tsp.	salt	2 ml.
1 or 2	slices fresh ginger root, peeled and finely chopped	1 or 2
1 lb.	bean sprouts, blanched	½ kg.
4	scallions, cut into 1-inch [2½-cm.] pieces	4
1 tbsp.	soy sauce	15 ml.
¼ cup	fish fumet *(recipe, page 164)*	50 ml.
1 tbsp.	cornstarch	15 ml.
3 tbsp.	water	45 ml.

Cut the fish fillets against the grain into ¼-inch [6-mm.] slices. In a wok or heavy skillet, heat 3 tablespoons [45 ml.] of the oil. Add the salt, then the ginger root, and stir fry for a few seconds. When the oil is nearly smoking, add the fish and stir fry gently until half done (about 1 minute on each side). Remove the fish.

Heat the remaining oil. Add the bean sprouts and stir fry for 1 minute. Add the scallions and soy sauce; stir the mixture a few times. Add the fumet and bring to a boil. Return the fish and cook, covered, over medium heat until done (approximately 2 minutes).

Meanwhile, blend the cornstarch and cold water into a paste; then stir it into the sauce to thicken it. Serve at once.

GLORIA BLEY MILLER
THE THOUSAND RECIPE CHINESE COOKBOOK

Oven-fried Fish

(Options: bass, bluegill, crappie, sea robin, scup)

	To serve 4	
2 lb.	fish fillets or small whole fish, cleaned	1 kg.
1 cup	fine dry bread crumbs or cornflake crumbs	¼ liter
½ cup	milk	125 ml.
	salt	
3 tbsp.	butter	45 ml.

Heat the oven to 500° F. [260° C.]. Generously butter an oblong baking dish large enough to hold your fish in a single uncrowded layer. On a large sheet of wax paper or foil, spread a mound of bread crumbs or cornflake crumbs. Pour the milk into a shallow dish large enough to dip the fish. Season the milk with salt. Dip each fish in milk, then in crumbs to coat them evenly. Place them flat in the buttered dish, the fish barely touching each other. Pour the melted butter over the fish. Bake until crisp, golden brown and tender when pierced gently with a fork—about 7 minutes.

RUTH CONRAD BATEMAN
I LOVE TO COOK BOOK

Fried Fish in Batter

(Options: cod, perch, snapper)

	To serve 6	
2 lb.	fish fillets	1 kg.
½ tsp.	salt	2 ml.
	Batter	
1½ cups	flour	375 ml.
1 tbsp.	baking powder	15 ml.
1 tsp.	salt	5 ml.
2	eggs	2
1 cup	milk	¼ liter
	fat for deep frying	

Season the fish fillets and cut them into serving-sized pieces or smaller pieces, if desired. If the pieces of fish are more than ½ inch [1 cm.] thick, make three or four slits in the sides of each. The fish will cook more evenly and quickly. To make the batter, mix and sift the dry ingredients. Beat the eggs well and stir the milk into the eggs. Pour the liquid into the dry ingredients and beat until smooth. Dip the pieces of fish into the batter and fry in deep fat at 375° F. [190° C.] until golden brown, turning once. This will take about 7 minutes. Drain and serve.

GOVERNMENT OF CANADA, FISHERIES & OCEANS
THE CANADIAN FISH COOKBOOK

Fish Sauté Meunière

Poisson Meunière

(Options: dolphin, flounder, sole, whiting)

	To serve 4	
4	fish fillets, steaks or whole small fish, cleaned	4
½ cup	milk	125 ml.
¼ cup	flour, seasoned with salt and pepper	50 ml.
	salad oil	
	pepper	
1 tbsp.	fresh lemon juice	15 ml.
2 tbsp.	chopped fresh parsley	30 ml.
4	lemon slices, peeled	4
4 tbsp.	butter	60 ml.

Dip the fish in the milk, then in the seasoned flour. Put about ¼ inch [6 mm.] of oil in a skillet and heat until very hot. Add the fish and cook until golden brown on both sides. Remove to a warmed serving dish, sprinkle with a little pepper, a few drops of lemon juice and a little chopped parsley. Place the slices of lemon on top. Cook the butter until it is hazelnut brown in color and pour it over the fish.

LOUIS DIAT
FRENCH COOKING FOR AMERICANS

Fish with Bacon, Hamburg-Style

Scholle "Hamburger Art"

(Options: flounder, halibut, pompano, sole, turbot)

The original version of this recipe calls for plaice, a popular European flounder.

	To serve 4	
2	whole fish (about 1¼ lb. [⅔ kg.] each), cleaned	2
2 tbsp.	fresh lemon juice	30 ml.
5	slices bacon, diced	5
	salt	
	flour	
½	lemon, cut into wedges	½
6 to 8	sprigs parsley	6 to 8

Sprinkle the lemon juice over the fish and leave them for 10 minutes. Meanwhile, fry the diced bacon in a large skillet. When the bacon is crisp, remove it and keep it warm, leaving the fat in the pan.

Sprinkle salt over the fish, and coat them with flour. Fry them in the bacon fat in the pan, allowing 3 or 4 minutes on each side, until the fish are golden brown all over. Take great care that the heat is not too high and that the fish, with their light dusting of flour, do not burn.

Arrange the fish on a warmed platter with their more golden sides (the undersides, which were originally white) uppermost. Sprinkle the bacon over them, place the pieces of lemon around them and garnish the dish with the parsley.

HEINZ KATZ
MARITIME LECKEREIEN
DAS FISCHKOCHBUCH VON DER WATERKANT

Fish Balls
Balik Koftesi

(Options: bluefish, cod, drum)

To serve 4

1	whole fish (¾ lb. [⅓ kg.]), cleaned	1
1	small onion, quartered	1
2	sprigs parsley	2
1	small carrot	1
2	slices lemon	2
1	bay leaf	1
5	peppercorns	5
	salt	
1	slice white bread with the crust removed, soaked in water and squeezed dry	1
2	eggs	2
2	scallions, including the green tops, chopped	2
2 tbsp.	finely cut fresh dill	30 ml.
2 tbsp.	chopped fresh parsley	30 ml.
1 tbsp.	dried currants, soaked in warm water for 15 minutes	15 ml.
2 tbsp.	shelled pine nuts	30 ml.
½ tsp.	ground allspice	2 ml.
	pepper	
½ cup	flour	125 ml.
1 cup	salad oil or shortening	¼ liter

Put 1½ cups [375 ml.] of water into a saucepan with the onion, parsley sprigs, carrot, lemon slices, bay leaf, peppercorns and salt. Bring to a boil. Add the fish, cover, and simmer for 10 to 15 minutes or until the fish is tender. Remove the fish from the pan and cool. Then remove all the skin and bones from the fish.

Place the fish in a bowl. Add the bread, eggs, scallions, dill, parsley, black currants, pine nuts, allspice, and salt and pepper to taste. Mash with a fork, working the mixture into a fairly smooth paste. Form the paste into croquettes about 2½ inches [6 cm.] long and 1 inch [2½ cm.] in diameter, and roll them in the flour.

Heat the oil in a heavy sauté pan and fry the croquettes until golden brown on all sides, shaking the pan frequently to prevent burning.

Serve hot or cold with a lettuce salad.

NESET EREN
THE ART OF TURKISH COOKING

Spanish Fish Balls
Albóndigas de Pescado

(Options: any firm, white-fleshed fish)

To serve 4 to 6

1 lb.	cooked fish, bones removed	500 g.
2	small onions, very finely chopped	2
¾ cup	fresh bread crumbs	175 ml.
2	eggs, lightly beaten	2
2 tbsp.	olive oil	30 ml.
3 tbsp.	chopped fresh parsley	45 ml.
1 to 2 tsp.	oregano	5 to 10 ml.
	salt and pepper	
1 cup	flour	¼ liter
4 to 5 tbsp.	lemon juice	60 to 75 ml.
	olive oil for frying	
1½ cups	fish fumet *(recipe, page 164)*	375 ml.
¼ cup	blanched almonds, toasted in a moderate oven for 10 minutes and pulverized in a mortar	50 ml.

Pound the fish flesh in a mortar. In a bowl, combine the fish, half the finely chopped onion, the bread crumbs, eggs, olive oil, 2 tablespoons [30 ml.] of the parsley and the oregano. Season with salt and pepper. Mix together thoroughly, then form the mixture into balls about the size of small eggs. Roll the fish balls in the flour, dip them in the lemon juice, then roll them again in the flour. In a frying pan, heat olive oil to a depth of about ¼ inch [6 mm.] and fry the fish balls until golden brown all over. Drain the fish balls and place them in a shallow casserole.

Add the fish fumet, salt, the remaining parsley and onion. Simmer, covered, for about 10 minutes. Add the almonds and simmer uncovered for an additional 5 minutes to thicken the sauce. Serve straight from the casserole.

CARMEN BUSTAMANTE
PETITS PROPOS CULINAIRES

Special Presentations

Arctic Char Mousse
Mousse d'Omble
(Options: pike, salmon, sturgeon)

A recipe from Alain Chapel, chef-proprietor of the restaurant La Mère Charles at Moinnay, near Lyon.

	To serve 2	
7 oz.	char fillets	200 g.
¾ cup	milk	175 ml.
2	eggs	2
1	egg yolk	1
	salt and pepper	
	Truffle sauce	
1	fresh truffle (or substitute preserved truffle, liquor reserved)	1
½ cup	fish fumet (recipe, page 164), reduced to 1 or 2 tbsp. [15 or 30 ml.]	125 ml.
1 tbsp.	butter	15 ml.
	freshly ground pepper	

Pound the char in a mortar, then press it through a very fine sieve. Add the milk, eggs and extra egg yolk, and season with salt and pepper. Mix together thoroughly; the batter will be quite liquid.

Pour the mixture into a buttered 1-quart [1-liter] mold, filling it to just below the brim. Set the mold on a trivet or rack in an ovenproof pan partly filled with hot water. Cover and bake in a preheated 325° F. [160° C.] oven for about 30 minutes, or until the center of the mousse is dry to the touch.

Meanwhile, prepare the sauce. If you are using a fresh truffle, skin the truffle and simmer the peelings in a saucepan with ½ cup [125 ml.] of water for 10 minutes. Strain the cooking liquid and return it to the pan. If you are using a preserved truffle, do not peel it, but bring the reserved liquor to a simmer in a small saucepan. Stir in the fumet and reduce until the liquid has a syrupy consistency. Melt the butter in a small pan. Slice the truffle fairly thickly, add the slices to the butter and sweat them over low heat for a few minutes until they are heated through. Toss the truffle slices and the butter into the reduced sauce.

Unmold the char mousse and coat it with the sauce. A sprinkling of freshly ground pepper gives the final touch to this delicate, easily prepared dish.

LES PRINCES DE LA GASTRONOMIE

Bass in Pastry
Bar en Croûte Brillat-Savarin
(Options: rockfish, salmon, trout)

The technique of skinning a fish is shown on page 20; wrapping fish in pastry is demonstrated on pages 82-83.

	To serve 6	
1	whole striped bass (6 to 8 lb. [3 to 4 kg.]), cleaned	1
1	small bunch fresh tarragon	1
½ tsp.	dried thyme	2 ml.
2	bay leaves, crushed	2
	salt and pepper	
	rough puff pastry (recipe, page 167, but double the quantities called for)	
1	egg, lightly beaten	1

Begin the skinning operation with a cut around the tail of the bass, just penetrating the skin; then make a similar incision along the full length of the back, or dorsal, surface. Lift the skin free with a knife point, then gently pull it downward from the back, rolling the flap off without breaking it. Bone the bass by cutting through the full length of the ventral, or under, side of the bass, but do not split the fish. The bass must remain whole. Sprinkle the herbs inside the fish. Season with salt and pepper inside and out.

Make two layers of pastry, each ⅛ inch thick, and place the fish in between the layers. Cut off the excess, making the remaining pastry follow the shape of the fish. Using a knife, decorate the pastry to create "scales." Brush the pastry all over with the beaten egg. Bake in a preheated 350° F. [180° C.] oven for 40 to 45 minutes.

A. J. MC CLANE
THE ENCYCLOPEDIA OF FISH COOKERY

Turban of Sole Fillets
Filets de Sole en Torsade
(Options: flounder, fluke, halibut, salmon, turbot)

Two kinds of fish fillets can be used in this dish, arranged in an alternating pattern (pages 80-81). The mousseline can be flavored according to taste (pages 78-79).

	To serve 6 to 8	
10	sole fillets	10
	salt and pepper	
3 cups	mousseline (recipe, page 166)	¾ liter
2 tbsp.	butter, melted	30 ml.
	velouté sauce (recipe, page 164)	

Butter a 2-quart [2-liter] savarin or ring mold. Season the fillets and use them to line the mold by arranging them crosswise, slightly overlapping, with the ends hanging over the sides of the mold. Pack the mousseline into the mold, and tap the mold to settle the contents. Fold the fillet ends over the mousseline and press them down to fix them in place.

Put the mold in a larger pan, and pour hot water into the pan to come halfway up the sides of the mold. Poach in a preheated 325° F. [170° C.] oven for 35 to 40 minutes, or until the surface of the turban is springy to the touch.

Take the turban out of the oven, allow it to rest for a few minutes, then turn it out onto a warmed round platter. Brush with the melted butter, and serve with velouté sauce.

PROSPER MONTAGNÉ
THE NEW LAROUSSE GASTRONOMIQUE

————◆◆————

Pompano Baked in Paper, Louisiana-Style

Pompano en Papillotes "La Louisiane"

(Options: flounder, snook, sole)

The technique of wrapping fish in paper appears on page 86.

To serve 2

2	whole pompano (about 1½ lb. [¾ kg.] each), cleaned, filleted and skinned	2
	court bouillon made with dry white wine (recipe, page 163)	
2 tbsp.	butter	30 ml.
1 tbsp.	finely chopped onions	15 ml.
1 tbsp.	finely chopped fresh mushrooms	15 ml.
1 tbsp.	finely chopped green pepper	15 ml.
1 tbsp.	finely chopped truffle	15 ml.
½ tsp.	finely chopped shallot	2 ml.
½ tsp.	finely chopped fresh chervil or parsley	2 ml.
½ tsp.	finely cut chives	2 ml.
½ tsp.	finely chopped celery leaves	2 ml.
½ tsp.	finely chopped fresh tarragon	2 ml.
1	garlic clove, finely chopped	1
	salt and pepper	
	fresh thyme	
	ground mace	
	grated nutmeg	
2 tbsp.	dry sherry	30 ml.

Poach the pompano in enough court bouillon to cover for 12 minutes. Drain, reserving the stock. Keep the pompano fillets hot. Prepare the stuffing as follows: heat the butter in a skillet, and stir in the onion, mushroom, green pepper, truffle, shallot, parsley or chervil, chives, celery leaves, tarragon and garlic. Season the mixture with the salt and pepper, thyme, mace and nutmeg and cook for about 5 minutes over

gentle heat, stirring almost constantly. Remove from the stove and stir in the sherry and enough of the strained fish stock to make the stuffing of a spreading consistency, rather on the moist side.

Place half of the stuffing over a pompano fillet; place the fillet on buttered wax paper or parchment paper. Adjust another fillet sandwich-style over the stuffing, bring the two edges of paper together and seal by folding the ends tight, allowing plenty of room around the fish fillets. Repeat with the two remaining fillets.

Lay the packages in a buttered shallow baking pan and place in a preheated 425 to 450° F. [220 to 230° C.] oven for 5 minutes. Serve at once, removing the paper at the table.

LOUIS P. DE GOUY
THE GOLD COOK BOOK

————◆◆————

Tamar Salmon in Pastry

(Options: bass, rockfish, trout)

To serve 6

2 lb.	salmon fillet	1 kg.
2 tbsp.	olive oil	30 ml.
	salt and freshly ground pepper	
1 to 2 tbsp.	fresh lemon juice	15 to 30 ml.
	rough puff pastry (recipe, page 167, but double the quantities called for)	
2	medium-sized onions or shallots, finely chopped	2
1 tsp.	chopped tarragon	5 ml.
1½ cups	fresh button mushrooms, thinly sliced	375 ml.
1	egg, beaten	1
6 tbsp.	butter, melted	90 ml.

Heat 1 tablespoon [15 ml.] of the olive oil in a large skillet. Season the salmon with salt, pepper and lemon juice. Place it in the hot oil and cook lightly on both sides without coloring. Take out the salmon and allow it to cool.

Roll out the pastry into an oblong, allowing enough width to fold over the salmon and seal the edges together, and enough length for sealing the ends. Heat the remaining oil in a saucepan and sweat the onions or shallots in it with half of the tarragon. Allow to cool.

Spread the onions or shallots on the center of the pastry, to the width and length of the salmon fillet. Place the mushrooms on top and season with salt and pepper. Then place the salmon on top of this filling. Brush beaten egg on the edges of the pastry and fold them up over the salmon; seal well. Grease a baking sheet, place the pastry-wrapped salmon on it, folded side down, and brush more beaten egg over the top. Bake for 1 hour in a preheated 375° F. [190° C.] oven. Serve with the melted butter mixed with the remaining tarragon.

CAROL WRIGHT
THE WEST COUNTRY

Rolled Stuffed Sole Fillets, Paillard-Style

Paupiettes de Soles Paillard

(Options: flounder, fluke, snapper, turbot)

This recipe is the creation of A. Deland, formerly head chef at the Restaurant Paillard. At the restaurant, the *paupiettes* were served on artichoke bottoms.

	To serve 4	
8	sole fillets	8
1½ cups	mousseline (recipe, page 166)	375 ml.
	salt and pepper	
1	onion, thinly sliced	1
1 cup	thinly sliced fresh mushrooms	¼ liter
1	bouquet garni	1
1 cup	fish fumet (recipe, page 164) or dry white wine	¼ liter
2	egg yolks	2
1 cup	heavy cream	¼ liter
Mushroom purée		
1 lb.	mushrooms, trimmed	½ kg.
1 cup	béchamel sauce (recipe, page 165)	¼ liter
	cream	
4 tbsp.	butter	60 ml.

To make the mushroom purée, rub the mushrooms through a sieve as rapidly as possible. Add the purée to béchamel sauce that has been thickened with a few tablespoons of cream. Boil this mixture down for a few moments and strain it through a fine sieve. Heat the purée once more, remove from the heat and blend in the butter.

Incorporate half of the mushroom purée into the mousseline. Season the fillets, spread them thinly with the mousseline and roll them up. Line a baking pan with the finely chopped onion and mushrooms, put in the bouquet garni and pack in the rolled fillets. If the pan is completely filled, the contact will keep the fillets from unrolling. Pour on the fumet or wine, cover the pan and cook in a preheated 350° F. [180° C.] oven for 12 minutes. Drain the *paupiettes,* arrange them in a deep, buttered dish, cover and keep them warm.

Strain the cooking liquor into a saucepan, and add the remaining mushroom purée. Mix the egg yolks with the cream, and add to the liquor. Bring just to a boil, whisking all the time. Adjust the seasoning. Coat the *paupiettes* with this sauce and serve immediately.

PROSPER MONTAGNÉ
THE NEW LAROUSSE GASTRONOMIQUE

Whole Boned Trout in Pastry

Truite Farci en Croûte

(Options: bass, perch, scup)

The technique of boning round fish is shown on pages 24-25.

	To serve 4	
4	small whole rainbow trout (about ¾ lb. [⅓ kg.] each), cleaned and boned	4
	salt	
	freshly cracked white pepper	
	fresh lemon juice	
1 cup	finely ground raw salmon	¼ liter
2	egg whites	2
1 cup	light cream	¼ liter
2 tsp.	salt	10 ml.
	cayenne pepper	
	melted butter	
⅓ cup	fish fumet (recipe, page 164)	75 ml.
4	dried currants	4
1	egg, beaten	1
	hollandaise sauce (recipe, page 165)	
Pastry		
2 cups	flour	½ liter
½ tsp.	salt	2 ml.
6 tbsp.	butter	90 ml.
2 tbsp.	olive oil	30 ml.
1	egg yolk	1
⅓ cup	ice water	75 ml.

Preheat the oven to 350° F. [180° C.]. Open the trout up from the back and sprinkle them with salt, pepper and a little lemon juice. Fold them over, leave for about 10 minutes, then rinse them in very cold water. Dry the trout well on paper towels, then sprinkle them again with a little salt, pepper and lemon juice and allow them to marinate.

Put the ground salmon in a small metal bowl over a bowl of crushed ice. With a wire whisk stir in the egg whites. Add

the light cream, drop by drop, beating all the time. Then add the salt and the cayenne pepper. Stuff this salmon mousse into the trout.

Arrange the stuffed trout on a buttered baking dish and brush them all over with melted butter. Pour the fish stock over them, cover with buttered wax paper and cook for 10 minutes in the oven. Remove the trout from the oven, drain, and chill them.

To make the pastry, set the oven at 375° F. [190° C.]. Put the flour and salt in a bowl. Add the butter and rub it into the flour until it resembles coarse cornmeal. Then add the olive oil, egg yolk and ice water. Work up quickly to a firm dough.

Divide the dough into four pieces, and roll out each piece large enough to encase a trout. Wrap each fish in pastry and secure the edges. Then, with a small knife and pastry pincers, make the markings of a fish on the pastry (fins, tail, head, etc.) and dot with a black currant for the eye.

Place the pastry-enclosed trout on a buttered baking sheet. Brush with beaten egg and bake until golden brown (about 20 minutes). Remove, arrange on a hot napkin on a platter and serve with a separate bowl of hollandaise sauce.

DIONE LUCAS AND MARION GORMAN
THE DIONE LUCAS BOOK OF FRENCH COOKING

Accompaniments

Savory Barbecue Marinade or Basting Sauce

¼ cup	olive oil	50 ml.
¼ tsp.	summer savory	1 ml.
¼ tsp.	fresh tarragon	1 ml.
¼ tsp.	finely chopped fresh parsley	1 ml.
¼ tsp.	dill seed, or branch dill, crushed	1 ml.
¼ tsp.	freshly ground black pepper	1 ml.
1 tsp.	freshly grated lemon peel	5 ml.
2 tbsp.	fresh lemon juice	30 ml.

Heat the oil in a small saucepan. Add the herbs, pepper and lemon peel, and let it brew over a very low heat for a few minutes. (Do not cook.) Stir in the lemon juice. Use hot as a basting sauce, or cold as a marinade for fish steaks.

Vary the seasonings according to preference. Melted butter or a mixture of oils may be used instead of olive oil.

FRANCES MACILQUHAM
FISH COOKERY OF NORTH AMERICA

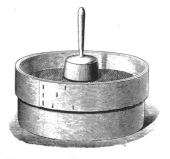

Montpellier Butter
Beurre Montpelier

The original version of this recipe calls for double the amounts given here.

Use this butter to decorate large fish, such as salmon and trout; it can also be used for smaller pieces and slices of fish.

To make about 3 cups [¾ liter]

½ cup	watercress leaves	125 ml.
½ cup	fresh parsley leaves	125 ml.
½ cup	fresh chervil leaves	125 ml.
½ cup	fresh chives	125 ml.
½ cup	fresh tarragon leaves	125 ml.
1	shallot, chopped	1
8 to 10	fresh spinach leaves, stems removed	8 to 10
2 tsp.	capers, washed, drained and squeezed dry	10 ml.
2 tbsp.	chopped sour pickle	30 ml.
1	garlic clove	1
2	anchovy fillets, soaked for 10 minutes, drained and patted dry	2
24 tbsp.	butter (¾ lb. [⅓ kg.])	360 ml.
2	hard-boiled egg yolks	2
1	egg	1
⅔ cup	oil	150 ml.
	table salt	
	cayenne pepper	

Put into a saucepan containing boiling water the watercress, parsley, chervil, chives, tarragon, shallots and spinach. Boil for 2 minutes, then drain, cool, press in a towel to expel the water, and pound in a mortar with the capers, pickle, garlic and anchovy fillets. Mix this paste with the butter, then add the egg yolks and raw egg, and finally pour in, by degrees, the oil. Strain through a very fine sieve, put the butter into a bowl and stir it with a wooden spoon to make it smooth. Season with salt and a little cayenne pepper.

AUGUSTE ESCOFFIER
THE ESCOFFIER COOK BOOK

Herb and Butter Sauce

Sauce Maréchale

This recipe is by Liliane Benoît of the restaurant Le Soubise, at Soubise in the Bordeaux region of France. The sauce is particularly good with sole, turbot and sea bass. Green peppercorns are unripened, and soft like capers. They are obtainable preserved in oil or water, or freeze-dried.

To make about 1 cup [¼ liter] sauce

1½ tbsp.	finely chopped shallots	22 ml.
1 tbsp.	chopped fresh parsley	15 ml.
1 tsp.	chopped fresh thyme	5 ml.
¼	bay leaf, crushed	¼
1	small sprig fennel, or 1 tsp. [5 ml.] fennel seeds	1
2 or 3	large basil leaves, crushed	2 or 3
1 tsp.	green peppercorns, crushed	5 ml.
1 cup	dry white wine	¼ liter
	salt	
20 tbsp.	unsalted butter (10 oz. [300 g.]), softened and cut into small pieces	300 ml.
1	lemon	1

Combine all the ingredients except the butter and lemon in a saucepan. Reduce slowly until almost a paste. Strain, and press on the residue in the sieve to extract all of the juices. You should have about 2 tablespoons [30 ml.] of essence.

Return the essence with three or four bits of butter to the saucepan, and cook over very low heat. Stirring with a whisk, add butter, bit by bit, until it is all incorporated. As you add the butter, also add a few drops of lemon juice. The sauce should be smooth and a bit thicker than heavy cream.

If the sauce must wait, let it go cold rather than trying to keep it in a double boiler. Reheat carefully. It is very fragile.

MADELEINE PETER
FAVORITE RECIPES OF THE GREAT WOMEN CHEFS OF FRANCE

Tartare Sauce

To make about 1 cup [¼ liter] sauce

2	hard-boiled egg yolks	2
	salt and pepper	
1 cup	olive oil	¼ liter
3 tbsp.	wine vinegar	45 ml.
1 tbsp.	very finely cut scallion tops or chives	15 ml.
2 tbsp.	mayonnaise *(recipe, page 166)*	30 ml.

Pound the egg yolks until quite smooth. Season, then beat in the oil and the vinegar gradually and by turns. When per-fectly smooth, add the scallion tops or chives blended with the mayonnaise.

THE WISE ENCYCLOPEDIA OF COOKERY

Green Sauce

La Pommade Verte

The cornichons called for in this recipe are small pickled cucumbers, obtainable where French foods are sold; you can substitute sour pickles.

This sauce can be served as an accompaniment to grilled or poached fish.

To make about 2 cups [½ liter] of sauce

1 cup	coarsely torn and tightly packed spinach leaves	¼ liter
1 cup	coarsely torn and tightly packed chard leaves	¼ liter
1 cup	coarsely torn and tightly packed sorrel leaves	¼ liter
2 tbsp.	finely chopped fresh parsley	30 ml.
2 tbsp.	finely chopped fresh chervil	30 ml.
2 tbsp.	finely chopped fresh tarragon	30 ml.
2 tbsp.	finely chopped capers	30 ml.
2 tbsp.	finely chopped cornichons	30 ml.
4	anchovy fillets, soaked in water for 10 minutes, patted dry and finely chopped	4
3	hard-boiled egg yolks	3
1	thick slice day-old French or Italian bread, crust removed, soaked in warm water and squeezed almost dry	1
1 to 1½ cups	olive oil	250 to 375 ml.
	salt and pepper	
1 tbsp.	wine vinegar	15 ml.

Blanch the spinach, chard and sorrel in boiling water. Drain, squeeze the leaves dry and chop them finely. Put them in a mortar with the parsley, chervil and tarragon, and add the chopped capers, cornichons and anchovies.

Pound in the egg yolks and soaked bread, then gradually work in ½ cup [125 ml.] of the oil, a few drops at a time. Work the mixture with the pestle until thoroughly smooth. Season with salt and pepper, beat in the vinegar and enough oil to give the sauce the consistency of mayonnaise.

C. CHANOT-BULLIER
VIEILLES RECETTES DE CUISINE PROVENÇALE

Aioli

Aioli, a garlic-flavored mayonnaise, is traditionally served with salt cod. The amount of garlic used is a matter of individual preference. To prevent curdling, both oil and egg yolks should be at room temperature before use.

	To serve 6 to 8	
8	garlic cloves	8
4	egg yolks	4
	salt	
2¼ cups	olive oil	550 ml.
1 tsp.	fresh lemon juice	5 ml.

Pound the garlic cloves in a mortar with a wooden pestle, and add the egg yolks, lightly beaten with a pinch of salt; then little by little, drop by drop, without ceasing to stir, and turning the pestle in the same direction and with the same rhythm, incorporate the olive oil until you produce a thick mayonnaise. If the aioli becomes too thick, add, before finishing, 2 teaspoons [10 ml.] or more of tepid water. At the end add the lemon juice.

An "accident" can happen if the oil is too cool in contrast to the room temperature, or if it is poured in too fast. The oil will then rise to the surface and the aioli will be spoiled. To reverse this disaster, pour the sauce into another bowl and clean the mortar and pestle. Crush a garlic clove in the clean mortar with a little salt, add a few drops of water and the yolk of an egg, and start the operation over again by adding, in small spoonfuls, the first aioli (the failure). Thus the sauce will be retrieved and your honor saved!

JEAN-NOEL ESCUDIER AND PETA J. FULLER
THE WONDERFUL FOOD OF PROVENCE

---◆◆◆---

Standard Preparations

---◆◆◆---

Milk and Lemon Court Bouillon

	To make 2 quarts [2 liters] court bouillon	
1 cup	milk	¼ liter
1¾ quarts	lightly salted water	1¾ liters
1	lemon, peel and pith removed, thinly sliced and seeds removed	1

Combine the milk and salted water in the pan that will be used for poaching the fish, and add as many lemon slices as you like. The court bouillon requires no cooking before being used as a poaching medium.

A Wine Court Bouillon

This court bouillon is a general-purpose poaching liquid for most fish. The amount of wine may be varied according to taste. Fennel leaves and a garlic clove may also be included.

	To make about 2 quarts [2 liters] court bouillon	
1	large onion, sliced	1
1	large carrot, sliced	1
1	large leek, sliced	1
1	rib celery, diced	1
12	sprigs parsley	12
2	sprigs thyme	2
2	sprigs dill (optional)	2
1	bay leaf	1
6 cups	water	1½ liters
	salt	
2 cups	dry white or red wine	½ liter
5 or 6	peppercorns	5 or 6

Put the vegetables, herbs and water into a large pan, and season with a pinch of salt. Bring to a boil, then reduce the heat, cover and simmer for approximately 15 minutes. Pour in the wine and simmer for an additional 15 minutes, adding the peppercorns during the last few minutes of cooking. Strain the court bouillon through a sieve into a bowl or a clean pan before using it.

Vinegar Court Bouillon

Use the same ingredients as for a wine court bouillon, but substitute ¾ cup [175 ml.] red or white wine vinegar for the wine. Add the vinegar to the pan with the vegetables, herbs and water, bring to a boil, cover and simmer for 30 minutes, adding the peppercorns for the last few minutes of cooking.

Fish Fumet

To make about 2 quarts [2 liters] fumet

2 lb.	fish heads, bones and trimmings, rinsed and broken into convenient sizes	1 kg.
1	onion, sliced	1
1	carrot, sliced	1
1	leek, sliced	1
1	rib celery, diced	1
1	bouquet garni	1
2 quarts	water	2 liters
	salt	
2 cups	dry white wine	½ liter

Place the fish, vegetables and herbs in a large pan. Add the water and season lightly with salt. Bring to a boil over low heat. With a large, shallow spoon, skim off the scum that rises to the surface as the liquid reaches a simmer. Keep skimming until no more scum rises, then cover the pan and simmer for 15 minutes. Add the wine and simmer, covered, for another 15 minutes.

Strain the fumet through a colander placed over a deep bowl. If the fumet is to be used for a sauce or for aspic, do not press the solids when straining lest they cloud the liquid.

Aspic

The technique of coating fish with aspic is demonstrated on pages 84-85.

To make about 1 quart [1 liter] aspic

1 quart	fish fumet *(recipe, above)*	1 liter
2	egg whites	2
2	eggshells, finely crushed	2
2 to 4 tbsp.	Madeira or other fortified wine	30 to 60 ml.
3 to 4 tbsp.	powdered gelatin	45 to 60 ml.

Strain the fumet into a bowl through a fine sieve lined with three or four layers of dampened cheesecloth or one layer of muslin. Place the bowl in the refrigerator for several hours to allow the fine solids in the fumet to form a sediment. Decant the clear liquid into a large saucepan and warm it over low heat.

In a small bowl soften 3 tablespoons [45 ml.] of the gelatin with 6 or 8 tablespoons [90 or 120 ml.] of cold water. Add a little of the warm fumet, then stir the softened gelatin into the fumet in the saucepan. When the gelatin is completely dissolved, remove the pan from the heat. Refrigerate a spoonful of the fumet. If the fumet does not set within 10 minutes, soften the remaining gelatin in 4 tablespoons [60 ml.] of water, warm the fumet again and stir in the gelatin.

To clarify the fumet, beat the egg whites until they form soft peaks and add them to the saucepan with the crushed eggshells. Place the pan over high heat and whisk the fumet to thoroughly incorporate the egg whites. Cook without stirring so that the whites will separate from the fumet and rise to form a curdlike layer on its surface. When a few bubbles begin to break the egg-white layer, remove the pan from the heat and set it aside for 10 minutes. Bring the fumet to a boil two more times, letting it stand off the heat for 10 minutes between each boil.

Strain the fumet into a bowl through a fine sieve lined with three or four layers of dampened cheesecloth or one layer of muslin. When all of the fumet has dripped through the cloth, test another spoonful in the refrigerator and add more softened gelatin if necessary. Leave the fumet in the bowl to cool to room temperature. Taste the cooled aspic for salt and add the Madeira. The aspic is now ready for use.

Fish Velouté Sauce

To make about 1 cup [¼ liter] sauce

2 cups	fish fumet *(recipe, left)*	½ liter
2 tbsp.	butter	30 ml.
2 tbsp.	flour	30 ml.

Melt the butter in a heavy saucepan over low heat. Stir in the flour to make a roux and cook, stirring, for 2 to 3 minutes. Pour the fumet into the pan, whisking constantly. Raise the heat and continue to whisk until the sauce comes to a boil. Reduce the heat to low, and move the saucepan half off the heat so the liquid on only one side of the pan simmers. A skin of impurities will form on the still side. Remove the skin periodically with a spoon. Cook the sauce for about 40 minutes to reduce it and to eliminate the taste of flour.

Savory Sabayon Sauce

To make about 1 cup [¼ liter] sauce

1¼ cups	fish fumet *(recipe, above left)*	300 ml.
3	egg yolks	3
16 tbsp.	unsalted butter (½ lb. [¼ kg.]), chilled and finely diced	240 ml.

In the top of a double boiler—or in a small saucepan if you are making a bain-marie—boil the fish fumet until it has been reduced to about 5 or 6 tablespoons [75 or 90 ml.]. Meanwhile pour water to a depth of about 1 inch [2½ cm.] into the bottom section of a double boiler or, for a bain-marie, into a large saucepan. Heat the water until it simmers, then reduce the heat to low. Place the top of the double boiler over the bottom; or set a rack or trivet into the bain-marie and place the saucepan on the rack or trivet.

Whisk the egg yolks into the reduced fumet. Add the butter, a handful at a time, whisking between each addition. Continue adding butter and whisking until all of the butter is incorporated and the sauce has the consistency of a light, foamy custard. Remove the double-boiler top or saucepan from the heat, and whisk the sauce for a further 30 seconds.

Basic White Sauce

Use this recipe whenever béchamel sauce is required.

To make about 1 ½ cups [375 ml.] sauce

2 tbsp.	butter	30 ml.
2 tbsp.	flour	30 ml.
2 cups	milk	½ liter
	salt	
	white pepper	
	grated nutmeg (optional)	
	heavy cream (optional)	

Melt the butter in a heavy saucepan. Stir in the flour and cook, stirring, over low heat for 2 to 5 minutes. Pour in all of the milk at once, whisking constantly to blend the mixture smoothly. Raise the heat and continue whisking while the sauce comes to a boil. Season with a very little salt. Reduce the heat to very low, and simmer for about 40 minutes, stirring every so often to prevent the sauce from sticking to the bottom of the pan.

When the sauce thickens to the desired consistency, add white pepper and a pinch of nutmeg if you like; taste for seasoning. Whisk again until the sauce is perfectly smooth, then add cream if you prefer a richer and whiter sauce.

White Butter Sauce

Beurre Blanc

To make 1 to 1 ½ cups [250 to 375 ml.] sauce

⅓ cup	dry white wine	75 ml.
⅓ cup	white wine vinegar	75 ml.
3	shallots, very finely chopped	3
	salt	
	pepper	
½ to ¾ lb.	unsalted butter, chilled and finely diced	¼ to ½ kg.

In a heavy stainless-steel or enameled saucepan, boil the wine and vinegar with the shallots and a pinch of salt until only enough liquid remains to moisten the shallots. Remove the pan from the heat and allow it to cool for a few minutes. Season the mixture with pepper.

Place the pan on a fireproof pad over very low heat and whisk in the butter, a handful at a time, until the mixture has a creamy consistency. Remove from the heat as soon as all of the butter has been incorporated.

Tomato Sauce

When fresh ripe tomatoes are not available, use 3 cups [¾ liter] of drained, canned Italian plum tomatoes.

To make about 1 cup [¼ liter] sauce

6	medium-sized ripe tomatoes, chopped	6
1	onion, diced	1
1 tbsp.	olive oil	15 ml.
1	garlic clove (optional)	1
1 tsp.	chopped fresh parsley	5 ml.
1 tsp.	mixed dried basil, marjoram and thyme	5 ml.
1 to 2 tbsp.	sugar (optional)	15 to 30 ml.
	salt and freshly ground pepper	

In a large enameled or stainless-steel saucepan, gently fry the diced onion in the oil until soft, but not brown. Add the other ingredients and simmer for 20 to 30 minutes, or until the tomatoes have been reduced to a thick pulp. Sieve the mixture, using a wooden pestle or spoon. Reduce the sauce further, if necessary, to reach the desired consistency. Adjust the seasoning.

Hollandaise Sauce

This sauce can be turned into a mousseline sauce by the addition of cream. Whip ¾ cup [175 ml.] light or heavy cream until foamy but not stiff, and stir it into the prepared hollandaise sauce, off the heat.

To make about 1 cup [¼ liter] sauce

3	egg yolks	3
1 tbsp.	cold water	15 ml.
16 tbsp.	cold unsalted butter (½ lb. [¼ liter]), finely diced	240 ml.
	salt and white pepper	
	cayenne pepper	
1 tsp.	strained fresh lemon juice	5 ml.

Pour water to a depth of about 1 inch [2½ cm.] into the bottom of a double boiler or a large saucepan or fireproof casserole if you are making a bain-marie. Heat the water until it simmers, then reduce the heat to low. Place the top of the double boiler over the bottom; or set a rack or trivet into the water bath and place the saucepan on the rack or trivet. Put the egg yolks and the cold water in the upper pan and beat the yolks until smooth. Whisk a handful of the butter into the yolks and beat until the butter has been absorbed; continue adding diced butter in this way until all of it has been used. Beat until the sauce becomes thick and creamy. Season the sauce to taste with salt, white pepper and cayenne pepper. Then add the lemon juice.

Béarnaise Sauce

To make about 1 cup [¼ liter] sauce

½ cup	dry white wine	125 ml.
¼ cup	white wine vinegar	50 ml.
2	shallots, finely chopped	2
	cayenne pepper or 1 small dried red chili	
1	sprig tarragon	1
1	sprig chervil	1
3	egg yolks	3
16 tbsp.	unsalted butter, cut into small bits and brought to room temperature	240 ml.
1 tsp.	finely chopped tarragon	5 ml.
1 tsp.	finely chopped chervil	5 ml.
	salt and freshly ground pepper	

Put the wine, vinegar and shallots in a fireproof earthenware casserole, a heavy enameled saucepan or the top part of a glass or stainless-steel double boiler set over hot, not boiling water. Add a pinch of cayenne or the chili, and the sprigs of tarragon and chervil. Place the pan over low heat and simmer the mixture for 15 to 20 minutes, or until only 3 to 4 tablespoons [45 to 60 ml.] of syrupy liquid remain. Strain the liquid into a bowl, pressing the juices from the herbs, then return the liquid to the pan.

Reduce the heat to very low and whisk in the egg yolks. After a few seconds, whisk in one third of the butter and continue whisking until it is absorbed. Repeat this procedure twice more, whisking until the sauce begins to thicken. Remove the pan from the heat and continue whisking: the heat of the pan will continue to cook and thicken the sauce. Stir in the chopped herbs and season the sauce with salt and pepper to taste.

Mayonnaise

To prevent curdling, all of the ingredients should be at room temperature. Mayonnaise will keep for several days in a covered container in the refrigerator. Stir the mayonnaise well before you use it.

To make about 2 cups [½ liter] mayonnaise

3 or 4	egg yolks	3 or 4
	salt and white pepper	
1 tbsp.	wine vinegar or fresh lemon juice	15 ml.
1 or 2 tsp.	Dijon-style prepared mustard (optional)	5 or 10 ml.
2 cups	oil	½ liter

Put the egg yolks in a bowl. Season with salt and pepper and add 1 teaspoon [5 ml.] of the vinegar or lemon juice, and the mustard if used. Mix thoroughly with a small whisk. Add the oil, drop by drop to begin with, whisking constantly. When the sauce starts to thicken, pour the remaining oil in a thin, steady stream, whisking rhythmically. Whisk in the remaining vinegar or lemon juice and taste for seasoning.

Mousseline

The recipe below gives proportions for a rich mousseline, suitable for forming into dumplings or quenelles and for use as a stuffing or as an ingredient in a molded fish dish. For a particularly delicate mousseline stuffing, the quantity of cream can be increased to 1½ cups [375 ml.].

A pinch of cayenne pepper, or ¼ teaspoon [1 ml.] of ground saffron dissolved in 1 teaspoon [5 ml.] of boiling water, may be added while pounding the fish. For texture and flavor, any of the following ingredients may be mixed into the purée after the cream has been incorporated: shelled, peeled and chopped pistachios; cooked and chopped shrimp or mussels; cooked mushroom-and-onion *duxelles;* sautéed chopped mushrooms; chopped fresh or preserved truffles.

To make about 2 cups [½ liter] mousseline

½ lb.	skinned fillets of hake, pike, salmon, sole or whiting, chopped	¼ kg.
	pepper	
1	large egg white	1
1 cup	heavy cream	¼ liter

Using a mortar and pestle, pound the fish to a smooth purée. Season with pepper and add the egg white, pounding until it is completely incorporated. Alternatively, reduce the fish to a purée in a food processor, using the metal cutting blade; add and blend in the pepper and egg white.

A little at a time, rub the purée through a fine-meshed drum or conical sieve, using a plastic pastry scraper for a drum sieve, a wooden pestle for a conical sieve. Pack the purée into a glass or metal bowl and press plastic film against the top surface. Place the bowl in a larger bowl containing crushed ice and refrigerate for at least 1 hour.

Remove the bowls from the refrigerator. Using a wooden spoon, work a little heavy cream into the mixture. Return the bowls to the refrigerator for 15 minutes. Continue beating in small quantities of cream, refrigerating for 15 minutes between each addition. Beat the mixture vigorously as soon as it becomes soft enough.

When about half of the cream has been incorporated, season the mixture with salt and refrigerate for a few minutes. Whip the remaining cream until it stands in soft peaks, then incorporate it thoroughly into the purée. Refrigerate until ready for use.

Short-Crust and Rough Puff Pastry

One simple formula produces dough both for plain short-crust pastry and for rough puff pastry. The difference is in how you roll it out.

To make enough pastry to cover or line an 8-inch [20-cm.] pie

1 cup	flour	¼ liter
¼ tsp.	salt	1 ml.
8 tbsp.	cold unsalted butter, cut into small pieces	120 ml.
3 to 4 tbsp.	cold water	45 to 60 ml.

Mix the flour and salt in a mixing bowl. Add the butter and cut it into the flour rapidly, using two table knives, until the butter is in tiny pieces. Do not work for more than a few minutes. Add half the water and, with a fork, quickly blend it into the flour-and-butter mixture. Add just enough of the rest of the water to allow you to gather the dough together with your hands into a firm ball. Wrap the dough in plastic wrap or wax paper and refrigerate it for 2 to 3 hours, or put it in the freezer for 20 minutes until the outside surface is slightly frozen.

To roll out short-crust pastry. Remove the ball of pastry dough from the refrigerator or freezer and put it on a cool floured surface (a marble slab is ideal). Press the dough out partially with your hand, then give it a few gentle smacks with the rolling pin to flatten it and render it more supple. Roll out the dough from the center, until the pastry forms a circle about ½ inch [1 cm.] thick. Turn the pastry over to flour both sides, and continue rolling until the circle is about ⅛ inch [3 mm.] thick. Roll the pastry onto the rolling pin, lift up the pin and unroll the pastry over the piepan. If you are using the pastry to line a piepan, press the pastry firmly against all surfaces and trim the edges. If you are using the pastry to cover a pie, trim the pastry to within ½ inch of the rim, turn under the edges of the pastry around the rim to form a double layer, and press the pastry firmly to the rim with thumb and forefinger to crimp the edges.

To roll out rough puff pastry. Place the dough on a cool, floured surface and smack it flat with the rolling pin. Turn the dough over to make sure that both sides are well floured. Roll out the pastry rapidly into a rectangle about 1 foot [30 cm.] long and 5 to 6 inches [13 to 15 cm.] wide. Fold the two short ends to meet each other in the center, then fold again to align the folded edges with each other. Following the direction of the fold lines, roll the pastry into a rectangle again, fold again in the same way and refrigerate for at least 30 minutes. Repeat this process two or three more times before using the pastry. Always let the pastry dough rest in the refrigerator between rollings.

Croutons

To prepare croutons as a garnish for delicate-tasting dishes, you can substitute clarified butter for the combination of butter and oil specified in this recipe. If the croutons are to accompany strong-flavored dishes, you may prefer to sauté them in plain olive oil.

To make about 1 cup [¼ liter] croutons

2	slices cut ½ inch [1 cm.] thick from a loaf of day-old, firm-textured white bread	2
4 tbsp.	butter	60 ml.
¼ to ½ cup	oil	50 to 125 ml.

Remove the crusts from the bread and cut the slices into cubes. Combine the butter and ¼ cup [50 ml.] of the oil in a large skillet. Melt the butter over medium heat, add the bread cubes and increase the heat to high. Turn the cubes frequently with a broad spatula so that they brown evenly on all sides, and add more oil to the skillet as necessary to keep the cubes from burning. Drain the croutons on paper towels before serving.

Batter for Deep Frying

The consistency of this batter may be varied by changing the proportion of liquid to flour. A thin batter will cook crisper and lighter, but some of it will be lost in the oil during frying; a thicker batter clings better, but tends to be more bready.

To coat 12 to 15 fish pieces, depending on size

1 cup	flour	¼ liter
	salt and pepper	
1 tbsp.	olive oil	15 ml.
1 cup	beer, water or milk	¼ liter
2	egg whites	2

Sift the flour into a bowl and season with salt and pepper. Make a well in the center of the flour. Add the oil, and gradually whisk in the beer, water or milk, working from the center outward. Whisk for only as long as it takes to produce a smooth batter: do not overwork the mixture.

Let the batter rest for about 1 hour at room temperature, lest it shrink away from the fish pieces during the deep frying and provide an uneven coating. Beat the egg whites until they form soft peaks, and fold them gently into the batter just before using it.

Recipe Index

All recipes in the index that follows are listed by English titles. Entries are organized by the names of the fish specified in the recipe titles and also by major ingredients called for in titles. At the end of the listing for each fish are the page numbers of recipes for which that particular fish — although not mentioned in the recipe titles — is an appropriate option. Sauces and stuffings are listed separately. Foreign recipes are listed under the country or region of origin. Recipe credits are on pages 174-176.

General Index/ Glossary

Included in this index to the cooking demonstrations are definitions, in italics, of special culinary terms not explained elsewhere in this volume. The Recipe Index begins on page 168.

Aioli, 34, 35; uses, 34
Anchovies, 41; cooking methods, chart 6; fish steaks larded with, 46; in Montpellier butter, 34, 35; northern, 12
Anchovies, salt: not to be confused with anchovy fillets canned in oil, salt anchovies are whole fish, imported in wooden crates from the Mediterranean. They are obtainable at Greek or Italian food stores.
Angler, 8, 11; cooking methods, chart 6
Arctic char: cooking methods, chart 6
Aromatic vegetables: in braise,

41, 42; in court bouillon, 28, 29; in papillotes, 86; puréeing, 42, 43; in stew, 48
Aromatics: all substances —such as vegetables, herbs and spices —that add aroma and flavor to food when used in cooking.
Aspic jelly, 28, 84-85; food decorated with, 84, 85; strained fumet for, 29, 84
Bain-marie, 34, 80; how to make, 34
Baking, chart 6-7, 9, 12, 51-57
Barbecuing. See Grilling, outdoor
Bass: channel, 10; cooking methods, chart 6; largemouthed, 15; smallmouthed, 15
Bass, sea, 11, 41, 52, 68; baked in lettuce-leaf wrapping, 54-55; black, 11; black, in stew, 48-49; boned through belly, 24-25; cooked in Chinese steamer, 38-39; giant, 11; small, 56; white, 10
Bass, striped, 11, 32; Atlantic, 8; braising, 42-43; pan-dressed, 16
Basting: pouring or spooning oil, fat or liquid over food to prevent it from

drying up during cooking; 42, 51, 52-53, 55, 58, 60
Batter: beer in, 73; -coated cod fillet, 62; for deep frying, 73
Beurre blanc, 34
Beurre manié: an uncooked sauce-thickener made by kneading together equal amounts of flour and butter; 42
Blanching: plunging food into boiling water for a short period. Done for a number of reasons: to remove strong flavors, such as the excess saltiness of some salt pork; to soften vegetables before further cooking; to facilitate the removal of skins or shells. Another meaning is "to whiten"; 46
Bluefish, 13, 27; cooking methods, chart 6, 51, 60
Bluegill, 15; cooking methods, chart 6
Boning: barbecued steaks, 60; flatfish through back, 56-57; poached fish, 31, 33; poached salt cod, 75; roundfish through back, 56-57; roundfish through belly, 24-25. See also Filleting
Bonito: cooking methods, chart 6,

46; Pacific, 13
Bouquet garni: a bunch of mixed herbs —the classic three being parsley, thyme and bay leaf —tied together or wrapped in cheesecloth, and used for flavoring stocks, sauces, braises and stews; 40, 44
Braise (braising), chart 6-7, 41-47
Bream, 15; cooking methods, chart 6
Broiling, chart 6-7, 9, 12, 51, 58-59
Buffalo: cooking methods, chart 6; smallmouthed, 14
Bullhead, 15; cooking methods, chart 6
Burbot: cooking methods, chart 6
Butter: for basting, 51; and bread-crumb coating, 70-71; clarifying, 65; cold, as sauce-thickener, 55; for frying, 63, 64, 75; Montpellier, 34, 35; in sabayon, 34; sauce (beurre blanc), 34; sauce, for fried fish, 65; sauce, made from poaching liquid, 37; in velouté sauce, 37
Butterfish, 13, 27; cooking methods, chart 6; skinning, 20
Butterfly fillets, 16

Recipe Credits

The sources for the recipes in this volume are shown below. Page references in parentheses indicate where the recipes appear in the anthology.

Académie Culinaire de France, *Cuisine Française.* © Éditions Universitaires aux droits des Éditions Le Bélier-Prisma, 1971. Published by Éditions Le Bélier-Jean-Pierre Delarge, Éditeur, Paris. Translated by permission of Éditions Le Bélier-Jean-Pierre Delarge, Éditeur(97).
Acton, Eliza, *Modern Cookery.* Published by Longman, Green, Longman and Roberts, London, 1860 edition(130).
Adam, Hans Karl, *German Cookery.* © The Wine and Food Society Publishing Company, 1967. First published by David and Charles (Holdings) Limited, Newton Abbott. By permission of Pitman Publishing Ltd.(101).
Ainé, Offray, *Le Cuisinier Méridional.* Imprimeur-Libraire, 1855(107).
Audot, L. E., *La Cuisinière de la Campagne et de la Ville ou la nouvelle Cuisine économique.* Published by Librairie Audot, 1881 (59th edition)(104, 127).
Ayrton, Elisabeth, *The Cookery of England.* Copyright © Elisabeth Ayrton, 1974. Published by Penguin Books Ltd., London. By permission of Penguin Books Ltd.(116).
Bar-David, Molly Lyons, *The Israeli Cook Book.* Copyright © 1964 by Crown Publishers, Inc., New York. Published by Crown Publishers, Inc. Used by permission of Crown Publishers, Inc.(155).
Barberousse, Michel, *Cuisine Provençale.* Privately published by Michel Barberousse, Seguret. Translated by permission of Michel Barberousse(117, 143).
Bateman, Ruth Conrad, *I Love to Cook Book.* Copyright © 1962 by The Ward Ritchie Press. Published by The Ward Ritchie Press. Used by permission of The Ward Ritchie Press(156).
Beard, James, *James Beard's New Fish Cookery.* Copyright © 1976 by James A. Beard. Published by Little, Brown and Company, Boston. Used by permission of Little, Brown and Company(113, 148).
Beeton, Mrs. Isabella, *The Book of Household Management* (1861). Reproduced in facsimile by Jonathan Cape Ltd., London(154).
Bertholle, Louisette, *Secrets of the Great French Restaurants.* Copyright © 1974 by Macmillan Publishing Co., Inc. Copyright © 1972 by Opera Mundi, Paris. Published by Macmillan Publishing Co., Inc. Reprinted by permission of Macmillan Publishing Co., Inc.(127).
Besson, Joséphine, *La Mère Besson "Ma Cuisine Provençale."* © Éditions Albin Michel, 1977. Published by Éditions Albin Michel, Paris. Translated by permission of Éditions Albin Michel(109, 154).
Blanchard, Marjorie Page, *Treasured Recipes from Early New England Kitchens.* Copyright 1975 by Harrington's In Vermont, Inc. Published by Garden Way Publishing Company in association with Harrington's of Richmond, Vermont, Inc. By permission of Writers House, Inc., author's agents(125).
Bocuse, Paul, *Paul Bocuse's French Cooking.* Copyright © 1977 by Random House, Inc. Published by Pantheon Books, Inc., New York. Reprinted by permission of Pantheon Books, a Division of Random House, Inc.(90).
Boni, Ada, *Italian Regional Cooking.* Copyright © 1969 by Arnoldo Mondadori. Published by Bonanza Books, a division of Crown Publishers, Inc. By permission of Arnoldo Mondadori Editore, Italy(127).
Bontou, Aloide, *Traité de Cuisine Bourgeoise Bordelaise.* Published by Feret et Fils Éditeurs, Bordeaux. Translated by permission of Feret et Fils Éditeurs(120, 141).
Borelli, Irène, *La Cuisine Provençale.* © Solar. Published by Solar, Paris 1975. Translated by permission of Solar(118, 133).
Borgström and Danfors, *Scandinavian Cookbook.* Published by Wezäta Förlag, Stockholm. By permission of Wezäta Förlag(120).

Born, Wina, *Het Groot Visboek.* © 1972 by J. H. Gottmer—Haarlem. Published by J. H. Gottmer—Haarlem. Translated by permission of J. H. Gottmer—Haarlem(94).
Bouzy, Michel, *Les Poissons-Crustacés-Coquillages.* Published by Blondel la Rougery, Paris. Translated by permission of Blondel la Rougery(107).
Boyd, Lizzie (Editor), *British Cookery.* Copyright © British Farm Produce Council and British Tourist Authority. Published by Croom Helm, London. By permission of British Farm Produce Council and British Tourist Authority(91, 106, 119, 153).
Brera, Gianni and Luigi Veronelli, *La Pacciada.* Copyright © 1973 by Arnoldo Mondadori Editore, Milan. Published by Arnoldo Mondadori Editore, Milan. Translated by permission of Arnoldo Mondadori Editore(150).
Brissenden, Rosemary, *South East Asian Food.* Copyright © R. F. and R. L. Brissenden, 1970. Published by Penguin Books Ltd., London. By permission of Penguin Books Ltd.(145).
Brody, Jerome, *The Grand Central Oyster & Restaurant Seafood Cookbook.* Copyright © by Jerome Brody and Joan and Joseph Foley. Published by Crown Publishers, Inc., New York. Used by permission of Crown Publishers, Inc.(110).
Brown, Cora, Rose and Bob, *The South American Cook Book.* First published by Doubleday, Doran & Company Inc., 1939. Republished in 1971 by Dover Publications Inc., New York(104).
Burros, Marian, *Pure & Simple.* Copyright © 1978 by Marian Fox Burros. Published by William Morrow & Company, Inc. Used by permission of William Morrow & Company, Inc.(138).
Caillat, A., *150 Manières d'Accommoder les Sardines.* Privately published, Marseilles, 1898(93).
Calera, Ana Maria, *La Cocina Vasca.* © Editorial "La Gran Enciclopedia Vasca," 1971. Published by La Gran Enciclopedia Vasca, Bilbao(91, 102).
Carnacina, Luigi and Luigi Veronelli, *La Buona Vera Cucina Italiana.* © 1966 by Rizzoli Editore. Published by Rizzoli Editore, Milan. Translated by permission of Rizzoli Editore(149).
Carrier, Robert, *The Robert Carrier Cookery Course.* © Robert Carrier, 1974. Published by W. H. Allen and Co. Ltd. By permission of W. H. Allen and Co. Ltd.(139).
Cass, Elizabeth, *Spanish Cooking.* Copyright © Elizabeth Cass, 1957. First published by André Deutsch Ltd., 1957. Also published by Mayflower Books Ltd., 1970. By permission of André Deutsch Ltd.(138).
Chanot-Bullier, C., *Vieilles Recettes de Cuisine Provençale.* Published by Tacussel, Marseilles. Translated by permission of Tacussel, Éditeur(111, 162).
Chantiles, Vilma Liacouras, *The Food of Greece.* Copyright © 1975 by Vilma Liacouras Chantiles. Published by Atheneum, New York. By permission of Vilma Liacouras Chantiles(132).
Chao, Buwei Yang, *How to Cook and Eat in Chinese.* Published by Faber and Faber Ltd., London. By permission of Faber and Faber Ltd.(155).
Chapelle, Vincent de la, *Le Cuisinier Moderne.* Paris 1735(140).
Cholcheva, Penka, *Kniga za Vseki den i Vseki Dom.* Published by Technika Publishing House, Sofia, 1978. Translated by permission of Jusautor Copyright Agency, Sofia(145).
Claudian, *A Table.* Published by Publications Périodiques, Paris, 1963. Translated by permission of Publications Périodiques(105).
Collin, Rima and Richard, *The Pleasures of Seafood.* Copyright © 1976 by Rima and Richard Collin. Published by Holt, Rinehart and Winston(88).
Colutta, Flavio, *Cucinae Vini della Toscana.* © Copyright 1974 Ugo Mursia Editore, Milan. Published by Ugo Mursia Editore. Translated by permission of Ugo Mursia Editore(92).
Correnti, Pino, *Il Libro d'Oro della Cucina e dei Vini di Sicilia.* Copyright © 1976 Ugo Mursia Editore, Milan. Published by Ugo Mursia Editore. Translated by permission of Ugo Mursia Editore(144).

Costantini, Simone, *Gastronomie Corse et ses Recettes.* Published by U Muntese, Corsica. Translated by permission of U Muntese(114).
Courtine, Robert J., *Mon Bouquet de Recettes.* © Les Nouvelles Éditions Marabout, Verviers, 1977. Published by Les Nouvelles Éditions Marabout, Verviers. Translated by permission of Les Nouvelles Éditions Marabout(91, 106).
Curnonsky, *Bons Plats, Bons Vins.* Published by Ponsot, Paris, c. 1950(95).
Cutler, Carol, *The Six-Minute Soufflé and Other Culinary Delights.* Copyright © 1976 by Carol Cutler. Published by Clarkson N. Potter, Inc. Used by permission of Clarkson N. Potter, Inc.(123, 152).
Dauzvardis, Josephine J., *Popular Lithuanian Recipes.* Published by the Lithuanian Catholic Press, Chicago, 1967. By permission of the Lithuanian Catholic Press(99).
David, Elizabeth, *French Provincial Cooking.* Copyright © Elizabeth David, 1960, 1962, 1967, 1970. First published by Michael Joseph Ltd., London, 1960. Also published by Penguin Books Ltd., London. By permission of Elizabeth David(108). *Summer Cooking.* Copyright © Elizabeth David, 1955. Published by Penguin Books Ltd., London. By permission of Penguin Books Ltd.(109).
Davidson, Alan, *Seafood of South-East Asia.* Copyright © Alan Davidson, 1977. Published by Federal Publications, Singapore. By permission of Federal Publications(125). *Mediterranean Seafood.* Copyright © Alan Davidson, 1972. Published by Penguin Books Ltd., London. By permission of Penguin Books Ltd.(134).
Davidson, Alan and Jane, *Dumas on Food.* Selections from *Le Grand Dictionnaire de Cuisine* by Alexandre Dumas translated by Alan and Jane Davidson. © Alan and Jane Davidson, 1978. Published by the Folio Society, London. By permission of the Folio Society(137).
De Croze, Austin, *Les Plats Régionaux de France.* Published by Éditions Daniel Morcrette, B.P. 26, 95270-Luzarches, France. Translated by permission of Éditions Daniel Morcrette(112).
De Gouy, Louis P., *The Gold Cook Book* (revised edition). Copyright 1948, 1969 by Louis P. De Gouy. Published by Chilton Book Company, Radnor, Pennsylvania. Reprinted by permission of Chilton Book Company(159).
de Lazarque, E. Auricoste, *Cuisine Messine.* Published by Sidot Frères, Libraires-Éditeurs, Nancy, 1927(89).
de Pomiane, Edouard, *Cuisine Juive: Ghettos Modernes.* Copyright 1929 by Albin Michel. Published by Éditions Albin Michel, Paris. Translated by permission of Éditions Albin Michel(88).
Dege, Hroar, *Fra Neptuns Gaffel.* Published by H. Aschehoug and Co., Oslo, 1966. Translated by permission of H. Aschehoug and Co.(116).
Derys, Gaston, *L'Art d'Être Gourmand.* Copyright by Albin Michel, 1929. Published by Éditions Albin Michel, Paris. Translated by permission of Éditions Albin Michel(137).
Deutsch, Herman B. and Deirdre Stanforth, *Brennan's New Orleans Cookbook.* Copyright © 1961 Brennan's Restaurant and Herman B. Deutsch. Published by Robert L. Crager & Co., New Orleans. Used by permission of Robert L. Crager & Co.(152).
Diat, Louis, *French Cooking for Americans.* Copyright 1941 by Louis Diat. Copyright © renewed 1969, by Mrs. Louis D. Diat. Published by J. B. Lippincott Company, New York. Reprinted by permission of J. B. Lippincott Company(94, 156).
Dougall, Anton B., *Kcina Maltija: Maltese Cuisine.* Copyright Anton B. Dougall M.C.F.A. (C.G.) 1974. Published by A. B. Dougall Co. Ltd., Malta. By permission of Anton B. Dougall Co. Ltd.(118).
Dubois, Urbain, *École des Cuisinières.* Published by Dentu, Paris, 1876(97).
Durand, Charles, *Le Cuisinier Durand.* Privately published by the author, Nîmes, 1843(143, 148).
Dyer, Ceil, *The Newport Cookbook.* Copyright © 1972 by Ceil Dyer. Published by Hawthorn Books, New York. Used by permission of Hawthorn Books(152).
Eren, Neset, *The Art of Turkish Cooking.* Copyright © 1969 by Neset Eren. Published by Doubleday & Company, Inc., New York. By permission of Neset Eren(128, 157).
Escoffier, Auguste, *Le Carnet d'Épicure.* (Magazine.)

1912, no. 10. Translated by permission of Pierre Escoffier(93). *The Escoffier Cook Book.* Copyright © 1969 by Crown Publishers, Inc. Published by Crown Publishers, Inc., New York. Used by permission of Crown Publishers, Inc.(144, 161).

Feng, Doreen Yen Hung, *The Joy of Chinese Cooking.* First published by Faber and Faber Ltd., London, 1952. By permission of Faber and Faber Ltd.(99).

The Fishermen's Wives of Gloucester/The Cape Ann League of Women Voters, *The Taste of Gloucester.* Copyright © 1976 Gloucester Cookbook Committee. Used by permission of the Gloucester Cookbook Committee(149).

Flower, Barbara and Elisabeth Rosenbaum, *The Roman Cookery Book, A critical translation of "The Art of Cooking by Apicius."* © E. Rosenbaum, 1958. Published by George G. Harrap and Co. Ltd., London. By permission of George G. Harrap and Co. Ltd.(133).

Foods of the World, *American Cooking; American Cooking: Creole and Acadian; American Cooking: The Eastern Heartland; American Cooking: The Melting Pot; American Cooking: Southern Style; The Cooking of China.* Copyright © 1968 Time-Life Books Inc.; Copyright © 1971 Time Inc.; Copyright © 1971 Time-Life Books Inc.; Copyright © 1971 Time Inc.; Copyright © 1971 Time Inc.; Copyright © 1968 Time Inc.; Published by Time-Life Books, Alexandria(103, 122, 126, 142, 143, 146, 151, 152).

Frederick, J. George and Jean Joyce, *Long Island Seafood Cook Book.* Copyright 1939 by Business Bourse, New York. Republished in 1971 by Dover Publications, Inc., New York. Used by permission of Dover Publications, Inc.(115).

Fuller, Peta J. and Jean-Noel Escudier, *The Wonderful Food of Provence.* Copyright © 1968 by Robert Rebstock and Peta J. Fuller. Published by Houghton Mifflin Company. Used by permission of Houghton Mifflin Company(106, 163).

Gosetti della Salda, A. (editor in chief), *La Cucina Italiana.* (Magazine.) Published by Casa Editrice "La Cucina Italiana." Translated by permission of A. Gosetti della Salda(128).

Gouffé, Jules, *Le Livre de Cuisine.* Published by Librairie Hachette, Paris, 1867(153).

Government of Canada, Fisheries and Oceans, *The Canadian Fish Cookbook.* By permission of Government of Canada, Fisheries and Oceans(156).

Government of Canada, *The Way to Cook Fish.* Copyright © 1975 Information Canada. Published by Department of Fisheries & Oceans. Used by permission of Government of Canada, Fisheries & Oceans, Fisheries Food Center(100, 154).

Graves, Eleanor, *Great Dinners from Life.* Copyright © 1969 Time Inc. Published by Time-Life Books, Alexandria(95).

Grigson, Jane, *Fish Cookery.* Copyright © Jane Grigson, 1973. Published by the International Wine and Food Publishing Company. Used by permission of Overlook Press, Inc.(113, 153).

Guérard, Michel, *Michel Guérard's Cuisine Minceur.* English translation Copyright © 1976 by William Morrow and Company, Inc. Published by William Morrow and Company, Inc., New York. Used by permission of William Morrow and Company, Inc.(129).

Guinandeau, Z., *Fez Vu par Sa Cuisine.* Published by J. E. Laurent. Translated by permission of Madame Guinandeau(124).

Heath, Ambrose, *Herrings, Bloaters and Kippers.* Published by Herbert Jenkins Ltd., London. By permission of the publisher, Herbert Jenkins Ltd.(140).

Jakobsson, Oskar, *Good Food in Sweden.* © 1968 G. L. A. and Oskar Jakobsson. Published by Generalstabens Litografiska Anstalt, Stockholm. By permission of G. L. A. and Oskar Jakobsson(113).

Jans, Hugh, *Bistro Koken.* Copyright © 1973 Unieboek b.v./C. A. J. van Dishoeck, Bussum. Published by Unieboek/C. A. J. van Dishoeck, Bussum. Translated by permission of Unieboek/C. A. J. van Dishoeck(118).

The Junior League of Tampa, *The Gasparilla Cookbook.* Copyright © 1961 The Junior League of Tampa, Inc.

Published by The Junior League of Tampa, Inc. Used by permission of The Junior League of Tampa(121).

Kahn, Odette, *La Petite et la Grande Cuisine.* © Calmann-Lévy, 1977. Published by Éditions Calmann-Lévy, Paris. Translated by permission of Éditions Calmann-Lévy(98).

Käkönen, Ulla, *Natural Cooking the Finnish Way.* Copyright © 1974 by Ulla Käkönen. Published by Times Books, a Division of Quadrangle/The New York Times Book Co. Reprinted by permission of Times Books, a Division of Quadrangle/The New York Times Book Co. (122, 123).

Karaoglan, Aida, *A Gourmet's Delight, Selected Recipes from the "Haute Cuisine" of the Arab World.* Copyright © 1969 Dar An-Nahar. Published by Dar An-Nahar, Beirut. By permission of Caravan Books(134, 138).

Katz, Heinz, *Maritime Leckereien, Das Fischkochbuch von der Waterkant.* © Ditzen Druck und Verlags—GmbH, Bremerhaven. Published by Ditzen Druck und Verlags—GmbH, 1976. Translated by permission of Ditzen Druck und Verlags—GmbH(156).

Knight, Jacqueline E., *The Cook's Fish Guide.* Copyright © 1973 by Jacqueline E. Knight. Published by E. P. Dutton & Co. Inc., New York. Reprinted by permission of E. P. Dutton & Co. Inc.(115, 147).

Kouki, Mohamed, *Poissons Méditerranéens.* Published with the collaboration of the Office National des Pêches, Tunis(111).

Labarre, Irène, *La Cuisine des Trois B.* © Solar 1976. Published by Solar, Paris. Translated by permission of Solar(117).

Lassalle, George, *The Adventurous Fish Cook.* Published by Pan Books Ltd., London, and Macmillan London Ltd. By permission of Pan Books Ltd.(134).

Leone, Gene, *Leone's Italian Cookbook.* Copyright © 1967 by Gene Leone. Published by Harper & Row, Publishers, Inc. Used by permission of Harper & Row, Publishers, Inc.(124).

Lucas, Dione and Marion Gorman, *The Dione Lucas Book of French Cooking.* Copyright 1947 by Dione Lucas. Copyright © 1973 by Mark Lucas and Marion F. Gorman. Published by Little, Brown and Company, Boston. Used by permission of Little, Brown and Company(96, 160).

McClane, A. J., *The Encyclopedia of Fish Cookery.* Copyright © 1977 by A. J. McClane and Arie de Zanger. Published by Holt, Rinehart & Winston. Used by permission of Holt, Rinehart & Winston(158).

MacIlquham, Frances, *Fish Cookery of North America.* Copyright © 1974 by Frances MacIlquham. Published by Winchester Press, New York. Reprinted by permission of Winchester Press(112, 161).

MacMiadhacháin, Anna, *Spanish Regional Cookery.* Copyright © Anna MacMiadhacháin, 1976. Published by Penguin Books Ltd., London. By permission of Penguin Books Ltd.(135).

McNeill, F. Marian, *The Scots Kitchen.* Published by Blackie and Son Limited, London. Reproduced by permission of Blackie and Son Limited(150).

Magyar, Elek, *Kochbuch für Feinschmecker.* Printed in Hungary, 1967. Published by Corvina Verlag, Budapest. Translated by permission of Dr. Bálint Magyar and Dr. Pál Magyar(92, 102).

Mallos, Tess, *Greek Cookbook.* Copyright © Tess Mallos, 1976. Published by The Hamlyn Publishing Group Ltd. By permission of The Hamlyn Publishing Group Ltd.(136).

Marshall, Mel, *Cooking Over Coals.* Copyright © 1971 Mel Marshall. Published by Winchester Press, Inc., New York. Used by permission of Winchester Press, Inc.(106).

Martin, Peter and Joan, *Japanese Cooking.* Copyright © 1970 Peter and Joan Martin. First published 1970 by André Deutsch Limited. Published by Bobbs-Merrill Company Inc.(146).

Massachusetts Seafood Council, *Seafoods 'N Seaports . . . a cook's tour of Massachusetts.* Massachusetts Department of Natural Resources in cooperation with The U.S. Bureau of Commercial Fisheries under P.L. 88-309(139).

Médecin, Jacques, *La Cuisine du Comté de Nice.* © Juillard, 1972. Published by Penguin Books Ltd., London,

1979. Translated by permission of Penguin Books Ltd.(145).

Menon, *La Cuisinière Bourgeoise.* Paris, 1745(103).

Miller, Gloria Bley, *The Thousand Recipe Chinese Cookbook.* Copyright © 1966 by Gloria Bley Miller. Published by Grossett & Dunlap, New York. Used by permission of Gloria Bley Miller(155).

Miloradovich, Milo, *The Art of Fish Cookery.* Copyright © 1949 by Milo Miloradovich. Published by Bantam Books, Inc., New York. Reprinted by permission of Doubleday & Company, Inc.(147).

Molchanova, O. P., et al., *Kniga O Vkusnoĭ I Zdorovoĭ Pishche.* Published by Pishchepromizdat Publishing House, Moscow, 1952(131, 136).

Molokhovets, Elena, *Podarok Molodȳm Khozyaikam.* Published in St. Petersburg, 1892(98).

Monselet, Charles, *Lettres Gourmandes.* Published by Jacques Grancher, Éditeur, Paris. Translated by permission of Jacques Grancher, Éditeur(123).

Montagné, Prosper, *The New Larousse Gastronomique.* English translation Copyright © 1977 by Hamlyn Publishing Group Limited. Published by Crown Publishers, Inc., New York. By permission of Crown Publishers, Inc.(158, 160).

Montagné, Prosper and A. Gottschalk, *Mon Menu—Guide d'Hygiène Alimentaire.* Published by Société d'Applications Scientifiques, Paris(121).

Muffoletto, Anna, *The Art of Sicilian Cooking.* Copyright © 1971 by Anna Muffoletto. Published by Doubleday & Company, Inc., N.Y. Reprinted by permission of Doubleday & Company, Inc.(97, 104, 131).

Muthachen, Rachel C., *Indian Regional Recipes (for Newly-Weds).* Copyright © 1969. Published by Jaico Publishing House, Bombay. Used by permission of Jaico Publishing House(100, 132).

Nightingale, Marie, *Out of Old Nova Scotia Kitchens.* Copyright 1971 by Marie Nightingale. Published by Pagurian Press Ltd. By permission of Pagurian Press and Mrs. L. A. Nightingale(149).

Nignon, Édouard, *Les Plaisirs de la Table.* Published by the author c. 1920. Translated by permission of Daniel Morcrette, B. P. 26, 95270 Luzarches, France(116).

Olney, Richard, *Simple French Food.* Copyright © 1974 by Richard Olney. Published by Atheneum, New York. Reprinted by permission of Atheneum and A. M. Heath & Company Ltd., Author's Agents(89, 114). *The French Menu Cookbook.* Copyright © 1970 by Richard Olney. Published by Simon & Schuster, New York. By permission of John Schaffner, Literary Agent(96, 129).

Orga, Irfan, *Cooking with Yogurt.* First published 1956 by André Deutsch Limited, London. By permission of André Deutsch Limited(130).

Ortiz, Elisabeth Lambert, *The Complete Book of Caribbean Cooking.* Copyright © Elisabeth Lambert Ortiz, 1973, 1975. Published by M. Evans and Company, Inc., New York. By permission of John Farquharson Ltd., Literary Agents(125).

Paddleford, Clementine, *How America Eats.* Copyright © 1960 Clementine Paddleford. Published by Charles Scribner's Sons, New York. Used by permission of Charles Scribner's Sons(148).

Pakhuridze, N. (Editor), *Blyuda Bruzinskoĭ Kukhni.* Published by Paneka Publishing House, 1972(101).

Peck, Paula, *Paula Peck's Art of Good Cooking.* © 1966 by Paula Peck. Published by Simon & Schuster, New York. By permission of Simon & Schuster, a Division of Gulf & Western Corporation(142).

Peter, Madeleine, *Favorite Recipes of the Great Women Chefs of France.* Copyright © 1977 by Editions Robert Laffont S.A. Copyright © 1979 by Holt, Rinehart and Winston. Reprinted by permission of Holt, Rinehart and Winston(135, 162).

Petits Propos Culinaires, © 1979, Prospect Books. Published by Prospect Books, Washington, D.C. By permission of the publisher(157).

Petroni, Paolo, *Il Libro della Vera Cucina Marinara.* © Copyright 1976 by Casa Editrice Bonechi—Via Cairoli 18b-Firenze. Published by Casa Editrice Bonechi. Translated by permission of Casa Editrice Bonechi(146).

Piruzyan, A. S., *Armyanskaya Kulinariya.* Published by Ekonomika Publishing House, Moscow, 1971(144).

Les Princes de la Gastronomie, © 1.2.1975—Les Éditions Mondiales. Published by Modes de Paris. Translated by permission of Les Éditions Mondiales(158).
Ray, Elizabeth (Editor), *The Best of Eliza Acton.* © Longmans, Green & Co. Ltd., 1968. Introduction Copyright © Elizabeth David 1968. Published by Penguin Books Ltd., London. By permission of Penguin Books Ltd.(108).
Reboul, J. B., *La Cuisinière Provençale.* Published by Tacussel, Marseille. Translated by permission of Tacussel, Éditeur(110).
Reynière, La, *200 Recettes des Meilleures Cuisinières de France.* © Éditions Albin Michel, 1977. Published by Éditions Albin Michel, Paris. Translated by permission of Éditions Albin Michel(130).
Sarvis, Shirley, *Crab & Abalone: West Coast Ways with Fish & Shellfish.* Copyright © 1968 by Shirley Sarvis and Tony Calvello. Published by Bobbs-Merrill Company Inc. By permission of Shirley Sarvis(119, 141).
Schrecker, Ellen and John, *Mrs. Chiang's Szechwan Cookbook.* Copyright © 1976 by Chiang Jung-feng and Ellen Schrecker. Published by Harper & Row, Inc. Used by permission of Harper & Row, Inc.(100).
Seranne, Ann, *Ann Seranne's Good Food & How to Cook It.* Copyright © 1972 by Ann Seranne. Published by William Morrow & Company, Inc. Used by permission of William Morrow & Company, Inc.(94).
Sokolov, Raymond A., *Great Recipes from The New York Times.* Copyright © 1973 by Raymond A. Sokolov. Published by Quadrangle/Times Books, New York. Reprinted by permission of Quadrangle/Times Books(108, 110).

Troisgros, Jean and Pierre, *The Nouvelle Cuisines of Jean & Pierre Troisgros.* Copyright © 1978 in the English translation by William Morrow and Company, Inc. Originally published under the title *Cuisiniers à Roanne.* Copyright © 1977 by Éditions Robert Laffont, S. A. Used by permission of William Morrow and Company, Inc.(151).
U.S. Department of Commerce, *Country Catfish.* Developed at the National Fisheries Education Center, National Marine Fisheries Service(147). *A Seafood Heritage.* Developed at the National Fishery Education Center, National Marine Fisheries Service(102, 143).
University of California Cooperative Extension, *California Seafood Recipes.* U.S. Department of Commerce, National Marine Fisheries Service(139).
Valente, Maria Odette Cortes, *Cozinha Regional Portuguesa.* Published by Livraria Almedina, Coimbra, 1973. Translated by permission of Livraria Almedina(105, 133).
Van der Meer, Janny and Beatrice R. Mansur, *Tanzanian Food with Traditional and New Recipes.* Published by the Food and Agriculture Organization of the United Nations. By permission of the Food and Agriculture Organization of the United Nations(154).
van Es, Ton, *Het Volkomen Visboek.* © 1975 by Meijer Pers b.v., Amsterdam, Holland. Published by Meijer Pers b.v. Translated by permission of Meijer Pers(90, 126).
Verdon, René, *The White House Chef Cookbook.* Copyright © 1967 by René Verdon. Published by Doubleday & Company, Inc., New York. Reprinted by permission of Doubleday & Company, Inc.(141).
Vermeersch, Fons, *Op Zoek Naar Spijs en Drank.* © Uitgeverij Lannoo, Tielten Utrecht. Published by Lannoo, Belgium. Translated by permission of Lannoo(115).

Wason, Betty, *Bride in The Kitchen.* Copyright © 1964 by Elizabeth Wason Hall. Published by Doubleday & Company, Inc., New York. Reprinted by permission of Doubleday & Company, Inc.(150).
The Wise Encyclopedia of Cookery. Copyright 1948 Wm. H. Wise & Co. Inc. Published by Wm. H. Wise & Co. Inc., New York. Used by permission of Grossett & Dunlap, Inc.(162).
Wretman, Tore, *Svensk Husmanskost.* © Tore Wretman, 1967. Published by Forum Publishers, Stockholm. Translated by permission of Tore Wretman(120).
Wright, Carol, *The West Country.* Copyright © Carol Wright, 1975. Published by Cassell & Company Ltd., an imprint of Cassell & Collier Macmillan Publishers Ltd. By permission of Cassell & Company Ltd.(159).
Zachary, Hugh, *The Beachcomber's Handbook of Seafood Cookery.* Copyright © 1969 by Hugh Zachary. Published by John F. Blair, Publisher, Winston-Salem. Used by permission of John F. Blair, Publisher(119, 121).
Zeitoun, Edmond, *250 Recettes Classiques de Cuisine Tunisienne.* Published by Jacques Grancher, Éditeur, Paris. Translated by permission of Jacques Grancher, Éditeur(140).
Zelayeta, Elena, *Elena's Secrets of Mexican Cooking.* Copyright © 1958 by Prentice-Hall, Inc. Published by Prentice-Hall, Inc., Englewood Cliffs, N.J. Used by permission of Prentice-Hall, Inc.(126).
Žeránska, Alina, *The Art of Polish Cooking.* Copyright © 1968 by Alina Žeránska. Published by Doubleday & Company, Inc., New York. By permission of Doubleday & Company, Inc.(136).

Acknowledgments

The indexes for this book were prepared by Anita R. Beckerman. The editors are particularly indebted to Pat Alburey, Hertfordshire, England; Gene Cope, Dr. Virginia Sidwell, National Marine Fisheries Service, Washington, D.C.; Bob E. Finley, National Marine Fisheries Service, Chicago; John D. Kaylor, National Marine Fisheries Service, Gloucester, Mass.; Jacqueline Knight, Williamsport, Pa.; and Jeremiah Tower, Berkeley, Calif.

The editors also wish to thank: Kevin Allen, Thomas J. Moreau, Warren F. Rathjen, National Marine Fisheries Service, Gloucester, Mass.; William O. Antozzi, Henry R. McAvoy, National Marine Fisheries Service, St. Petersburg, Fla.; James W. Ayers, National Marine Fisheries Service, Little Rock, Ark.; Dr. Robert Balkovic, John Dassow, Conrad Mahnken, National Marine Fisheries Service, Seattle; Beverly Barton, James Brooker, National Marine Fisheries Service, Washington, D.C.; Alvin Bennof, Giant Food, Inc., Washington, D.C.; John Bridge, Estuary Products, Essex, England; James R. Bybee, Howard Ness, Doris Robinson, National Marine Fisheries Service, Terminal Island, Calif.; Don Caldwell, Canadian Embassy, Washington, D.C.; Dr. Daniel Cohen, Dr. Stanley Weitzman, National Museum of Natural History, Smithsonian Institution, Washington, D.C.; Pamela Davidson, Jennifer Davidson, London; Christopher Dewees, Dr. Robert J. Price, Dept. of Food Science & Technology, Univ. of Calif., Davis; Cecile Dogniez, Paris; J. Audrey Ellison, London; Dr. Edward Epremian, National Academy of Science, Washington, D.C.; Dr. George Flick, Mary C. Holliman, Dept. of Food, Science and Technology, Virginia Polytechnic Institute and State Univ., Blacksburg; Bertha Fontaine, National Marine Fisheries Service, Pascagoula, Miss.; Dorothy Frame, London; Diana Grant, London; Carter and Debbie Harrison, Carlisle, Ark.; Dr. Murray L. Hayes, Northwest and Alaska Fisheries Center, Seattle; Maggie Heinz, London; Marilyn Hellinger, Maryland Seafood Council, Annapolis, Md.; Marion Hunter, Surrey, England; Arlene Joyce, National Marine Fisheries Service, Baltimore, Md.; Dr. Robert Lackey, Virginia Polytechnic Institute and State Univ., Blacksburg; Joseph F. Lèdner, National Marine Fisheries Service, N.Y.; Bob Martin, Sport Fishing Institute, Washington, D.C.; William H. Massmann, Dr. Charles Walker, William M. Zarbock, Fish & Wildlife Service, Washington, D.C.; Agneta Munktell, London; Al McDonald, Cannon Seafood, Inc., Washington, D.C.; C. J. Newnes, London; Craig Phillips, National Aquarium, Washington, D.C.; Dr.·A. E. Reynolds, Food Science Dept., Michigan State Univ., East Lansing; Shirley Sarvis, San Francisco; E. B. Smith, Norfolk, England; Dr. Gary Stauffer, National Marine Fisheries Service, La Jolla, Calif.; J. M. Turnell & Co., London; Eileen Turner, Sussex, England.

Picture Credits

The sources for the pictures in this book are listed below. Credits for each of the photographers and illustrators are listed by page number in sequence with successive pages indicated by hyphens; where necessary, the locations of pictures within pages are also indicated—separated from page numbers by dashes.
Photographs by Aldo Tutino: 16, 18, 20, 21—top and center, 30—top, bottom center and right, 31, 38-39, 42-43, 48-50, 52-53—top, 58, 59—bottom, 60-61, 65—bottom, 66-71, 73, 74-75—top, 78-79, 82-83, 86.
Photographs by Alan Duns: cover, 4, 19—top right and bottom, 21—bottom, 22-26, 28—center and right, 29, 30—bottom left, 32-33, 36-37, 40, 44-47, 52-53—bottom, 54-55, 56-57—top, 59—top, 64, 65—top, 72, 76, 80-81, 84-85.
Photographs by Tom Belshaw: 19—top left and center, 28—bottom left, 34-35, 56-57—bottom, 62, 74-75—bottom.
Other photographs: Louis Klein, 2.
Illustrations (alphabetically): Biruta Akerbergs, 17. Mary Evans Picture Library and private sources, 88-167. Thomas L. Kronen, courtesy The National Marine Fisheries Service, Chicago, 9—top (2), fourth from top, and bottom left. Rod Ruth, courtesy The National Marine Fisheries Service, Chicago, 8, 9—all except top (2), fourth from top, and bottom left, 10-15.

Library of Congress Cataloguing in Publication Data
Time-Life Books.
   Fish.
   (The Good cook, techniques and recipes)
   Includes index.
   1. Cookery (Fish) I. Title. II. Series.
TX747.T55 1979   641.6'9'2   79-1196
ISBN 0-8094-2864-4
ISBN 0-8094-2863-6 lib. bdg.
ISBN 0-8094-2862-8 retail ed.

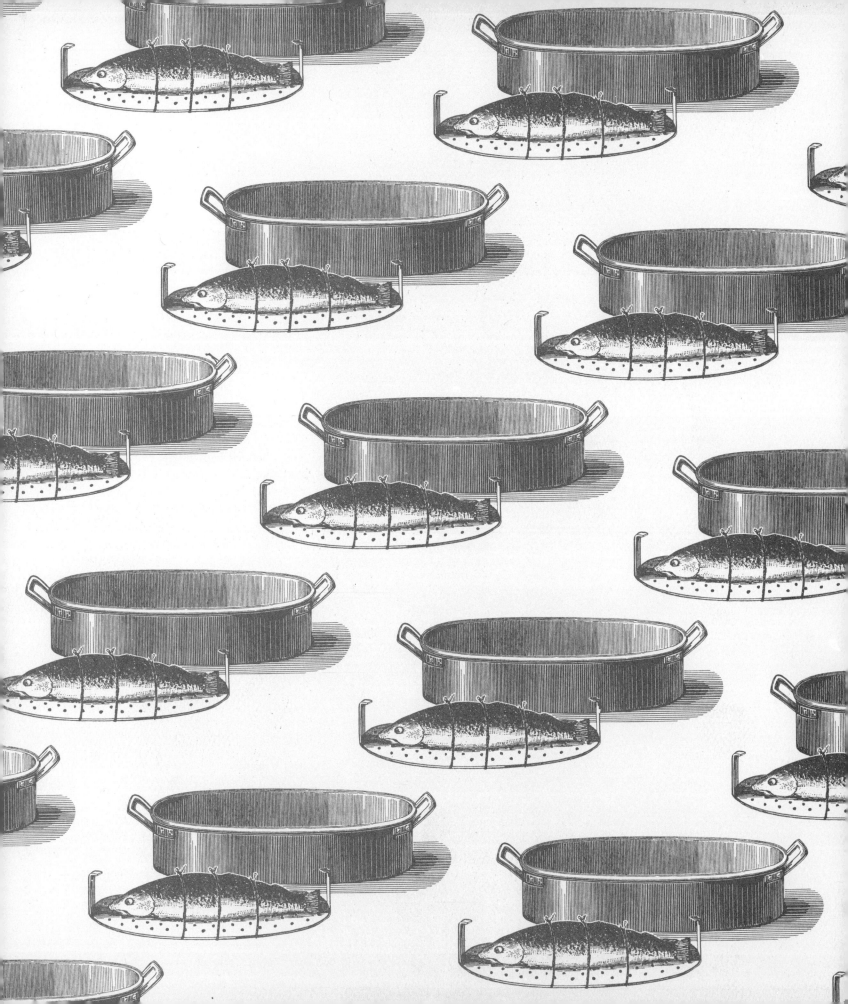